HUMAN INTELLIGENCE, Learning & Behaviour

G. A. Mohr, PhD (Cambridge)
CEO, Transworld Research & Innovation (TRI)
World Hons Mult. incl. Marquis Who's Who in the World, 2000-2001
Nominated for World Innovation Foundation (London) by Chairman

Richard Sinclair
BA (Monash), Dip.Bus.Sci. (IASC), Director, TRI

Edwin Fear
Dip.Bus.Sci. (IASC), Director, TRI

Copyright © 2017 GA Mohr, Richard Sinclair & Edwin Fear, 2017

All rights reserved worldwide.

No part of this publication may be reproduced, stored in a retrieval system, or transmitted in any form or by any means, electronic, mechanical, photocopying, recording, or otherwise, without the prior written permission of the publisher.

Publisher:
Inspiring Publishers
PO. Box 159 Calwell ACT Australia 2905
Email: publishaspg@gmail.com
http://www.inspiringpublishers.com
National Library of Australia Cataloguing-in-Publication entry.

Author: Mohr, G. A. (Geoffrey Arnold), 1946.

Title: **Human Intelligence, Learning & Behaviour/**
    Dr Geoff Mohr; Richard Sinclair, Edwin Fear, co-authors

ISBN: 9781925477733 (pbk)

Notes: Includes bibliographical references.

Subjects: Learning, Psychology of.
        Psychology, Comparative. Intellect. Human behavior.

Other Creators/Contributors: Sinclair, Richard & Fear, Edwin

HUMAN INTELLIGENCE, Learning & Behaviour

Also by G. A. Mohr

A Microcomputer Introduction to the Finite Element Method

A Treatise on the Finite Element Method

Finite Elements for Solids, Fluids, and Optimization

The MBS: A Course in Management Science

Finite Elements & Optimization for Modern Management

Natural Finite Elements using Basis Transformation

The Pretentious Persuaders,
A Brief History & Science of Mass Persuasion

Curing Cancer & Heart Disease,
Proven Ways to Combat Aging, Atherosclerosis & Cancer

The Variant Virus, Introducing Secret Agent Simon Sinclair

The Doomsday Calculation, The End Of The Human Race

The War of the Sexes, Women Are Getting On Top

Heart Disease, Cancer, & Aging:
Proven Neutraceutical & Lifestyle Solutions

2045: A Remote Town Survives Global Holocaust

The History & Psychology of Human Conflict

Elementary Thinking for the 21st Century

The 8-Week+ Program to Reverse Cardiovascular Disease

Also by G. A. Mohr, Richard Sinclair & Edwin Fear

The Evolving Universe: Relativity, Redshift and Life from Space

World Religions: The History, Psychology, Issues & Truth

World War 3: When and How Will It End?

The Brainwashed: From Consumer Zombies to Islamism & Jihad

TABLE OF CONTENTS

Preface 7

Chapter 1 The Human Brain 11

Chapter 2 Language and Learning 27

Chapter 3 Conditioning, Memory & Brainwashing 41

Chapter 4 The Psychology of Attitudes 63

Chapter 5 Raising a Smarter Child 81

Chapter 6 Real IQ 100

Chapter 7 Psychology & Psychiatry 115

Chapter 8 Education 132

Chapter 9 Learning Life Skills 152

Chapter 10 The Mass Media 166

Chapter 11 The Psychology of Advertising 180

Chapter 12 Have You Been Brainwashed? 201

Chapter 13 The Psychology of Habits.......................... 211

Chapter 14 Human Conflict 221

Chapter 15 Reverse Evolution 241

Chapter 16 Keeping Your Brain Active 273

Chapter 17 The Relativity of Intelligence 285

Chapter 18 Conclusions..296

References..307

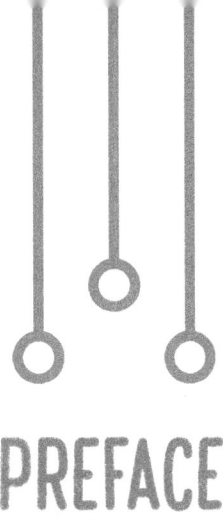

PREFACE

*I'm looking for signs of intelligent life on the
planet and I'm not doing very well.*
Reply by the first author when asked in Cambridge in 1975:
"What are you doing here?"

No brain no pain.
Overheard by the first author in the Engineering
faculty tea room at Auckland University circa 1981.

The original idea that led to this book was for a book about the human brain. Thus Chapter One begins with that subject, with some logic the next three chapters discussing language and learning, how memory works, conditioning and 'brainwashing', and attitude formation and measurement.

Chapter 5 discusses ways in which young children can be made more intelligent, Chapter 6 focusing mainly on the notion of 'Real IQ' or 'effective IQ', calculation of which includes such factors as creativity and continued learning.

Chapter 7 briefly discusses psychology and psychiatry, the main emphasis being upon psychological disorders that affect brain function adversely.

Chapter 8 discusses education, focusing mainly on the many problems in the education system today, particularly the degree to which education had been 'drawn out' from an excessive and slow 12 years at school to an increasing array of tertiary courses, many of which are largely superfluous and are simply 'cash cows' for Universities, TAFE colleges, and the growing number of private providers.

Chapter 9 discusses the important topic of learning real life skills such as choosing a career, and how to survive in hierarchical organizations and the consumer society.

Chapters 10 and 11 discuss the mass media and advertising industries that 'brainwash' us with religious, political and other propaganda, and reduce us to consumer zombies.

Chapter 12 follows up this theme to ask: Have You Been Brainwashed, a tabular example of Likert scaling being given to assess this.

Chapter 13 discusses the psychology of habits, that is, how we form habits good and bad by, for example, imitative and social learning.

Chapter 14 discusses the vexatious issue of human conflict, of which we have such a long and troublesome history, now being in the midst of 'World War 3' as the authors discuss in a recent book (Mohr, Fear & Sinclair, 2015). To throw some light upon just why humans engage in so much conflict Mohr's attitudinal model of conflict is presented in some detail (Mohr, 2014b).

Chapter 15 then discusses reverse evolution of mankind, pointing out that reductions in IQ have been observed over the past century, and discussing the many reasons why this has occurred, and is continuing to occur.

Chapter 16 discusses several ways in which to keep one's brain 'young' by keeping it active, keeping physically healthy, improving diet, and dealing with such issues as aging of the brain and Alzheimer's disease.

Chapter 17 discusses the 'relativity of intelligence', presenting a couple of further examples (in addition to those in earlier chapters) of how higher IQ, especially the Real IQ defined in Chapter 6, increases learning efficiency, concluding with estimates of the RIQ of a few famous people.

Finally, Chapter 18 briefly summarizes the book, also extending Mohr's attitudinal model of conflict slightly to show that there is a positive feedback loop involving group differences and contacts.

I am grateful to those with whom I have been able to discuss my work from time to time, including, of course, the co-authors Richard Sinclair and Edwin Fear.

Thanks also to the publishers who have been most helpful and done an excellent job.

Geoff Mohr, Melbourne, 2017.

Chapter 1
THE HUMAN BRAIN

> We must, however, acknowledge, as it seems to me,
> that man with all his noble qualities . . . still bears in
> his bodily frame the indelible stamp of his lowly origin.
> Charles Darwin, *The Descent of Man* (1871), ch. 23.

EVOLUTION OF THE HUMAN BRAIN

Bacteria were the first organic life form on the planet. There are two theories as to how they first appeared:

(a) Nitrogenous rains formed the first organic compounds in warm vents at the bottom of the ocean, these developing into bacteria.
(b) Dormant bacteria came to the Earth on meteorites, springing to life in these warm vents. The authors favour this theory in their book The Evolving Universe (Mohr, Sinclair & Fear, 2014).

Next plants developed in these hot springs, eventually making their way to the land. Around this time fungi developed, presumably from bacteria (there seems no other possibility), some scientists believing that bacteria can also transform into viruses (Cantwell, 1990).

Then bacteria merged somehow to form larger organisms in the sea, this process of evolution continuing to produce larger and larger creatures in the sea, brains developing in such creatures as fish to allow them to control their bodily functions.

Then the fins of some fish species developed in such a way as to allow them to move onto the land, beginning the evolution of land-based animals.

The remarkable process of evolution continued to allow birds to take to the air, their two-legged nature placing them on the same early branch of the tree of evolution as man.

With the evolution of apes came chimpanzees, with which we share 96% of the same genes and somewhat similar social and other behaviours such at that of alpha males and tribal conflicts.

Comparisons of blood proteins and the DNA of the African great apes with that of humans indicates that the line leading to modern people did not split off from that of chimpanzees and gorillas until comparatively late in evolution, perhaps 6 million to 8 million years ago.

Fossils of the first hominines, the australopithecines, have been discovered dating to 5 million years ago. This genus seems to have become extinct about 1.5 million years ago, but before doing so one of seven species of australopithecines, Australopithecus africanus, evolved into the genus Homo between 1.5 and 2 million years ago.

The earliest evidence of stone tools comes from sites in Africa dated to about 2.5 million years ago. These tools have not been found in association with a particular hominine species.

Around 1.7 to 1.9 million years ago two new species of large brained, small-toothed hominines emerged, Homo ergaster in Africa and Homo erectus in Asia. Later H. erectus skulls possess brain sizes in the range of 1100 to 1300 cc (67.1 to 79.3 cu in), within the size variation of Homo sapiens.

A number of archaeological sites dating from the time of Homo erectus reveal a greater sophistication in tool making than was found at the earlier sites. Evidence found at the cave site of "Peking Man" in northern China, suggests that H. erectus used fire.

The remains of the foundations of an oval structure built by a Homo erectus group were found at the Terra-Amata site in France, and within this structure there was a fireplace (Weiss and Mann, 1978).

The Homo species spread widely and by 350,000 years ago planned hunting, fire making, wearing of clothes, and probably burial rituals, were well established.

Between 200,000 and 300,000 years ago, Homo sapiens evolved.

The Neanderthals or Homo sapiens neanderthalensis had similar DNA to modern man and occupied parts of Europe and the Middle East as early as 120,000 years ago. They lived only in family groups, the men being hunter-gatherers to feed the family.

The Neanderthals left cave paintings which were an important evolutionary advance. These often depicted a simple activity, perhaps a precursor to the highly pictorial hieroglyphic script of the ancient Egyptians (Egerton Eastwick, 1896).

Though Neanderthals had 10% larger brains than modern man, there is some evidence that the part of the cerebral cortex devoted to language and thinking in modern man was underdeveloped in Neanderthal man, casting some doubt on whether Neanderthal man was capable of modern spoken language. Thought by some to be a different evolutionary branch, the Neanderthals disappeared from the fossil record about 30,000 years ago.

Differing in appearance, modern humans or Homo sapiens sapiens evolved in southern Africa or the Middle East perhaps 90,000 to 200,000 years ago and 70,000 years ago began to spread to all parts of the world, reaching Europe about 40,000 years ago, soon outnumbering, perhaps interbreeding with, and finally supplanting the local, earlier Homo sapiens populations.

Like chimpanzees, homo sapiens sapiens formed tribes and there is evidence of religion, recorded events and art dating from 30,000 to 40,000 years ago implying the advanced language and ethics required for the ordering of social groups.

THE STRUCTURE OF THE HUMAN BRAIN

In the human brain the upper layer, the cerebrum, is the largest part of the brain and its external layer is called the cerebral cortex. The outer portion is grey because it contains billions of nerve cell bodies, and the inner portion is white from the tangle of axons coated in myelin sheaths.

The cerebral cortex makes up 76% of the human brain and provides the information processing necessary for language, reason and creative thought. It is the larger frontal cortex of man that gives him greater intelligence and far more complex language than other animals.

There are only two main types of cells in nerve tissue:

[1] The actual nerve cell is the neuron, the 'conducting' cell that transmits impulses and is the structural unit of the nervous system.
[2] Neuroglia, or glia for short, the word 'neuroglia' meaning 'nerve glue'. These are nonconductive and maintain homeostasis, form myelin, and provide support and protection for neurons in the central and peripheral nervous systems. Homeostasis is the metabolic equilibrium actively maintained by several complex biological mechanisms that operate via the autonomic nervous system to offset disrupting changes.

The human brain has circa 10 billion neurons and circa 50 trillion neuroglia. Each neuron has three basic parts: the cell body (soma), one or more dendrites, and a single axon. The soma is from 10 to 25 micrometres in diameter and is often not much larger than its nucleus.

Neurons are quite complex and very numerous, and are the core components of the brain and spinal cord of the central nervous system (CNS), and of the peripheral nervous system (PNS).

Dendrites branch many times into a complex 'dendritic tree' with thousands of 'spines'. An axon, also called a nerve fibre when myelinated, may branch hundreds of times. Axons and dendrites in the CNS are about one micrometer thick and sensory neurons can have axons that run from the toes to the posterior column of the spinal cord, or more than 1.5 metres in adults.

In the brain messages are transferred from the axon terminals of one neuron to the dendrites of another via connections called synapses, memories being stored in the dendritic spines.

Neuron structure and size varies considerably, for example unipolar neurons having a single 'tree' for the axon and dendrites, whereas multipolar neurons have several tree-like structures to accommodate the axon and numerous dendrites.

Neurons can also be classified by function:

(a) Afferent neurons or sensory neurons transmit information from tissues and organs to the CNS.
(b) Efferent neurons or motor neurons transmit signals from the CNS via nerve fibres to the effector cells of muscles or glands to stimulates contraction or secretion.
(c) Interneurons connect neurons in different regions of the CNS.

THE NERVOUS SYSTEM

Figure 1.1. shows the structure of the nervous system (Sweeney, 2009). The central nervous system consists of the brain and the spinal cord and it interprets sensations and issues commands in the form of motor responses, which are based on current sensations, reflexes, and experiences.

The peripheral nervous system comprises the axons that branch from the spinal cord and carry nerve impulses to and from the brain.

The autonomic or 'involuntary' nervous system is based in the midbrain's pons and medulla and it regulates the functions essential for life, such as heart function and breathing.

The sympathetic branch puts the body on alert and supplies it with energy in response to fear or excitement. The

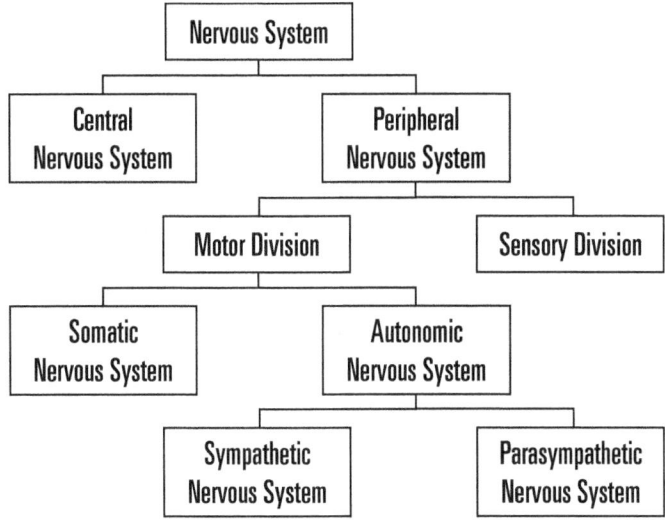

Figure 1.1. *Divisions of the nervous system. Each division is responsible for the collection of and response to different stimuli.*

parasympathetic branch relaxes the body, lowering heart rate, breathing rate, and blood pressure.

CHEMICAL EFFECTS

Neurons release neurotransmitters that bind to chemical receptors of which there are three types:

[1] Excitatory, causing an increase in firing rate.
[2] Inhibitory, causing a decrease in firing rate.
[3] Modulatory, causing long-term effects unrelated to firing rate.

Table 1.1 shows the key neurotransmitters, their location, and function.

Table 1.1. Neurotransmitters.

Neurotransmitter	Location	Function
Acetylcholine	Nervous system parts associated with motion, including the brain's motor cortex	Makes muscles contract. Also plays a role in attention, memory, and sleep.
Dopamine	Brain and the peripheral nervous system	Body motion and reward experiences, including pleasure.
Endorphins	Brain, pituitary gland, and spinal cord	Powerful, natural opiates, that block pain
Gamma-aminobutyric acid (GABA)	Retina, spinal cord, hypothalamus, and cerebellum	Commonest neurotransmitter – quiets neurons.
Glutamate	Brain and spinal cord	Activates cells for learning and memory.
Norepinephrine	Brain and peripheral nervous system	Regulates moods, blood pressure, heartbeat and arousal
Seretonin	Brain stem, cerebellum, pineal gland, and spinal cord	Crucial for sleep and appetite. Linked to depression and anxiety.

The cell membrane of the axon and soma contain voltage-gated ion channels that allow neurons to generate and propagate an electrical signal or 'action potential'. These signals are generated and propagated by charge-carrying ions including sodium (Na^+), potassium (K^+), chloride (Cl^-), and calcium (Ca^{2+}). Several types of stimuli can activate a neuron by causing ion-specific channels to open, allowing ions to flow through the cell membrane and change its potential.

Thicker axons carry action potential more rapidly, many of them having myelin insulating sheaths to increase the efficiency and effectiveness of impulse transmission (Sweeney, 2009).

Conduction of nerve impulses in on an 'all or none' basis, that is, if a neuron responds at all, it must respond completely. Thus greater intensity of stimulation doesn't produce a stronger signal but can produce a higher frequency of firing.

Many drugs, besides pharmaceutical ones, affect the brain, for example (Sweeney, 2009):

[1] LSD "binds so tightly to serotonin receptors" that very small amounts greatly affect the brain, causing hallucinations and sometimes psychosis.
[2] Marijuana's active ingredient, delta-9-tetrahydrocannabinol (THC) inhibits the release of glutamate and GABA, reducing communication between certain neural networks. In contrast, caffeine has the opposite effect, slightly raising cognitive function.
[3] Morphine affects the cerebral cortex without affecting the lower parts of the brain.
[4] Cocaine stimulates the whole brain, but particularly its emotional centres.

STORAGE CAPACITY OF THE HUMAN BRAIN

Each of circa 10 billion (10×10^9) neurons in the brain can have from 1,000 to 10,000 dendritic spines, so that, assuming 1,000 spines, there are about 10 trillion (10×10^{12}) spines. Assuming each spine can store 1 byte of information, the total brain capacity is 10 Terabytes (10×10^{12} bytes).

Because of the level of 'noise' in the brain, however, each bit of information must be stored redundantly in as many as 100 spines, so if the average 'redundancy' is 10 spines, the effective capacity of the brain is 100 Gigabytes (100 × 10^9 bytes).

The brain must have 'spare capacity', however, so that only part of the brain is used, so a conservative estimate of 'effective' brain capacity might be about 50 GB.

Note, however, that some estimates of the number of neurons in the brain are as high as 100 billion, giving an effective brain capacity of 500 GB.

This we might compare with a fairly good, but not top of the range, PC which today would have at least 5 GB of RAM (random access memory), and a hard disk storage capacity of at least 500 GB.

The number of neurons in the brain varies greatly between species, the nematode worm having only 302 neurons, whereas the fruit fly has circa 100,000 neurons.

As might be expected, some studies have found a correlation of 0.40 or more between brain size (measured by MRI or CAT) and IQ, the correlation being higher in adults than in children (Mackintosh, 2011).

It is generally assumed that the humans have evolved with relatively large brains in order to provide the large amount of semantic memory required for our advanced languages. Animals, of course, rely largely on 'visual memory', and one might expect that visual memory requires more storage capacity than language. We learn and remember language, however, in a largely visual fashion, thus recognizing both letters of the alphabet and words or 'word parts' in visual fashion, so that, indeed, a substantially larger brain is required for the semantic memory required to store language.

THE MEMORY SYSTEM

Figure 1.2 shows the multi-store or Atkinson-Shiffrin information processing model of memory (Atkinson and Shiffrin, 1968). In this, the sensory register, located in a part of the brain called the thalamus, processes information from sensory channels associated with vision, hearing and other senses.

The visual sensory register can hold 10 - 20 bits of information for only about 1 second, whereas the auditory sensory register can hold information for up to 4 or 5 seconds.

Of the up to 20 bits of information that our visual registers can accommodate with a brief glance, for example an array of letters of the alphabet, we can only remember four or five of them, this number being called the span of apprehension.

As a consequence most information in the sensory registers is lost but that to which sufficient attention is paid is

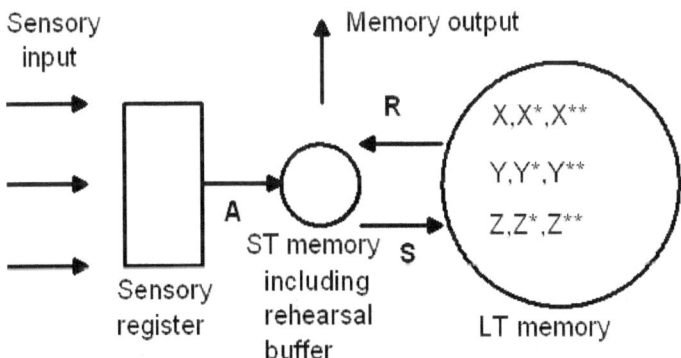

Figure 1.2. *Information processing model of memory.*

transferred to the short-term-memory (STM), located in a part of the brain called the hippocampus. Here it is held for about 20 - 30 seconds and some of it is processed by being rehearsed in the rehearsal buffer, the rest being lost.

This model fits everyday life fairly well. For example, when somebody tells you a phone number and you are interrupted while dialling it you are likely to forget it because it will be lost from STM. This is because the STM holds only about 5 - 9 items and, under certain conditions, as few as two or three.

Sternberg (1966) conducted an experiment that illustrates how memory, in this case STM, works. He showed a group of people sets of from 1 to 6 digits and seconds later asked them if the set contained a particular digit. Response times were closely proportional to the number of digits shown, demonstrating that the coding of the set in STM was searched serially or one digit at a time.

In the rehearsal buffer such processes as repetition of the information link it to information already stored in memory and then pass it to long-term-memory (LTM) where it remains for periods of days up to a lifetime. In LTM information is consolidated, a process that may take from half an hour up to months. If consolidation is somehow interrupted some memory loss occurs.

An important part of the process of LTM processing is long-term potentiation (LTP) in which chemical 'dosing' strengthens neural connections.

Thus the strength of a memory depends upon the type or amount of attention paid to the stimuli. Attention to physical characteristics is encoded less than the sounds of words, whilst emotional content enhances encoding, sometimes leading to 'flashbulb' memories which may include minute details of extremely emotional moments.

Similarly, memories that in LTM that have recently been accessed are 'dosed' chemically so that they are easier to recall again in the near term, whereas memories that have not been accessed for a long time are difficult to recall, taking from a few minutes up to several hours to recall.

Most LTM information is stored in the cerebral cortex, the 'thinking' part of the brain which is much more developed in humans than in other species.

Simple passive repetition of information, or maintenance rehearsal, is not sufficient to ensure that items are passed to LTM. The active process of elaborative rehearsal, involving reorganization of the material and attaching meaning to it is more likely to pass information to LTM.

There are four types of LTM:

[1] Procedural memory or implicit memory is 'knowing how' to perform some skill, often learnt by procedural or implicit learning.
[2] Declarative memory is 'knowing that' or memory of data or facts and events.
[3] Episodic memory of prior life experiences is a type of declarative memory. 'Flashbulb' memories are clear episodic memories of unique and highly emotional events, an example being the movie footage of the 'twin towers' collapsing after the 9/11 attacks.
[4] Semantic memory such as words and language rules is another type of declarative memory which involves more 'preprocessing' in STM than episodic memory.

In such processing, even inherently organized material is subjectively organized by the learner into categories. Up to a point, it is found that the more categories used the better the material can be recalled.

Semantic memory uses constructive processes to store information in an organized manner, often into a hierarchical structure of categories and sub-categories.

Recall of the information then occurs by reconstructive processes. With these speed of recall depends upon the hierarchical level at which information is recalled, more general 'heading' information being recalled more rapidly than specific information.

Thus, when we have difficulty remembering a person's name, for example, we often can only remember one or more names similar in some respect such as their first letter and then finally remember the required name anything from seconds to days later.

Memory processing also makes much use of images and concrete images are easily formed for words like 'cat' whilst abstract images for words like 'mercy' are more difficult to form.

Australian aborigine elders, for example, remember centuries of tribal history by associating important events with environmental features and recall and pass on this history by 'walking through' these places.

Information stored in LTM is easier to recall if it is stored with retrieval cues which are associated with 'blocks' of information. Individual items within these blocks are then stored with 'tags'.

How easily information is recalled later depends much upon how well it has been associated with images, categorized and provided with cues.

An example of how images affect information recall from LTM occurs if witnesses who saw a speeding car crash are asked:

"How fast do you think the car was going when it _ _ _ _?" with the final verb having such variations as contacted, hit, and crashed.

Speed estimates will increase in the order of these three verbs by as much as 25% because the new information in the wording of the question conflicts or interferes with the memory and associated images of the event in LTM.

Information that has been stored in a well-organized fashion can sometimes be recalled by redintegration, the process by which some event such as a 'leading question' unlocks a rapid sequence of memories that may be connected by a chain of associations.

This is the ideal situation when we read an exam question. One or more words in the question quickly trigger recall of a stream of relevant information. If the exam is the usual written answer one we tend to forget part of the answer before we can write it down.

CONCLUSION

Humans make a wide array of tools, we cook food, we build houses, roads and bridges, we heat and cool our buildings, we build ships, cars and aircraft, and man has walked on the moon. It is advanced language, in particular, that sets us apart from other animals and allows us to do these things, communicating our ideas to successive generations so that our knowledge and skills have advanced for many thousands of years. Language and learning, therefore, are discussed in the following chapter.

In the foregoing chapter the basic structure of the human brain was discussed, showing that our senses transfer and store information in the dendritic spines of the neurons, perhaps in the synapses at the ends of these spines.

It was estimated that our brain capacity was comparable to that of a modern PC, though some writers estimate human brain capacity to be an order greater than this, if not more.

Having made such a comparison, however, it is interesting to note that humans are gradually being replaced by computers in the workplace, examples being self-service at petrol stations, supermarket checkouts and bank ATMs.

Further examples are the ever growing multitude of security cameras, drones used to gather military intelligence, cruise missiles for bombing raids, and driverless cars.

Such developments have led to the question: Will humans ultimately be replaced by robots?

As in the long term that would require robots to build and perform maintenance on other robots that seems highly unlikely, indeed, impossible.

What seems more likely, however, is that thanks to overpopulation, resource depletion, pollution, and perhaps nuclear war, man will before very long become extinct, just as many other animals species already have, and continue to do so. Indeed, in the book The Doomsday Calculation it is predicted that this could occur by the end of the millennium (Mohr, 2012c).

☺☹☻☺☹☻☺☹☻☺☹☻☺☹

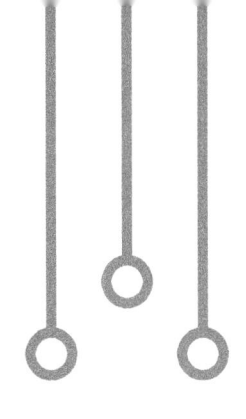

Chapter 2
LANGUAGE AND LEARNING

Some people have argued that language is what makes the human species different from other species.
Roger Bell and Ralph Hall,
Impacts: Contemporary Issues & Global Problems,
The Jacaranda Press, Milton QLD (1991).

Language is the autobiography of the human mind.
Friedrich Max Müller,
Quoted in Scholar Extraordinary
(Nirad Chaudhuri, 1974).

THE DEVELOPMENT OF LANGUAGE

Despite his larger brain size, there is some doubt whether Neanderthal man had developed language. Doubtless the roots of language lie in the 30 different vocal sounds made by vervet monkeys (Insight, 1982), no doubt related to lallation or meaningless mumbling in infants. Given some encouragement they are then ready to learn such 'baby talk' as

> da da, ma ma, wee wee
> gee gee, puff puff, bow wow

The messages in any language are built up from a small catalogue of elementary speech sounds which are combined to form words from which sentences are built up.

Generally, these words are arbitrary and do not sound like or have any other relationship with the things they represent but there are a few exceptions such as some of the words for animal noises (a phenomenon called onomatopoeia).

Language involves a duality of patterning (Foss and Hakes, 1978) in which it relates two different forms of representation: an external phonological system for sound and an internal semantic system for meaning. These two systems are related by a language's syntactic system.

We understand a sentence spoken to us because our brain stores it temporarily in our short-term-memory (STM) and compares it to the word and language rules stored as semantic memory in our long-term-memory (LTM). If we rehearse the message in STM it may be stored in LTM.

How we understand language

The way in which text is remembered provides an insight into why key words are important in the memory process. It is believed that text is not stored in memory literally but as a number of propositions, each of which has a relational term for which there are arguments (using the latter word in the same way it is used in connection with mathematical functions, especially when they are used in computer programs).

The sentence "Tom hit Jack", for example, is remembered as

(HIT, TOM, JACK)

If later "Tom apologized for hitting Jack" this is stored as

((APOLOGIZE, TOM), (HIT, TOM, JACK))

with the simple proposition of the original memory embedded in a complex one. Here the 'strong' word HIT acts as a key word and it is linked directly to the word TOM in long-term memory.

There is no doubt that a deer can remember events such as, "Lion killed deer" as a visual memory stored in episodic memory. As a result the declarative memory 'danger' would be added to the neuron in LTM storing the image of a lion, or perhaps to a newly formed adjacent neuron.

Some clue to how humans developed language is found by observing that howler monkeys have massively developed larynxes and hyoid bones (the bone that supports the tongue) so that their spectacular howls can be heard for miles.

Somehow, somewhere, humans gradually evolved with the physical attributes required to produce a variety of sounds and began to associate these with objects, passing this knowledge on to following generations.

As noted in Chapter 5, Krech's remarkable environmental enrichment experiments with rats demonstrated vividly that the gradually growth in the development of human language was undoubtedly largely responsible for the evolution of the large cerebral cortex that distinguishes modern man from other species.

THE SPREAD OF LANGUAGE

Somehow language spread with the migration of early humans, perhaps during the Agricultural Revolution, so that some languages have similar words, for example for father:

> pater (Latin), padre (Italian), pere (French)
> vater (German), father (English)

Just as European languages are rooted in Greek and Latin, oriental languages have roots in ancient Chinese and languages in the Middle East have roots in the ancient Babylonian and Egyptian languages.

There are now, of course, many languages and many more dialects. As a rule of thumb, two people speak the same

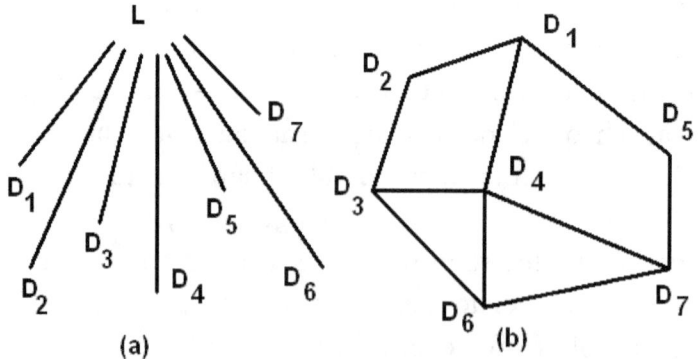

Figure 2.1. Language and dialects: (a) according to the notion of pure language; (b) a more accurate representation.

language if they are mutually intelligible. Two exceptions are the Chinese dialects Mandarin and Cantonese which are not mutually intelligible. Another is that Norwegians can usually be understood by Swedes.

Language, however, is not a 'pure' thing such that any variation from it is impure or substandard, as depicted in Fig. 2.1(a). From the point of view of modern linguistics Fig. 2.1(b) is the more nearly correct picture and it avoids linguistic chauvinism, a notion that has often led to one group of people trying to impose their language on another. This view also corresponds to way in which language spread globally.

LANGUAGE DEVELOPMENT IN INFANTS

At birth the human brain is relatively large compared to the body. Almost all the neural cells that will ever be available are present but only a basic network of the axons and dendrites that connect neurons together exists. At the outset these connections develop as the infant learns basic perception and motor skills, the long axons that extend from the brain cells then receiving signals from receptor cells, such as the small hair cells in the inner ear, or sending signals to effector cells in the muscles.

This development in the bulk of the brain parallels that in all animal species and is that necessary for basic functioning and survival.

What sets humans apart, however, is the considerable development of the cerebral cortex, the envelope of brain cells that covers the brain. This is where our thinking and storage of abstract memory information such as language occurs.

Development of the articulatory mechanisms required for controlled speech and the cortical mechanisms that control them is a slow maturational process that occurs in Broca's area of the frontal cortex. It has been suggested that babbling, however, is a sub cortical process.

Semantic memory of language is stored in Wernicke's area of the temporal lobe of the cerebral cortex.

Figure 2.2(a) shows a small part of the cerebral cortex of a newborn child in which long axons extend from the neurons and form branches. Fine terminal arbors at the end of these branches connect at synapses to the short dendrites surrounding other neurons. Figure 2.2(b) shows considerably more dendrites and branching of the axons at the age of one

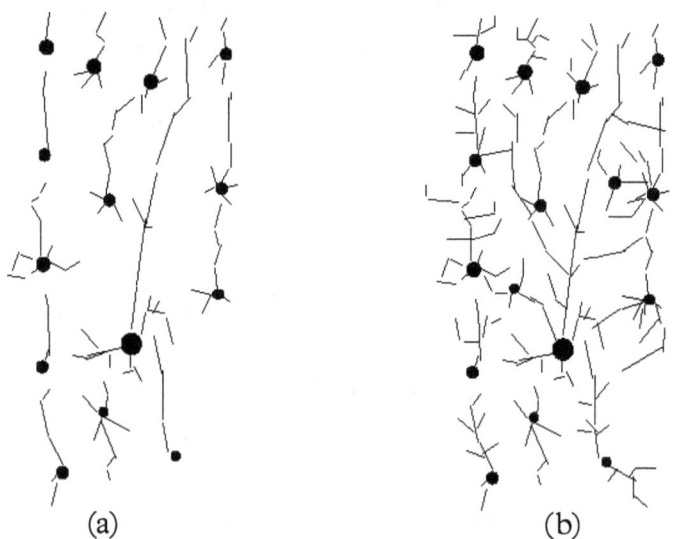

Figure 2.2. Postnatal development of the human cerebral cortex around Broca's Area (language related): (a) newborn; (b) 1 month.

month (Foss & Hakes, 1978). At the age of 24 months the neural network is a good deal denser.

The network continues to develop in following years and the neurons, while not increasing in number, do increase in size.

In addition, the motor nerve pathways that control such activities as speech production must gradually develop sheaths of the protein myelin that prevent 'short-circuiting' of impulses between nerve tracts.

As a result of this gradual brain development each human characteristic is developed at a different rate.

Eye coordination, for example, develops much more rapidly than speech. Nevertheless, for the first few months the infant may smile at any moving object such as a dummy head whereas later it may be upset by the faces of strangers.

Packard (1978) cites an example of the importance of timing in which two Harvard researchers studied the way kittens learnt to recognize shapes and patterns, a physiological ability that develops in the fourth week. If the kittens were blindfolded for this week they effectively became blind for life. Thus there appear to be periods when the infant's brain is highly receptive so that it is easiest to change a child's intelligence for better or worse before the age of four.

IMPRINTING

Imprinting is an important part of the early learning process in higher animals that plays a significant part in brain development.

Konrad Lorentz, an Austrian ethologist, demonstrated this by being the first moving object seen by ducklings after hatching. He waddled in a squatting position and quacked and soon the ducklings assumed him to be their mother and followed him about and flew to him when he quacked.

In other famous experiments baby monkeys have been persuaded to accept a foam-rubber dummy monkey complete with feeding bottle as their mother and kittens have been imprinted to accept as fellow kittens rats placed in their cage.

It has been suggested that the most critical period for imprinting in humans is from six weeks to six months and in this period the human infant develops attachments, particularly to its mother.

As the experiment of blindfolding four week-old kittens demonstrated, neural links in the brain close at certain ages for every function. Similarly, it is difficult to become a top musician if you start late.

Imprinting occurs, at least to some extent, in the learning of languages, so that becoming truly bilingual gets more difficult as one gets older. When older it is well nigh impossible to master a second language with the same ease, fluency and accent as the first.

Much of our language learning is stored as semantic memory, one of four basic long-term-memory types discussed earlier in this chapter. Semantic memory is very stable so that the meanings of words or the rules for their use may never be forgotten.

Some experiments have shown that semantic memory stores information in logical hierarchies which go from general categories to specific ones, so that clusters of words with related meanings are stored in the same location in the brain.

Much of this stable memory base for language and other knowledge is founded by imprinting at a very early age and it is important to take advantage of this in educating young children.

MODELLING

According to some experts the critical period in a child's intellectual, social and emotional development is between eight and eighteen months.

During this period, in particular, much of a child's learning is by modelling or imitative learning, also referred to as learning by observation.

It is desirable, therefore, for parents and others to use controlled modelling with infants in order to give them a head start in learning language and other skills.

After only four weeks babies begin to mimic the mother's mouth movements in speech and babbling begins at about two months, followed by laughter at about three months.

At six months lallation begins, that is, the baby utters repeated sounds such as 'ma ma' or 'ba ba'. At 10 months the baby begins to try to copy sounds made by the parents and by the end of the first year it may have learnt one or two real words.

In the first years much of the effort in training children is directed at development of survival skills such as eating, learning to walk and potty training. Modelling plays an important part in this, for example in the process of learning to walk, where the infant has had plenty of opportunity to watch the actions of adults.

Learning in a child's first year could be much advanced, therefore, by conscious and careful use of modelling, that is, demonstration of skills to be developed such as development of effective and clear speech.

In these early efforts use could be made of pictures and objects with which to associate the baby's first word efforts, for example the mother pointing to herself when vocalizing ma-ma.

Much of the time we also instinctively use conditioning, that is, repetitive presentation of items associated with simple skills to be learnt, often followed by praise when satisfactory progress is made.

At this early stage the cot can become the infant's first learning centre and objects that might be helpful to its learning can be placed within the infant's field of view, for example a picture of a dog in order to teach the word 'bow-wow'.

Here advantage might usefully be made of a TV set to play tapes or DVDs of simple movies, for example involving objects the words for which are to be learnt, perhaps including the numbers 1 to 4.

Demonstrating the possibilities for abstract learning at an early age, chimpanzees have been found better able to recognize the symbols for the numbers 1 to 4 than groups of objects up to four in number.

The important point, however, is that a good deal of patience is needed in the education process, particularly at the outset. Time is taken for memories to develop and fix and it is perhaps best to be a month or two ahead of the child's expected capabilities in trying to inculcate knowledge and skills for, as we all know, in later life it can be years after getting a certain idea that we actually get around to acting on it.

What is certain, however, that the sooner a mother begins to talk to her baby the better and, to a lesser extent perhaps, the same no doubt applies to many other areas of early learning.

GROUP MODELLING

At around the third month the baby recognizes the mother and smiles at her. Before this point it will be amused by many objects, including strangers, but now attachments have been formed by imprinting and it may be upset by strangers.

Within the first year, therefore, it would make good sense to involve the infant in play groups involving small groups of mothers and infants. In these early efforts at group activities can be attempted and the child can begin its social development.

Packard (1978) raised the interesting possibility of the use of professional people to teach by modelling.

These people would be trained to know the periods during which learning of various areas of knowledge areas can best be commenced and in how best to use modelling techniques to initiate that learning. Such people would then visit the home or attend play group sessions.

Packard noted that an experiment with a form of group modelling was undertaken at New York Medical College. This began with twenty pairs of mothers and babies when the babies were only four weeks old and lasted three years at the end of which the children were compared with those of a control group. The children in the experimental group were a good deal more advanced in language and other skills than the control group.

Indeed, some experts doubt the competence of the modern family for child rearing and believe that more professional efforts are essential to help develop emotional stability and intellectual development in infants.

VOCABULARY GROWTH IN EARLY CHILDHOOD

When children reach the age of one the pace at which learning can take place greatly increases.

Much of what has already been learnt will have been learnt by modelling, for example the ability for form words. Other skills like that of standing upright and then walking will have been learnt in part by conditioning and the associated reinforcement of praise as progress towards the objective is made.

Table 2.1. Words learnt with age.

Age (years)	Words learnt
1	3-5
1.25	15
1.5	25
1.75	100
2	250
2.5	450
3	900
4	1550
4.5	1900
5	2100
5.5	2300
6	2550

Now learning can be accomplished with a host of aids such as pictures, simple books and educational toys.

In addition, more formal processes such at those of rote learning of words can be used. At the outset the words to be learnt should carefully chosen, for example objects within the child's everyday environment to allow associative processes to help fix the words in long term semantic memory.

By this formative age the child has been out and about a good deal and optimistic attempts have been made to teach it many words of which it will have learnt only a few.

As shown in Table 2.1, however, word learning occurs at a quite rapid rate from here on, to the point at which a basic command of language has been obtained at age five.

Whilst the first year is instrumental in learning to begin to talk, in the second year a comparatively massive growth in vocabulary occurs. Thereafter the rate of increase is approximately linear but slows down as the child comes to grip with a widening range of subjects at school.

By the time they have learnt to read a little, however, children are able to learn things by cognitive learning which processes and stores abstract information.

Latent learning occurs when subjects are exposed to a body of information, rather than in small parts, and they then apply that information later on, perhaps in a test.

A laboratory example of this is that an experimental group of rats allowed to roam a maze will then do better in learning to get through it for a reward than a control group with no prior experience of the maze.

At school children are taught by presenting them with visual and verbal information to learn subjects in discrete 'blocks'. Here cognitive and latent learning occur and revision exercises and tests are used to reinforce and correct their knowledge.

CONDITIONING

Much early learning occurs by

(a) Imprinting, that is selection of a person to imitate.
(b) Imitative learning, that is, imitation of others.

Parents and teachers also use a good deal of conditioning, that is, repetitive presentation of information to be learnt, accompanied by occasional doses of positive and negative reinforcement. Conditioning, therefore, is discussed in more detail in the next chapter.

Imitative learning and modelling are important until middle age, if not beyond. Advertisers can rely on it to allow social learning to occur in groups of children so that only a few of them may be directly influenced by an advertisement but some of their friends and classmates are then likely to copy them resulting in a pyramid effect.

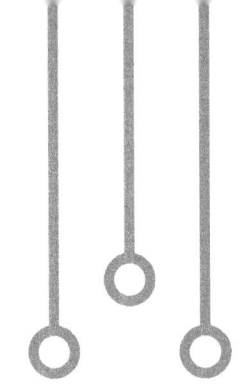

Chapter 3
CONDITIONING, MEMORY AND BRAINWASHING

*The real persuaders are our appetites,
our fears and above all our vanity.
The skilful propagandist stirs and coaches
these internal persuaders.*
Eric Hoffer, *The Passionate State of Mind* (1955).

INTRODUCTION

The preceding chapter dealt briefly with modelling which plays a crucial part in the early learning of infants. Mention was also made of how we also instinctively use conditioning, for example repetitive presentation of items associated with simple skills to be learnt, often followed by praise when satisfactory progress is made.

Conditioning is a fundamental learning process but it also has applications in psychotherapy, for example behaviour modification using aversion therapy, and thence more sinister ones in 'brainwashing' prisoners of war or crime suspects to obtain information from them or to make them 'switch sides'.

In the modern era, however, it is more relevant to everyday life than ever as conditioning is used to some extent in advertising to repetitively expose people to a brand name. They quickly develop recognition of the brand and, before long, some degree of acceptance, if not approval.

Much of the excessively long and drawn out education process is also conditioning for obedience and routine. Military training, of course, is one of the more extreme examples of conditioning. Some understanding of the mechanics of conditioning is therefore well worthwhile in an age when we are confronted with it almost at every turn.

CLASSICAL CONDITIONING

Classical conditioning, or learning by association, was first demonstrated by Ivan Pavlov's celebrated experiments with dogs in the 1890s.

In these he noted that a caged dog's mouth salivated when it saw food on a pan swung within its reach. Here the food is the *uncontrolled stimulus* (US) and salivation is the dog's *uncontrolled reaction* (UR)

Next, a bell was rung shortly before presentation of the food and the dog's saliva collected in a cup to measure the amount. Here the bell is the *controlled stimulus* (CS).

It was found that the after a few repetitions of the paired stimuli of bell and food the dog would begin to salivate with the ringing of the bell alone, this being the *controlled reaction* (CR).

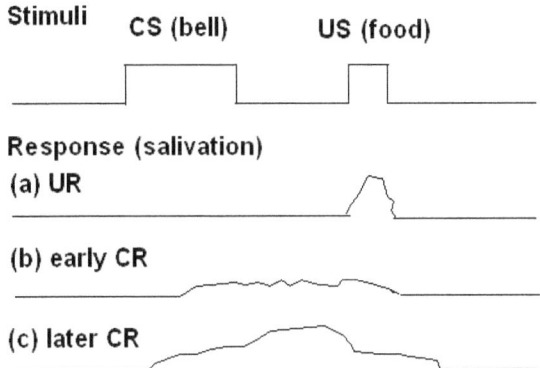

Figure 3.1. Pavlov's classical conditioning experiment:
(a) Bell precedes food presentation.
(b) Bell the only stimulus.
(c) US resumed temporarily - then only CS giving result shown.

Similar results can be obtained with almost any stimulus that consistently evokes a reflex response such as electrical shock. A dog or a human given a mild shock to a leg will quickly withdraw the leg.

If the electrode giving the shocks is attached to the leg, on the other hand, flexion of the leg will occur in response to shock, the US. Then when a prior conditioned or 'neutral' stimulus is given as warning conditioned response is developed and remains after the US is removed.

After many trials the results can be graphed as a *learning curve*. Typically this takes the form shown in Figure 3.2 where the curve gradually flattens as the number of trials increases.

Here the US and CS remain paired. If the US is removed, however, *extinction* occurs and the response (the CR) decreases. Then, if the US is again added after the CS, the

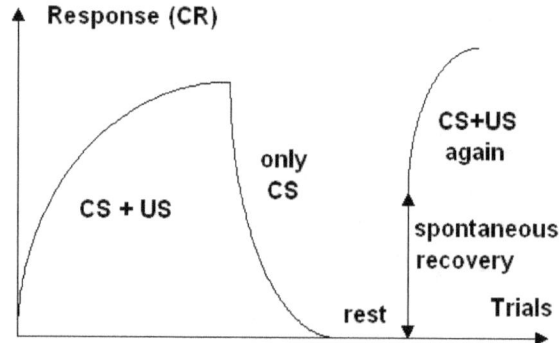

Figure 3.2. Conditioning, extinction and recovery.

response recovers, the initial amount of response being called the *spontaneous recovery*.

Advertising often uses classical conditioning by repeatedly associating a product with positive ideas and images, thereby encouraging people to have positive feelings towards the product itself.

OPERANT CONDITIONING

Operant conditioning, or learning by consequences, is characterized by the use of *reinforcement* which encourages a response in which the subject *operates* in some way, rather than just exhibiting a passive reflex response as in classical conditioning.

The classical experiments in operant conditioning were conducted in the 1940s by Skinner, a Harvard psychologist. In these he placed a rat in a box in which there was a lever that delivered food to it when pressed.

Initially the lever was operated from outside and soon the rat learnt the association between seeing the lever move and the appearance of food.

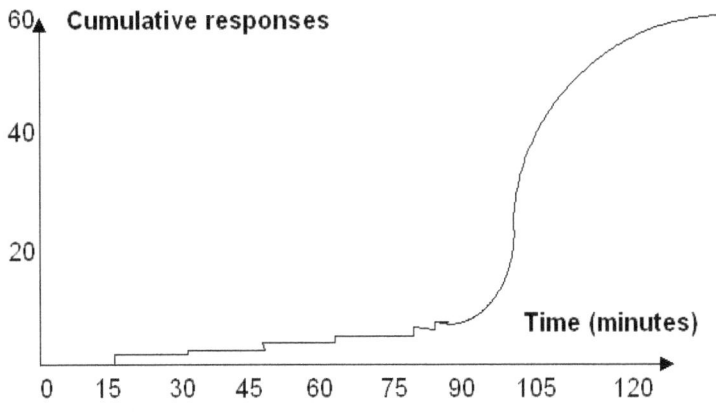

Figure 3.3. Operant conditioning responses by rat in Skinner Box. First response at 15 minutes, second at 30, third at 45, but after 75 minutes the rate of response becomes high.

After a while it operated the lever itself to obtain food and continued to do so with increasing frequency as it became more familiar with the routine, as shown in Figure 3.3.

In the result of Figure 3.3 the rat in the 'Skinner Box', as it came to be called, took 15 minutes to successfully operate the feed lever. Four more intervals of about 15 minutes occurred before following operations when, the rat having fully learnt the procedure, the rate of operation accelerated markedly.

We instinctively use operant conditioning in bringing up children, the reinforcement to encourage desired actions being smiles and vocal approval.

Note that the timing of reinforcement is important. In a Skinner box, for example, the greater the time delay between the rat pressing the lever and the delivery of the food the longer it will take the rat to associate the two events and thus learn the feeding operation.

As with classical conditioning, *extinction* occurs when reinforcement ceases. This 'unlearning' process may be stronger still when *negative reinforcement*, typically some form of punishment in the educational context, is used.

Conditioned physical responses may be accompanied by emotional feelings or responses and many of our feelings are developed by conditioning.

In the case of classical conditioning *conditioned emotional responses* (CERs) may develop. Indeed, our feelings about many people and other things in our lives develop in this kind of way.

Advertising is also a case in point where an ad reminds us of a familiar product, evoking feelings of recognition and approval whilst the implications for education are all too obvious.

GENERALIZATION AND DISCRIMINATION

When alternative conditioned or 'signal' stimuli are used in classical conditioning the subject may learn to *discriminate* between them and respond more strongly to one than the other.

In Pavlov's classical experiments, for example, he found that dogs also responded to a buzzer as a CS instead of a bell, but less strongly.

This is called *generalization* and the more similar the alternative CS the better the response. Sometimes, however, the conditioned responses occur when a new but similar CS is used that has never been paired with the US previously.

In this way a child can develop a fear of dogs after being bitten by a black dog. It may then generalize that fear into a phobia about other harmless black objects.

When two stimuli are used but pairing of the US or 'reward' is not maintained with the second stimulus the subject develops *discrimination* and begins to learn to ignore the second stimulus.

BEHAVIOUR SHAPING

In operant conditioning *shaping* can be used to speed up the process. In Skinner's rat experiment, for example, shaping might begin by remote operation of the 'food lever' only when the rat gets close to it, gradually decreasing the distance of the rat from the lever before the lever is operated. Then the lever is only operated when the rat touches the lever. Next the lever is only operated when the rat attempts to depress it.

Thus behaviour shaping involves reinforcing *successive approximations* to the desired behaviour pattern.

In this way conditioning can be accelerated and quite complex patterns of behaviour can be taught, a familiar example being circus bears that have been taught to ride bicycles in this way (Lindzey, Hall, & Thompson, 1978).

Packard (1978) reported that up to 20% of teachers in the eastern USA were systematically using behaviour modification techniques that involved systematic use of rewards and punishments in their classrooms.

Two teachers in Montana went too far by extending the 'Skinner box' idea to a four-foot high box for miscreant students. It had no lighting and no ventilation other than two small holes for observation. The relatives of a retarded child that had been locked in this box complained and the teachers were sacked.

A better example of a method of behaviour improvement was employed by a team of 'behaviour shapers' from the University of Kansas. They had the teacher play a 'game' in which the class was divided into two teams and the team which incurred fewer violations of several rules for class behaviour was given various rewards. The investigators reported good results.

Objections to such applications of behaviour shaping are that they focused on restricting behaviours such as talking in class whereas advocates of 'open' classrooms encourage a freer learning environment.

The advent of the PC in schools, however, has brought a highly mechanized learning process, some aspects of which progressive educators are pleased with.

With the use of appropriate teaching software, PCs become a 'teaching machine' with which students can learn at their own pace and receive instant reinforcement for correct answers.

REINFORCEMENT SCHEDULES

To this point we have assumed reinforcement, when used, was applied on a continuous basis, that is, after each response.

In operant conditioning reinforcement can also be made according to some fixed schedule. Examples include:

[1] The *fixed-ratio schedule* gives reinforcement after a certain number of responses.

Conditioning, Memory and Brainwashing | 49

[2] The *fixed-interval schedule* where reinforcement is given after a fixed interval of time, regardless of how many responses are made.

[3] In *variable-ratio* schedules reinforcement might come, for example, after three, then six responses, then three again. Similarly *variable-interval schedules* vary the time intervals between reinforcement.

Another obvious alternative is *random interval reinforcement*, that is, choosing an average interval and multiplying it by a random number between 0 and 1 produced by successive applications of a random number generator such as the RND( ) function of BASIC and other computer programming languages.

As might be expected, extinction is slower after cessation of scheduled reinforcements. This is the situation in human life where, for example, parents can only occasionally reward or punish a child's behaviour.

The result is that we may continue doing things we were shaped to do early in life long after reinforcement has ceased.

PRIMARY AND SECONDARY REINFORCEMENT

A primary reinforcer, or unconditioned reinforcer, is effective for an untrained subject, for example food as a positive reinforcer or electric shock as a negative reinforcer.

A secondary reinforcer, or conditioned reinforcer, must be learnt by being paired with a primary reinforcer.

In a Skinner box, for example, a gong could be sounded every time the primary reinforcement of food was obtained. As in classical conditioning, the subject would associate the gong with the food and soon it would become an effective secondary reinforcer.

A better example occurs in child rearing where parents typically reward children for good behaviour with food treats or presents as primary reinforcers, accompanied by praise as secondary reinforcement. Ultimately the secondary reinforcement of praise may become the most frequently used and important form of reinforcement.

Contiguity of reinforcement, that is the time interval, is also important. The smaller the interval in time between the two reinforcements to be associated, the sooner the secondary reinforcement is learnt.

UNDERSTANDING THE WORKINGS OF THE BRAIN

THE ROLE OF CHEMICALS

An example of the power of conditioning is cited by Packard (1978).

This came about from experiments with flatworms whose brains have only about 400 cells. The worms were conditioned to "scrunch up" when seeing a light go on when this was followed by electrical shocks. It was found that when the worms were cut in half, or even several pieces, the pieces regenerated brains that remembered the conditioning.

Similar results were then obtained with various species of vertebrates.

Even more startling was the 'memory transferability' achieved by making soup of the brains of rats conditioned to shun darkness and feeding it to hamsters. The injected hamsters soon began to shun darkness!

This led before too long to the suggestion that students should eat their professors!

Later Georges Ungar and co-workers detected a peptide compound¶ in the brain of a conditioned rat that caused it to avoid darkness.

[¶ Peptides link chains of up to thousands of amino acid molecules to form *polypeptides*. Proteins are naturally occurring polypeptides].

They pooled the brains of 4000 rats to obtain a sample of this compound large enough for analysis and synthesis of the compound (Ungar et al., 1972).

Subsequently Ungar's group reported discovering several other brain peptides that seemed to transfer learning from one animal to another.

THE ROLE OF ELECTRICITY

That electrical stimuli in the brain play an important part, however, was demonstrated graphically by Jose Delgado by rigging a bull for radio-triggered mild electrical stimulation of a part of its brain (Delgado, 1971). He then stood in front of the animal. When it charged the tiny electrode in its brain was triggered and the bull stopped. After triggering the stimulation several times the bull was so pacified that it allowed witnesses of the experiment into the ring without charging them.

In humans electrodes implanted in the brain have been found to cause recall of long forgotten memories.

It has been found that the speed of conduction of impulses or *action potentials* in nerves is approximately proportional to the square root of the fibre diameter, a result familiar in cable theory (Schmidt-Nielsen, 1979). In myelin coated axons, however, the conduction speed is approximately proportional to the fibre diameter.

THE 'STRENGTH' OF MEMORIES

Memory storage is sometimes so effective and indelible that sometimes we can't forget things we would like to such as bad habits.

Sometimes *motivated forgetting* suppresses memories of traumatic experiences but this generally occurs subconsciously and we are not able to control the repression process at will.

One clue is that when we do consciously forget certain things we quickly dismiss them from our thoughts as soon as they enter them. When happier thoughts cross our minds, on the other hand, they may linger a little longer and almost involve a euphoria comparable to that which might be induced by small doses of tranquilizers like alcohol.

In other words we use processes like elaborative rehearsal to 'tag' memories with appropriate emphasis as important, good, bad and so on.

It is also clear that we have different 'layers' of memory so that past memories are in 'background memory' and take from seconds to days to recall.

Presumably items in foreground memory are chemically tagged and, over time, the pathways and neurons that store them become depleted in these markers.

Supporting this view, research in Sweden found changes in RNA in rat's brains compared to those of a control group after they had been given a learning task.

Such work clearly demonstrates that, just as DNA stores genetic coding, macromolecules of RNA play an important role in memory processes.

EFFECT OF EXPERIENCE

The environment enrichment experiments with rats of Krech's group at Berkeley are mentioned in Chapter 5. These were perhaps the first physical evidence that the brain is modified by experience.

MEMORY STRUCTURE

Figure 3.4 shows a proposed structure in which the brain stores information about animals as categories and sub-categories with properties attached to each 'node' in the structure (Collins et al., 1969).

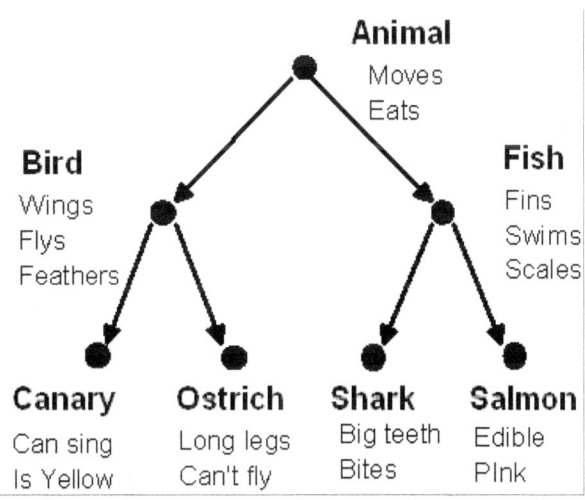

Figure 3.4. Hierarchical organization of the mental lexicon.

Some experimental results do not fit this model, for example Ripps et al. (1973) found that people were quicker to agree to the truth of the statement: *A cat is an animal* than they were to the truth of the statement: *A cat is a mammal.* They argued that MAMMAL should be closer to CAT than ANIMAL in the hierarchy.

More important, however, is that the word ANIMAL is much more frequently used than the word MAMMAL and frequency of reference to a memory certainly does enhance the speed of recall.

The present author would also argue that the brain almost certainly must store memories in a *precedence network* based on the order in which learning occurs.

In such a network a memory search that succeeds in finding a 'connection' or *common* property shared by a 'new' item in short term memory and an item in long-term memory might then store the data on the new item in the same physical area.

Then, for example, the first live animals that most children encounter might well be cats or dogs so that they will begin forming the memory structure shown in Figure 3.5.

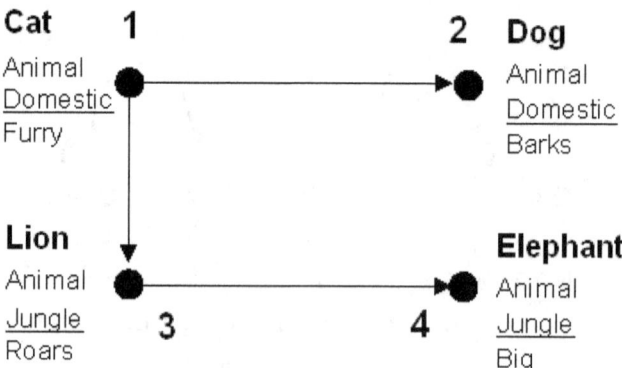

Figure 3.5. Precedence memory network.

Here four memories have the *common property* 'animal' and cat is the first animal encountered by an infant and thence the first memory stored (at node 1, perhaps one or more brain cells). The second memory is dog, the third lion, and so on. Then cat and dog are associated by the property *domestic* (in the child's language perhaps 'house' or 'nearby') whilst lion and elephant are associated by the common property *jungle*.

Such memories have a considerable visual 'content' and the ease of recall of a memory will depend its 'strength' which will depend on such factors as the degree of elaboration with which it was committed to long-term memory and the frequency and 'recency' with which the memory has been revisited.

NETWORK MODELS OF THE BRAIN

As noted in Chapter 1, long axons extend from neurons and their terminals connect to the short dendrites of other neurons in the brain.

Such networks can be modelled using the *Finite Element Method* (FEM). As a very simple example Figure 3.6 shows a direct current (DC) network with four resistance *elements* connecting four *nodes* (corresponding to a group of neurons storing a memory item) and this corresponds to the simple *precedence memory model* of Figure 3.5.

The numerical FEM model for this 'structure' is obtained by summing matrices for each element formed by using Ohm's Law to write the current flow in each element ij as

$$Q_{ij} = (V_i - V_j)/R_{ij}$$

where V_i and V_j are the voltages at nodes i and j at each end, and R_{ij} is the *resistance* of the element.

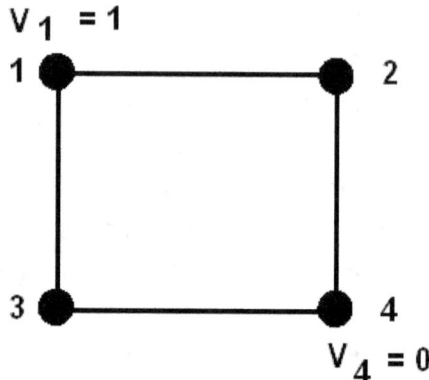

Figure 3.6. FEM model of simple DC network
Resistances 12, 13, 24, 34 all = 1.
Potential at node 1 is 1 and at node 4 it is 0.

$$\left\{ \begin{array}{c} Q_{ij} \\ -Q_{ij} \end{array} \right\} = (1/R_{ij}) \begin{bmatrix} 1 & -1 \\ -1 & 1 \end{bmatrix} \left\{ \begin{array}{c} V_i \\ V_j \end{array} \right\}$$

Then writing the two equations for current flow at each end of the element as a matrix we obtain

Doing this for each element and writing the entries from their *element matrices* in a *system matrix* in positions corresponding to the node numbers for each element we obtain the system equations:

$$\{Q\} = \left\{ \begin{array}{c} Q_1 \\ Q_2 \\ Q_3 \\ Q_4 \end{array} \right\} = \begin{bmatrix} G_{12}+G_{13} & -G_{12} & -G_{13} & 0 \\ -G_{12} & G_{12}+G_{24} & 0 & -G_{24} \\ -G_{13} & 0 & G_{13}+G_{34} & -G_{34} \\ 0 & -G_{24} & -G_{34} & G_{24}+G_{34} \end{bmatrix} \left\{ \begin{array}{c} V_1 \\ V_2 \\ V_3 \\ V_4 \end{array} \right\}$$

where $G_{12} = 1/R_{12}$ is the reciprocal of the resistance, or *conductance* of element 12.

This *assembly* process for the system matrix is easily done by a computer program and the matrix problem can be solved using a short matrix solution routine (Mohr, 1992).

First, either input or output currents must be specified at some nodes to 'force' current flows. Alternatively, voltages are specified for at least two nodes, one of these being a 'datum' potential which is often zero.

This is done in the present example, in the program calculating equivalent current 'loads' by multiplying the columns in the system matrix for 'specified voltage nodes' by the voltage specified at them and adding the result to the load matrix $\{Q\}$ or array V( ) in the program.

Then the problem is solved to determine the nodal voltages or potentials and the element currents are calculated using

$$Q_{ij} = (V_i - V_j)/R_{ij}$$

A short QBASIC[1] program that assembles and solves this problem is given below. Here key notation is

NN(,)	matrix storing the element node numbers
R( )	matrix storing the element resistances
C(,)	the system matrix
V( )	the nodal voltages
NP	number of nodes
NE	number of elements
NS	number of nodes with specified voltage
a$, b$	format specifier strings
X, S	temporary numbers

---

[1] QBASIC was included with DOS 5 and has been used in recent books on PCs. With a first line 'Show' added the same code lines can be used in VB if attached to a form but now a separate (text) file is needed to read the data.

The program reads the data in lines 3, 5 and 9, 'deploying' the element matrices into the system matrix in lines 6 and 7 and modifying the RHS 'load' vector V( ) for the specified voltages in line 11.

Then only lines 14 to 20 are required to solve the problem using Gauss-Jordan reduction, a standard method of inverting matrices, also applying this to the load vector V( ) to obtain the solution directly (Przemieniecki, 1968).

Here X is first used to store the *pivot* for 'row division' operations (line 14) and then used to store the 'row multiplier' (line 17) for the row subtraction operations (line 19) and doing these on the RHS vector V( ) (line 17) as well yields the solution.

Note that the RHS line numbers are not part of the program.

```
DIM NN(20, 2), R(20), C(20, 20), V(20)                        1
a$ = "###": b$ = "######.###"                                 2
READ NP, NE, NS                                               3
FOR K = 1 TO NE                                               4
READ I, J, R: NN(K, 1) = I: NN(K, 2) = J: R(K) = R            5
C(I, I) = C(I, I) + 1 / R: C(I, J) = C(I, J) – 1 / R          6
C(J, I) = C(J, I) – 1 / R: C(J, J) = C(J, J) + 1 / R          7
NEXT                                                          8
FOR K = 1 TO NS: READ N, S                                    9
FOR I = 1 TO NP                                              10
C(N, I) = 0: V(I) = V(I) – S * C(I, N)                       11
C(I, N) = 0: NEXT I                                          12
V(N) = S: C(N, N) = 1: NEXT                                  13
FOR I = 1 TO NP: X = C(I, I): V(I) = V(I) / X                14
```

```
FOR J = I + 1 TO NP: C(I, J) = C(I, J) / X: NEXT        15
FOR K = 1 TO NP: IF K = I THEN GOTO NEXK                16
X = C(K, I): V(K) = V(K) – X * V(I)                     17
FOR J = I + 1 TO NP                                     18
C(K, J) = C(K, J) – X * C(I, J): NEXT J                 19
NEXK: NEXT K: NEXT I                                    20
PRINT " Node Voltage"                                   21
FOR I = 1 TO NP                                         22
PRINT USING a$; I; : PRINT USING b$; V(I): NEXT I       23
PRINT " Element Current"                                24
FOR K = 1 TO NE: I = NN(K, 1): J = NN(K, 2)             25
Q = -(V(J) – V(I)) / R                                  26
PRINT USING a$; I; J; : PRINT USING b$; Q: NEXT         27
DATA 4,4,2                                              28
DATA 1,2,1, 1,3,1, 2,4,1, 3,4,1                         29
DATA 1,1, 4,0                                           30
```

The data appended to the program (lines 28 - 30) is for the problem of Figure 3.6 for which the solution is $V_2 = V_3 = 0.5$ and currents = 0.5 for each element.

The foregoing program also proves very useful for modelling hierarchical networks in Chapter 9.

FEM network models lend themselves to 'structural' models of memory such as that of Figures 3.4 and 3.5.

That the resulting numerical model is a matrix suggests that some form of database model might also be used to model memory storage in the brain, not a particularly startling idea!

Another possibility is to combine the two model types so that each node in Figure 3.6 is a database of some category like those in Figure 3.4 and the links between the nodes are the *joins* between common *fields* in these databases.

As there are billions of neurons in the human brain, however, we can only hope to model its memory processes on a small scale.

LONG-TERM POTENTIATION

The resistance of each element in Figure 3.6 can be compared to the *frequency* of use of a path in the brain's network and the voltage at each node can be compared to the *strength* of a memory 'image' or information 'bundle' stored in a neuron.

In practice a signal between two neurons is an electrical impulse passed along the axon of the first to the dendrites of the second via a synaptic junction. At this junction neurotransmitter chemicals pass the signal across a 'synaptic gap.' Evidently these chemicals react with RNA or peptide macromolecules in the neurons that play a role in memory *coding*.

In the case of classical conditioning, therefore, with frequent 'dosing' in this way the storage of a memory is made more permanent, an effect called *long-term potentiation* (Vander et al., 1994). Therefore, a more realistic FEM model of a neural network might include a capacitance property for nodes so that the charge stored at these could model the strength and/or recency of a memory.

BRAINWASHING

The term 'brainwashing' derives from a Chinese word and BW was first used by the Chinese military on Americans captured in the Korean War in trying to convert them to communist ideology using 'The Three D's' method:

[1] *Debilitation*: 'Softening up' by sleep and food deprivation.
[2] *Dread*: Rough treatment and threats of torture or death.
[3] *Dependency*: The subject realizes that they are dependent upon the brainwashers for survival and is treated as converted and allowed to mix with other converts who complete the persuasion process.

The American Heritage Dictionary of English defines brainwashing as:

1. *Intensive, forcible indoctrination, usually political or religious, aimed at destroying a person's basic convictions and attitudes and replacing them with an alternative set of fixed beliefs.*
2. *The application of a concentrated means of persuasion, such as an advertising campaign or repeated suggestion, in order to develop a specific belief or motivation.*

In line with the second definition, most people now believe that a great deal of brainwashing is done via the mass media. In the present work, therefore, the term *brainwashing* is generalized to include implanting ideas where none existed before, not just changing a person's ideas. This is important in view of the predilection of advertisers to target children of all ages when they are open-minded, if not naive, and thus willing to try new things.

In this context advertising needs only to succeed in a small percentage of the target age group and *social learning*, a form of imitative learning, will occur and ensure that other members of the target group follow the lead of those first persuaded by the advertising.

The results are nothing short of spectacular, of course, as young children are persuaded en masse what to wear, how to act, and to smoke, drink Coke, buy mobile phones, etc.

This, indeed, is *conditioning* on a grand scale.

As well as in advertising, conditioning techniques are used in the many stages and areas of life mentioned in Chapters 2 and 3, whilst the psychology of attitude formation is discussed in the next chapter, the mass media and advertising being discussed in Chapters 10 and 11.

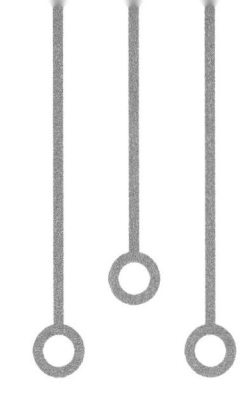

Chapter 4
THE PSYCHOLOGY OF ATTITUDES

The body of science described in this book could only have been developed in democratic societies, where attitudinal influence is the form of control that is most often relied upon.
Alice H. Eagly and Shelly Chaiken,
The Psychology of Attitudes (1993).

INTRODUCTION

The preceding chapter discussed conditioning which has important application in education where forcing pupils to sit out each day conditions them for productive life. Some aspects of conditioning are also involved, of course, in advertising and other forms of persuasion.

In the present chapter a brief introduction to the mechanics of attitude and belief formation is given. Of particular importance in advertising, *mere exposure research* and attitude measurement are also discussed.

Forbes' *contact hypothesis* regarding interactions between ethnic communities is briefly considered, this being of considerable importance in relation to religious persuasion, and, therefore, also having some relevance to advertising.

THE FORMATIVE YEARS

The period from age 12 to 30 has been termed the *critical period* for formation of attitudes and it can be divided into two parts (Morgan et al., 1979):

(a) Adolescence, during which parental, educational, peer group, advertising and sociological influences are largely responsible for development of most of the attitudes a person will form through life.
(b) Young adulthood is a time when commitments such as choosing a vocation and marriage occur, and one in which attitudes tend to *crystallize* or 'freeze' for life.

In part this crystallization may involve attempts at *cognitive consistency* in which we tend to make our attitudes relatively consistent with one another and thus avoid *cognitive dissonance* or conflicting attitudes.

An example of this might be that a person who goes to considerable effort to maintain good health, for example by exercising regularly and maintaining a healthy diet, is less likely to smoke or condone doing so.

Heider's *balance theory* is of the cognitive consistency type and assumes that we try to maintain consistent and balanced or harmonious relationships with other people and our environment. According to this theory we would not marry a person with whom we disagreed on major issues about which we felt strongly, such as abortion (Morgan et al., 1979).

That attitudes do indeed crystallize or 'firm up' in young adulthood was confirmed by a US survey of women college students in the 1930s which, when followed-up 20 years later, found that for most issues on the 'conservative-liberal' dimension the women's attitudes, except for a slight "conservative drift" typical of older people, remained the same as they had been in their twenties (Newcomb, 1963).

That attitudes tend to firm up in adolescence and young adulthood has, of course, important implication for marketing along the lines of 'get-em young and get-em for life,' an aim exemplified very well by the quotation that opens Chapter 11.

EXPECTANCY-VALUE MODELS OF ATTITUDE AND BELIEF FORMATION

The most popular models of attitude formation towards an object, action, or event, are the expectancy-value models of attitude formation which are expressed as a summation of evaluations of each of several attributes of the object of the form:

$$\text{Attitude}, A = \sum_{i=1}^{n} e_i v_i \quad (4.1)$$

where e_i is the *expectancy* about the object for attribute i, that is its score on a simple scale as to the subjective probability or extent to which the object has this attribute, v_i is the *value* or 'evaluation' of the attribute on a similar scale, and n is the number of attributes considered (Eagly & Chaiken, 1993).

For example, a person is reasonably sure that a new soft drink Choke a Dope has nice taste and is trendy but considers that it is too expensive. Using scales of 0 to 10 for e_i and -10 to 10 for v_i he might thus rate the soft drink as follows:

Attribute 1 (taste): $e_1 = 5/10$, $v_1 = 7/10$

Attribute 2 (trendy): $e_2 = 6/10$, $v_2 = 5/10$

Attribute 3 (price): $e_3 = 10/10$, $v_3 = -5/10$

giving an attitude score

$$A = (5 \times 7 + 6 \times 5 + 10 \times -5)/100 = 15/100 = 0.15$$

whereas a 'moderately good' score in which 5/10 is given for each expectancy and value would yield $A = 0.75$, whilst a 'middling' score of zero for each rating v_i would, of course, yield $A = 0$.

In practice there might, of course, be many more attributes and, perhaps, we might average the score as $A = {}_{i=1}S^n\, e_i\, v_i\, /n$, giving 0.05 in the foregoing example, and such scores have been found to correlate well with attitudes assessed by evaluative semantic differential items (Eagly and Chaiken, 1993).

INFORMATION INTEGRATION MODELS OF ATTITUDE FORMATION

The information integration theory of attitude formation calculates the response to a series of stimuli i as

$$R = w_0\, s_0 + {}_{i=1}S^n\, w_i\, s_i \qquad (4.2)$$

where w_i and s_i are respectively the weight and scale of a person's attitude to a set of n items of information, and w_0 and s_0

are the weight and scale value of the person's initial attitude (Eagly & Chaiken, 1993).

Here the scale value of information is its location on the evaluative dimension and the weight is its *importance* or psychological impact in relation to the individual's judgment.

Simple summation models such as that of Eqn 4.2 emphasize the importance of using multiple 'selling points' in advertising.

If the sum of the weights is required to be one then the model becomes an averaging model, but averaging models are more generally expressed as

$$R = (w_0 s_0 + {}_{i=1}S^n w_i s_i)/(w_0 + {}_{i=1}S^n w_i) \qquad (4.3)$$

The initial attitude parameters w_0 and s_0 may in some instances, that of religion being perhaps the best example, represent 'intergenerational' attitudes acquired from a very early age from family and society at large.

Such initial attitudes, of course, may involve *prejudice*, for example ethnocentricity or racism, and, as history shows, such prejudices are often firmly rooted and perhaps could only be modelled by assigning them an exceptionally large weight.

More important in the modern consumer society, however, is social or imitative learning and in this context w_0 and s_0 represent initial attitude acquired by social learning from a peer or social group.

For example, a person believes that Christianity provides good moral codes (attribute 1) and that Christ did exist and provide a good exemplar of how we should live (attribute 2), but doubts that God really exists (attribute 3). Even if God did exist, however, in view of man's disastrous history he has a low evaluation of this last attribute, so that, using scales 0 to 10 for both w_i and s_i, he might thus rate Christianity as follows:

Attribute 0 (initial attitude):
$w_0 = 5$, $s_0 = 5/10$ (i.e. 'halfway' values)

Attribute 1 (morality): $w_1 = 8/10$, $s_1 = 8/10$

Attribute 2 (good life model): $w_2 = 8/10$, $s_2 = 8/10$

Attribute 3 (God): $w_3 = 2/10$, $s_3 = 1/10$

giving a response score

$$R = [(5 \times 5 + 8 \times 8 + 8 \times 8 + 2 \times 1)/100]/[(5 + 8 + 8 + 2)/10]$$
$$= [155/100]/[25/10] = 1.55/2.3 = 0.674$$

whereas a 'middling evaluation score' with 5/10 for both the weights and scale values for attributes 0-3 would give $1/2 = 0.5$.

In contrast to simple summation models such as Eqn 4.2, averaging models emphasize the need to have a limited number of effective selling points in advertising.

Set size effect can be demonstrated by assuming all weights = 1 and an initial attitude score of 50 on a scale of 0 to 100. Then if all further pieces of information have a score of 100 the resulting weighted average score for k additional attributes is

$$R = (50 + 100k)/(1 + k) \qquad (4.4)$$

giving the values 50, 75, 83.3, 87.5, . . . for 0, 1, 2, 3, . . . pieces of information, resulting in the hyperbola converging towards the asymptote $R = 100$ shown in Fig. 4.1.

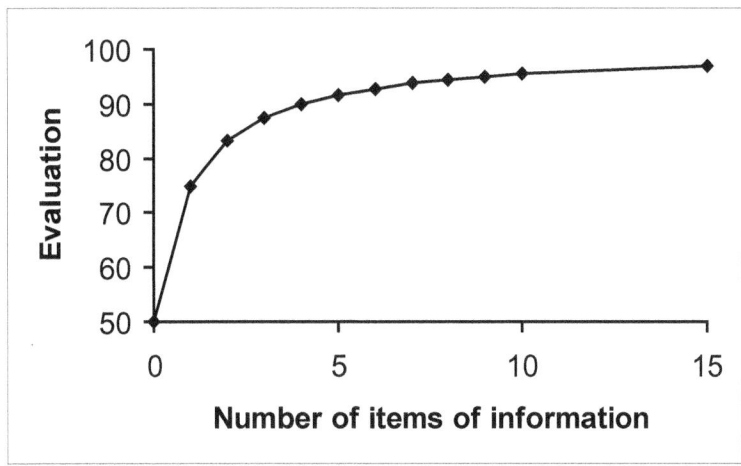

Figure 4.1. Theoretical set-size effect.

As might be expected, this hyperbolic result takes the same general shape as a learning curve, emphasizing that there is a diminishing return for each additional piece of information about a given subject, albeit with the unrealistic assumption that every piece of information has the same weight (w_i).

The *three hit theory* of advertising, namely that three consecutive ads are needed to make people aware of a product, its relevance, and its benefits, would give (with $k = 3$) $R = 87.5$ (on a scale 0 to 100) in Equation 4.4, or $R = 75$ if there is no initial attitude, i.e. $s_0 = 0$ so that the number 50 in the numerator is omitted.

This is a reasonably good result and, indeed, of some relevance, the present author often finds that it takes three goes to remember items of information, presumably because they were not retained in the short term memory register (see Figure 1.2) long enough in the first instance.

THREE-VALUE MODEL

A more general 'three-value' model is obtained by combining the expectancy-value and information integration models to obtain

$$R = b_0 w_0 s_0 + {}_{i=1}S^n b_i w_i s_i \qquad (4.5)$$

so that three ratings are associated with each attribute (Mohr, 2012a):

(1) A *belief* b_i or subjective probability or extent to which the object has the attribute (=e_i in Eqn 4.1).
(2) A *weight* or importance rating w_i (=w_i in Eqn 4.2).
(3) An evaluation or *scale value* s_i (=v_i in Eqn 4.1 and s_i in Eqn 4.2).

For example, a woman considers a dress that she has tried on in a ladies fashion shop is 'trendy' and her scores for this attribute might be

(1) $b_i = 7/10$ (she is fairly sure that it possesses this attribute).
(2) $w_i = 8/10$ (trendiness is quite important for a new dress).
(3) $s_i = 9/10$ (she rates it as very trendy).

Whilst a good deal more difficult to use in practice, this model does emphasize that it is sometimes desirable to consider both *belief* and *importance* considerations in assessing attitudes.

LOGICAL FORMATION OF ATTITUDES

McGuire (1960) proposed that people maintain beliefs that are connected by the rules of formal logic. Whilst most of our early attitude formation is via parents, education, peer groups, advertising, etc., it is at least sometimes true that we take 'time out' to think about things and may reassess an attitude, trying to do so in a logical way.

As a simple example consider a confectionery product with the three attributes T = tastes OK, N = looks nice, and P = price is OK, and a positive attitude to the product is denoted as A.

Using a little symbolic logic in which $\rightarrow$ mean 'implies', $\wedge$ means 'and', $-$ means 'not', and denoting A = attitude to the product is OK, we can write

$$\sim P \rightarrow \sim A$$

i.e. if the price is not OK then nor is attitude to it.

If $\vee$ means 'or' we might also write

$$(T \wedge P) \vee (N \wedge P) \rightarrow A$$

i.e. if taste and price are OK, or if the product looks nice and the price is OK, then attitude is OK.

The example is a little trivial, however, but no doubt we do indeed sometimes re-evaluate an attitude and use a little logic in doing so, but, generally, our attitudes are formed by the educational, imitative and information integration processes.

There is, however, scope for educators, religions, and advertisers to try and win us over with a little simple logic along the lines, for example, of: "You like to be comfortable so why not try - - -", an approach compatible with the cognitive consistency theory of attitude formation.

THE CONTACT HYPOTHESIS

Forbes (1977) proposed that ethnocentricity of different ethnic groups tended to be increased by cultural differences and (presumed negative) contact between them, expressing the ethnocentrism within two groups A and B as

$$E_a = a_1 C_t D_t \qquad (4.6a)$$
$$E_b = b_1 C_t D_t \qquad (4.6b)$$

where a_1 and b_1 are assumed to be positive, and are measures of the latent tendency of each group to respond ethnocentrically to each other, C_t is the amount of contact between the two groups at time t and D_t is the magnitude of the cultural differences between the two groups at time t.

He further proposed that the amount of contact and the cultural differences between the groups depended upon their proximity, incentives for contact such as trade, and upon the ethnocentrism of the groups, expressing this as

$$C_{t+1} = C_t (1 + g)/(1 + a_2 E_a + b_2 E_b) \qquad (4.7)$$
$$D_{t+1} = D_t (1 + a_3 E_a + b_3 E_b)/(1 + hC_t) \qquad (4.8)$$

where g is a factor that represents all the factors that determine growth or decline in contact other than the repulsive ethnocentrism and cultural differences of the two groups.

In equations 4.7 and 4.8 ethnocentricity decreases contact and increases cultural differences, as might be expected.

The denominator of the last equation ensures that cultural differences are reduced by contact so long as h is positive (the normal situation).

Contact theory has obvious application in marketing, PR and other activities involving persuasion, for example,

[1] It emphasizes that attitude changes with contact or, in general, information transfer, as we have already seen in Fig 4.1, for example.

If contact is 'positive', however, rather than negative as has generally been the case throughout man's sorry history, then equations 4.6 could be modified to reflect this by writing them in the form

$$E_{a,t+1} = E_{a,t} - a_1 C_t + a_4 D_t$$

where a_1 and a_4 are positive. Indeed, it might be hoped that the latter situation might be more likely in today's age of electronic communication and high speed travel. Moreover, it is in this situation that such equations might be applicable to advertising with E = 'resistance.'

[2] It reminds us that ethnic or 'local' considerations are important in international marketing of a product.
[3] It reminds us of the importance of targeting advertising towards an appropriate demographic for a product, and that cultural differences exist between teenagers and their parents and, more so, their grandparents.

MERE EXPOSURE RESEARCH

Persuasion studies on message repetition usually focus on the effects of repeated exposure to *information* about attitude objects. In a classic monograph Zajonc dealt merely with the objects themselves. Figure 4.2 illustrates the increase in attitude favourability with repeated exposure to three types of stimuli, showing a somewhat asymptotic behaviour similar to that of learning curves (Eagly & Chaiken, 1993).

This result is comparable to the size effect seen in Figure 4.1 insofar as increasing response is seen with increasing amounts

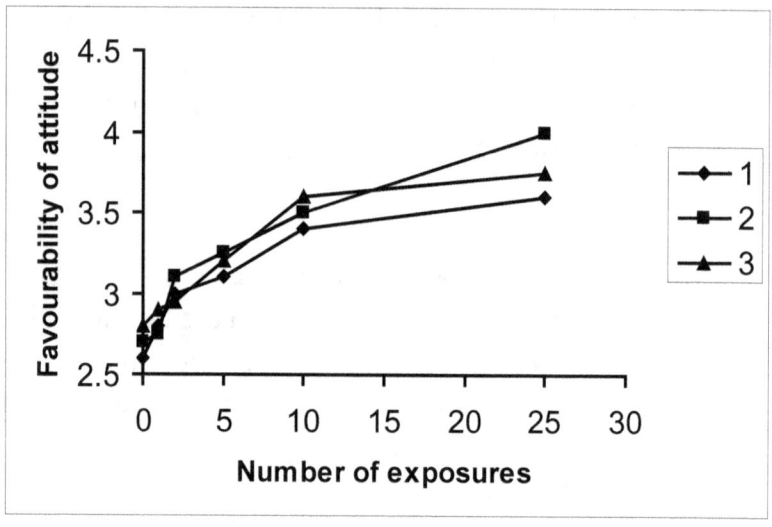

Figure 4.2. Increase in attitude favourability with increasing number of exposures to:
1. Turkish nonsense words.
2. Chinese-like characters. 3. Photographs.

of information, albeit repetition of the same information in the case of mere exposure.

Contact hypothesis, however, should be remembered here because it reminds us that oft repeated attempts at persuasion can also be irritating and result in negative attitudes, and some especially loud, haranguing radio and TV advertisements are good examples of this.

Implications of mere exposure in education are obvious, principally that students grow accustomed to new and perhaps difficult at first subjects, if not blasé about them, given time and repeated classroom exposure to them.

The latter observations might remind us that with repeated exposure we become accustomed to, if not hardened to, 'bad things' in life. For example, this is how children endure an excessive number of hours and years in classes and how adults endure jobs which may be, in reality, exceedingly tedious, arduous and boring.

It is also how, unfortunately, individuals become accustomed to essentially bad things such as cigarettes, alcohol, and drugs, perhaps in that order. This is, of course, good news for purveyors of such products.

MEASUREMENT OF ATTITUDES

One of the earliest methods of psychophysical scaling was Thurston's *method of equal-appearing intervals*. In this a panel of judges rates each of a set of attributes of an object (for example a new product) according to an ascending scale such as 0 - 10. Then the mean value of the ratings of all judges is the scale value of the attribute on the attitude dimension. For example, Table 4.1 shows the scale values that might be established for a new soft drink Choke a Dope.

Then for surveys, the mean of the scale values of the attributes selected by respondents is their assessment of an object. To obtain more reliable results attributes that are rated inconsistently by the judging panel are not used for surveys.

Likert's *method of summated ratings* was designed to be much easier to use than the method of equal-appearing intervals but to be at least as reliable. In this approach a large pool of items which are chosen intuitively for their relevance to the attitude object is used (Likert, 1961).

These items usually consist of statements of belief but statements about behaviours or affective reactions can also be used.

Table 4.1. Example scale values for new soft drink Choke a Dope.

Attribute	Value on scale 0 - 10
I don't like it.	0
It makes me feel ill.	1
It is very sweet and must have lots of sugar.	2
It has a nice colour.	3
The bottle looks nice.	4
My friends like it.	5
it is trendy.	6
The price is good.	7
It tastes nice.	8

Typically each item is presented to respondents in a multiple-choice format such as:

1. Strongly disagree.
2. Disagree.
3. Undecided.
4. Agree.
5. Strongly agree.

Then, for example, a survey on attitudes towards women might contain questions like:

(a) Swearing is more objectionable from a woman.
(b) Intoxication in women is worse than in men.

With scores from 1 - 5 given to each of perhaps a dozen or so such questions the total score is then obtained for each respondent.

Desirably an initial pool of items should be pilot tested on a group of people to eliminate ambiguous and non-discriminating items which tend to result in neutral responses. This can be done by examining the *item-total score correlations*, each of which correlates the respondents' scores on an item with their scores summed over all the items. Then a good item will have a positive correlation and better items have higher correlations.

Likert Scaling is widely used, for example to assess the response to political advertising campaigns, and a simple example of it is given in Chapter 12.

GUTTMAN SCALING

This approach gives stimulus-person scaling simultaneously and results in a matrix of data called the *Guttman scalogram*. For example, suppose we have five rods of from 5 to 7 feet in length (the exact lengths are not known) and ask each respondent to place a one in the Guttman scalogram matrix shown in Table 4.2 when they are taller than a

Table 4.2. Guttman scalogram.

Persons	Stimuli (rods)				
	C	E	B	D	A
2	1	1	1	1	0
4	0	1	0	1	0
3	1	1	0	1	0
6	0	0	0	0	0
5	0	1	0	0	0
1	1	1	1	1	1
*e.g. person 2 is taller than C, E, B, D but not A					

Table 4.3. Reordered Guttman scalogram.

Persons	Stimuli (rods)					Score
	A	B	C	D	E	
1	1	1	1	1	1	5
2	0	1	1	1	1	4
3	0	0	1	1	1	3
4	0	0	0	1	1	2
5	0	0	0	0	1	1
6	0	0	0	0	0	0

particular rod. This raw data is then reorganized to give the result in Table 4.3.

Table 4.3 is obtained by placing the column with least ones at the left, the column with the most ones at the right, and so on. Then the row with the maximum number of ones is placed at the top (this is for person '1' in our example and hence this is the tallest person) and that with the least ones is placed at the bottom.

The result is an upper diagonal matrix, as shown in Table 4.3, resulting in a score for each person shown on the right side in Table 4.3, this giving the ordinal ranking for each person.

The preceding example of Guttman scaling was for physical stimuli, when a perfect upper triangular matrix resulted. Generally, however, this is not the case when attitudinal stimuli are considered.

An example is Bogardus' social stimulus scale, illustrated in Table 4.4, in which respondents are asked to judge how closely they would relate to people of various nationalities or races.

Table 4.4. Bogardus' social stimulus scale.

	Acceptance level					
	Would marry	As a friend	Would give a job	Allow as citizen	OK as visitor	No contact
Armenians						
Bulgarians						
Canadians						
etc.						

Such attitudinal stimuli do not yield a perfect upper triangular matrix but it has been suggested that when about 90% of the non-zero entries do appear on or above the diagonal that this *coefficient of reproducibility* value is acceptable.

The Guttman scalogram has the advantage that the degree to which the reordered response matrix is 'triangularized' gives an immediate indication of the reliability of a survey. More complex to use, it is generally only usable for relatively small surveys, such as in-house surveys of consumer groups in advertising offices where it is an ideal tool.

CONCLUSION

Effective persuasion is all about changing attitude (where this, indeed, is necessary) so that some understanding of theories of attitude formation as cumulative or integrative processes is most important.

The later chapter on advertising (Chapter 11) discusses the important trio of cognitive, attitudinal, and behavioural responses and also McGuire's Reception-Yielding model of attitude formation, one that is particularly applicable in such contexts as advertising and religion.

Very relevant to attitude also is the vexatious question of ethnic conflict and, indeed, the equations of Forbes' contact hypothesis do emphasize that, over time, attitudes change. Moreover, models like that of contact hypothesis could be applied to the effects of advertising.

The results of mere exposure research compellingly indicate how attitudes to new stimuli tend to improve given repeated exposure to them, the bottom line being that it is by such means that we are reduced to consumer zombies from cradle to grave.

Finally, measurement of attitudes is, of course, especially important in many areas such as consumer and political campaign surveys. Though perhaps only applicable to relatively small surveys, the Guttman scalogram is useful because the degree of triangularization of the reordered response matrix gives an immediate indication of the accuracy of a survey.

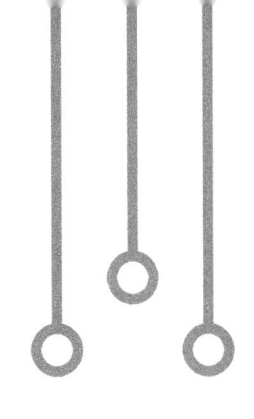

Chapter 5
RAISING A SMARTER CHILD

In the present writer's survey of Army recruits (Vernon, 1951), for example, the average I.Q. of those who were only children, or who had but one sibling, was about 106; but with each additional child sibling the figure declined till those from families of 13 and over averaged only 87.

Philip Vernon,
Intelligence and Attainment Tests (1960).

INTRODUCTION

As noted in the quotation above, having only one or two children makes them more likely to have a higher IQ, doubtless because of the greater resources and attention able to be given to the children.

Indeed, China's one child policy of the last couple of decades may be further proof of this because average intelligence in that part of Asia is now, at circa 100.25, slightly above that for the UK and USA, which have experienced declines over the last century (Vernon, 1960).

Man's population is also at least double what is sustainable with any degree of comfort (Mohr, 2012c), so having only one or two children is the only sensible course on that score.

In addition, care should always be taken in family planning, waiting until financial and emotional stability of the relationship is assured before having children.

It should also be noted that, as Lynn and Vanhaven (2002) point out, we have dysgenic fertility trends so that the least intelligent people have the most children.

Carlo Cipolla (1974) pointed out that our population growth graph went almost vertical with the coming of the industrial revolution and implored that what we needed was 'quality not quantity,' a phrase the first author recalls his fifth grade teacher Miss Bachelard repeating often.

In seeking a compatible partner intelligence is a key criterion. Then couples with higher intelligence might expect at least equally intelligent children, the desirable outcome.

Couples should also be aware of epigenetic marking before having children because traits such as obesity are passed on in that way. Thus it is also possible that traits such as exercising or thinking a lot might be passed on also.

ENRICHED LEARNING ENVIRONMENTS

Modern man is distinguished from other creatures by having a larger cerebral cortex, the centre for our thinking and language. This larger cortex must have evolved by the adaptive processes inherent in Darwin's theory of natural selection.

Clues to just how this occurred were given by the work of social psychologist David Krech and his group at UC Berkeley (Packard, 1978).

In this they provided a group of rats with an "enriched environment" of large cages with various things rats enjoy such as slides, wheels and the like. Then a maze with a sugar reward at the end was added. This had a dark and a lighted alley and the rats soon learnt which led to the sugar.

Then the maze lighting was reversed regularly so that the rats had to relearn the 'sugar route'.

A second control group of rats lived normally and a third group was kept in a deprived dark and noiseless area.

After 90 days it was found that the 'enriched' rats had developed thicker cerebral cortexes!

This was perhaps the first evidence that the brain is modified by experience. The enrichment conditions caused the following changes (Atrens and Curthoys, 1982):

[1] The size of the cerebral cortex was increased.
[2] The size of the cortical neurons increased.
[3] The size and number of synaptic contacts increased.
[4] The quantity of acetylcholinesterase, the compound responsible for breakdown of the neurotransmitter acetylcholine, increased.

Therefore, the rats which had experienced environmental enrichment were apparently anatomically and biochemically superior to those which had endured a deprived environment.

This 'rats result' provided laboratory evidence that environmental enrichment could physically and chemically alter the brain. This ability of neural tissue to change because of its activation is called *plasticity*.

It seems likely, therefore, that as early man discovered fire, began to make tools and advanced in many other ways his brain gradually evolved into that of *homo sapiens sapiens* or modern man.

The 'rats result' also provided laboratory evidence that environmental enrichment might be able to reverse the deficiencies in brain development resulting from an environmentally deprived childhood.

The conclusion, of course, is that, just as physical exercise is good for your body, mental exercise helps develop the brain, perhaps in synergy with an enriched physical environment that includes physical activities involving some intelligence and skill.

Maria Montessori provided evidence that an enriched environment accelerates human learning ability by taking poor children in Rome and placing them in stimulating classrooms with many interesting puzzles and objects to work with. The children were reading enthusiastically by three or four and were well into geometry by five or six.

If follows that the investment of a modest amount of money in setting up and equipping a personal learning centre for a child might be a wise one.

Increasingly the child will have learnt to spend time in this engaged in learning activities such as looking at picture books, drawing, learning to write, and so on.

Parents should also have made a point of not only supervising this important activity at least intermittently but also joining in for a substantial session of one-on-one instruction.

By now the child is capable of discussing its problems and progress and asking questions that might help solve problems and assist progress. Therefore, the parent should make a point of allowing a time period of at least several minutes every few days in which to talk with the child in this way.

The importance of the home environment was emphasized in a study by Bradley and Caldwell (1967) in which an inventory of favourable factors in the home was compared to the results from a test of the infant's development:

A group of 77 normal children was given an infant development test and a home assessment inventory at age 6 months, and the Stanford-Binet at age 3 years.

It was found that the home inventory predicted IQ at age 3 better than the infants' own mental development at 6 months!

Children with increasing scores had mothers who were involved with them and provided appropriate play materials; those with decreasing scores tended to live in homes where material things and daily events were disorganized.

Much of the correlation between home environment and IQ development can be ascribed to heredity but a study by Skodal and Skeels (1949) showed that improved environment increased children's IQs by an average of 20 points above that of their mothers.

EARLY BRAIN DEVELOPMENT

Rapid early brain development was discussed in Chapter Two and the effect of enriched environment was discussed in the foregoing section. It follows that the first few years of a child's life provide a 'window of opportunity' to increase its intelligence greatly and give it a head start in life.

To do this one should:

[1] Create an *enriched learning environment*, carefully placing intellectually stimulating pictures, toys and books in the child's bedroom as well as in a corner of a family room such as a lounge or meals area. These areas should then be used for educational activities such as learning the alphabet and numbers, initially, of course, guided by a parent who should encourage the child to indulge in learning activities on their own, for example forming words using a 'plastic alphabet.'

[2] Use encouraging language and attitudes to enhance learning. Research has shown that children who are treated affectionately make more myelin and thus have higher IQ, and this can be related to the well-known *teacher expectancy effect* in which children who do better in class get better marks and praise, encouraging them to do even better.

[3] Provide brain-enhancing nutrition. For example, DHA (docosahexaenoic acid) is found in the placenta and in breast milk, and is best for building myelin. DHA is an omega-3 long-chain polyunsaturated fat that makes up as much as 25% of the fat in the brain, and is added to most infant formulas. Indeed, incidence of ADHD has been found to be much greater in children with lower blood levels of DHA (Perlmutter & Colman, 2006).

After infancy, omega-3 fish oil, along with a children's multivitamin tablet are useful supplements for young children.

As discussed in the following section, antioxidants have been found to improve IQ in the young and thus are also recommended.

[4] Avoid dietary excitotoxins, chemicals added to food that overly stimulate the brain, causing surges in brain activity that may harm healthy cells. Hyperactive children are especially susceptible to the effects of excitotoxins. The most damaging chemicals that should be avoided include:
  (a) Aspartame, an artificial sweetener (NutraSweet).
  (b) MSG (monosodium glutamate), used in many processed foods and also in Asian cooking.
  (c) Hydrolyzed vegetable protein, used as a flavouring agent and a filler in processed foods.

[5] Implement a program of 'IQ building' activities, noting that IQ tests include questions testing verbal, spatial and numerical ability. If a child has a problem with numbers, for example, early detection and correction of this will prevent far greater problems later.

These activities IQ building activities should include:
  (a) Board games.
  (b) Puzzles.
  (c) 'Intelligent' electronic games on 'toyshop PCs'.
  (d) Writing exercises, gradually building these from very short sentences to longer ones.
  (e) Maths exercises, beginning with counting and moving on to addition and subtraction, and then multiplication and division.

[5] Limit TV. Between the ages of 1 and 3 there is a strong correlation between the amount of TV viewing and the risk of ADHD (Perlmutter & Colman, 2006).

[6] As discussed in a following section, by the second year they should be involved in small learning groups supervised by a specialist teacher so that they can begin real learning.

[7] In the third year they should begin kindergarten for at least a couple of days a week and these learning efforts should continue. By now they have a modest vocabulary and are capable of *cognitive learning* which processes and stores *abstract* information.

[8] As soon as possible get the child interested in music. At first this might be soothing 'relaxation music' to help the infant child sleep, later moving on to children's music related to nursery rhymes such as 'London Bridge is falling down', and before too long to classical music such as Mozart of Beethoven to try and instil a lifelong interest in 'halfway intelligent' music before the child is overwhelmed by 'pop music', much of which is trivial and performed in a ridiculous, if not quite insane, screaming fashion.

ANTIOXIDANTS TO IMPROVE IQ IN THE YOUNG

Dr A.C. Kubala et. al. divided 351 students into two groups, those with higher, and those with lower vitamin C levels. Those with higher C levels were 4.5 points higher in IQ (Holford, 2009).

In another study, Patrick Holford, Stephen Schoenhaler, John Yudkin, Hans Eysenck and Linus Pauling gave 30 children a special multivitamin and mineral supplement and 30 others a placebo.

After 8 months the supplement children's average non-verbal IQ[2] was 10 points higher, with some children being up to 20 points higher. Several other studies have had similar findings.

Another study of 200 teenagers in Dakota found that 20 mg (but not 10mg, the RDI being 7 mg) of zinc increased memory accuracy and attention spans (Holford & Colson, 2008).

Contrastingly, MIT researchers found that children with diets high in refined carbohydrates such as sugar, white bread and sweets, had IQ up to 25 points lower (Schauss, 1983).

Some of the studies that have made such findings have sometimes included infants, improved IQ from diet improvements showing up a few years down the track. Thus, pregnant women would be wise to ensure that their diets are as healthy as possible and include some of the key nutrients discussed in this chapter.

As might be expected, therefore, a healthy diet with appropriate vitamin and mineral supplements will also help reduce age-related memory loss.

SMALL LEARNING GROUPS

Packard (1978) raised the interesting possibility of the use of professional people to teach by modelling.

These people would be trained to know the periods during which learning of various areas of knowledge can best be

---

[2]Non-verbal IQ is more fluid and susceptible to brain chemistry, while the verbal IQ is more influenced by teaching.

commenced, and in how best to use modelling techniques to initiate that learning. Such people would then visit the home or attend play group sessions.

Packard noted that an experiment with a form of group modelling was undertaken at New York Medical College. This began with twenty pairs of mothers and babies when the babies were only four weeks old and lasted three years at the end of which the children were compared with those of a control group.

The children in the experimental group were a good deal more advanced in language and other skills than the control group.

Indeed, some experts doubt the competence of the modern family for child rearing and believe that more professional efforts are essential to help develop emotional stability and intellectual development in infants.

As an example of this, Weiss and Mann (1978) refer to a project in Milwaukee that found that children given more attention by the mother or a specially trained teacher, showed markedly higher IQ.

TWO HEADS ARE BETTER THAN ONE

It is, of course, better when both parents take an active part in a child's home learning. Having two teachers 'on the same page' about everything taught will, of course, reinforce the child's learning efforts.

In addition, variation from a woman's softer touch to a man's perhaps more goal-oriented approach can help with progression through longer learning tasks.

It has been found that correlation of intelligence with parent's occupation is slightly less then that for genes (Vernon, 1960), there being, of course, a correlation between occupations and intelligence in any case.

More important, regardless of a parent's occupation, if one of their roles is active teaching of the child that may have a far more important bearing on the child's IQ development than the parent's occupation outside the home.

A sound routine for home learning should be established, perhaps involving a combination of day care or learning groups and home sessions once or twice a day and of duration ranging from half an hour to an hour, depending on the child's age.

ENHANCING THE LEARNING PROCESS

The home learning process can be enhanced by such means as the 'Superlearning' recommended by Ostrander and Schroeder (1979). This involves encouraging physical and psychological relaxation with quite background music, slow breathing exercises, and visualizing nice scenes to achieve a reflective and receptive frame of mind.

Then the child is encouraged to affirm: "I can do it."

Here, developing a positive attitude is comparable to the 'teacher expectancy effect' where it is found that students who already get good marks are encouraged to do even better by a combination of the positive results, the confidence they obtain from these, and the 'expectation' and confidence the teacher shows about their ability. Here 'hope' plays an important part, and students who become accustomed to getting low marks tend to lose hope, and without hope, of course, life is much less bearable.

With the scene set, the parent/teacher reads the material aloud at a careful pace while the child reads it silently. This is repeated again with quiet background music and the child is then tested on the material.

HOME SCHOOLING

In the USA home schooling has increased markedly in recent decades. The number of home-schooled children grew from just a few thousand in the early 1970s to 1.1 million in 2003, having increased 30% between 1999 and 2003 (Penn, 2007).

In 2000, only 52 percent of colleges had formal admission policies for home-schooled students, but by 2005 85% did, in that year a study showing that home-schooled students scored 81 points higher than the national average on the SAT (Penn, 2007).

Though home-schooled children were only 2% of school-age children, they were 12% of the students in the National Spelling Bee and in three out of seven years a home-schooled child won the National Geography Bee (Penn, 2007).

In 2001, a home-schooled boy from Montana completed high school at 15. Not feeling ready for college, he wrote the novel *Eragon* which become a best-seller and was released as a movie in 2006 (Penn, 2007).

Certainly, therefore, children taught well at both home and school should do better!

The author remembers a little rainy Sunday afternoon home instruction and thus, for example, being able to count to 100 at age 4. By age 9 and in grade 4 he was equal top of the class in arithmetic and did fairly well thereafter, finishing school and his first degree with first class honours.

He also remembers going to an expensive private school where there was far too much emphasis on extra-curricular activities, in part to impress upon the parents that they were getting their money's worth, but that he would have preferred more freedom to develop his own lifestyle.

In addition, as always at school, if not University, there is total reliance on rote learning of standard academic material, and little or no instruction on life skills, for example how to deal with such issues as sex, bullying, smoking, and booze (to which list one would now add drugs, of course).

Teenagers should also be taught how to decide as soon as possible upon a realistically achievable career goal and advised on how to achieve it. They should also be instructed how to survive in the workplace, for example how to deal with bullying workmates or bosses.

MORE ADVANCED HOME LEARNING

The 'early learning' areas discussed above should be increased in level, moving from toys to more advanced books, puzzles and games, and perhaps including a PC with language and maths programs designed for the age of the child.

At circa 10 or 11 it should be possible to introduce a child to simple algebra, for example:

$$x = 4$$
$$y = 2$$
$$x + y = ?$$

$$x \times y = ?$$
$$x/y = ?$$

At age circa 12 or 13 it should be possible to introduce a child to simple calculus, for example:

(a) A car has travelled distance x_1 at time t_1, and distance x_2 at time t_2, so the average speed during that time interval is:

$$\delta x/\delta t = (x_2 - x_1)/(t_2 - t_1).$$

(b) At any time during this journey the speed is calculated as:

$$s = dx/dt = \text{the limit of } \delta x/\delta t \text{ as } \delta t \text{ approaches zero}$$

Then if x is a function of time it can be expressed as

$x = a + bt + ct^2$, where a, b and c are constants.

Then we *differentiate* this function with respect to t to obtain:

$$s = dx/dt = b + 2ct$$

so that the speed is increasing linearly with time.
Then the acceleration is calculated as:

$$A = d^2x/dt^2 = ds/dt = 2c$$

Then, without rushing it too much, *integration* should be taught to calculate (for example) areas.

ABILITY DIFFERENCES BETWEEN MEN AND WOMEN

As we evolved as hunter-gatherers and thus with men and women having somewhat different roles it follows that men and women must have developed and passed on through the generations somewhat different skill levels for various activities.

For example, the men being the hunters were stronger and developed greater aggression needed for hunting.

Women, on the other hand, were largely responsible for child rearing, pretty much a full-time job when little was known about preventing conception. Thus women had many children but because child mortality rates were very high relatively few of them survived to adulthood. Raising children, of course, involves a very different skill set indeed from that of hunting.

With the Agricultural Revolution new and increasingly diverse occupations emerged and men, of course, took up these and all but a few women were still left with the task of caring for a family.

It was thus men who developed philosophy, arts, science and technology and built towns and cities, all too often fighting wars to defend them against advancing armies directed by power-hungry rulers.

Less than three hundred years ago the Industrial Revolution began, bringing with it machines and factories that greatly changed lifestyles. Again, all the inventions that came with the Industrial Revolution were made by men.

Advanced education was then required to train people for new occupations in society such as law, medicine and engineering. Almost invariably this was for men, of course, though, no doubt because of their traditional caring role with families, it was always women that were apprenticed as nurses and midwives.

So it was that, only about a hundred years ago, Cambridge University only had male academic staff and students.

Some part of all this evolutionary history must have been passed on in the differing DNA for men and women. In addition, just as epigenic marking passes on traits such as obesity, so to it must be able to pass on traits such as higher level thinking and the like.

Morgan et al. (1979) conclude on differences between men and women:

[1] "Girls excel in verbal ability." "Group differences average about 4 points on a verbal IQ measure."
[2] "Boys excel in visual-spatial ability. This superiority appears consistently in adolescence and adulthood, not earlier, and reaches an average level of about 6 points on an IQ-like measure."
[3] "Boys excel in mathematical ability." "It averages somewhat less than the difference in spatial ability and may be related to it."
[4] "Males are more aggressive. This sex difference has been observed in many lower species as well as most, if not all, human cultures. It can be observed very early, as soon as social play begins. Most male aggression is directed toward other males."

Thus Vernon (1960) observed that:

There are, it should be noted, considerable sex differences, female being relatively superior in spelling and inferior in arithmetic [results for 15-year olds]. *Many surveys of intelligence and attainments have also demonstrated that the range or spread of ability (as distinct from the average performance) is slightly more restricted in girls.*

Consistent with this, Mackintosh (2011) notes that a meta-analysis of studies of differences in maths performance between men and women concluded that men were 'more variable' than women but obtained higher average scores on maths tests. He concludes, however, that:

(a) "The two sexes do not differ consistently in average IQ (different test batteries can show male advantage, female advantage, or no difference) and that conclusion is not simply an artefact of any deliberate policy by IQ testers to eliminate items that favour one sex or another."

(b) "But males and females do differ reliably in certain components of IQ – the most salient of these differences being that men outscore women on most tests of spatial ability, while women outscore men on tests of perceptual speed and short-term memory."

CONCLUSION

Children's brains develop most rapidly in the earliest years and maximum advantage should be taken of this by teaching them as much as possible at home. To that end a child should have a personal learning centre reflective of the Montessori tradition and both parents should take part in routine educational sessions. In these it is best to encourage and teach a child to rise above the expected level of learning for their age by, for example, teaching them simple maths at an early age.

The first author recalls an example of this, a boy he went to school with from years 9 to 12. This boy must have had special instruction from an early age because he was precocious in maths to the point of studying year 12 maths while in year 8. Not surprisingly, he went on to be a Professor of Mathematics.

In addition, it is best to have the child join learning groups at least occasionally, perhaps run by an educator trained for the purpose. Failing that, friends and neighbours with children of the same age group can be found to help run regular 'play and learn' sessions.

Noting that studies have found that schools have only about a 30% influence over a child's learning, and the success of home schooling in the USA, some degree of home schooling is worth considering, whilst minimizing the distance children have to travel to school is also worthwhile where possible.

Whilst getting a child used to a PC early on is worthwhile, try, however, to prevent children becoming addicted to PC games without any educational benefit, particularly noisy war games and the like. Similarly, try and discourage excessive use of mobile phones and the Internet, encouraging limited use of the latter for educational information purposes only, and not for pointless browsing and 'tweets' etcetera.

Note that sound diet and appropriate supplementation can help increase IQ, a recent study in Finland of children in grades 1,2 and 3 finding that those who ate fruit, vegetables, fish and whole grains did far better in standardized tests than those with poor diets.

Studies have found correlations between IQ scores and formal tests of reading, mathematics or other subjects (including graded school exams) range from 0.40 to 0.70 (Mackintosh, 2011).

Finally, note that when a group of children are given an assignment or test of significant length, the more intelligent children will finish it faster, of course, speeding up as they get near the end, whilst the less intelligent children will tend to slow down towards the end of the test. When the test is marked, therefore, the more intelligent will have completed it much more quickly and will also have obtained higher marks.

Chapter 6
REAL IQ

Nutrition, hormones, blood circulation, and myriad other variables influence the activity of brain genes, and all are sensitive to genetic inheritance and to environmental variables.
Lynch G, Granger R, *Big Brain, The Origins and Future of Human Intelligence,* Palgrave Macmillan, Houndmills, Basingstoke (2008).

Genius is one percent inspiration and ninety-nine percent perspiration.
Thomas A. Edison, newspaper interview quoted in *Golden Book,* April 1931.

BIOLOGY

Study of the biology of earth's many life forms has gone on for several hundred years. Perhaps the greatest breakthrough was the discovery and modelling of DNA (deoxyribonucleic acid), a large biochemical that had first been isolated in 1871.

The Canadian physician Oswald Avery proved in 1944 that DNA affects hereditary traits. Previously the general consensus was that proteins carried the hereditary information that cells need to split off from others and grow.

In February 1951 Linus Pauling published a paper in which he demonstrated the helical structure of proteins and proposed that this might be common to many large and complex molecules in nature. In 1953 American biochemist James Watson and British biophysicist Francis Crick proposed the double helix structure of DNA (White, 2002).

This great step in biology was important in the understanding of human heredity and disease. It is also particularly helpful in the difficult task of unravelling the complexities of cancer, a process involving cells with mutations 'outgrowing' ordinary cells.

BIOCHEMICAL LEARNING AND EVOLUTION

Two further research results indicative of the biochemical nature of learning processes have been obtained:

(a) The work by George Ungar's group (Ungar et al., 1972) in which peptides in rats conditioned to shun darkness were isolated. These peptides seemed able to transfer the conditioning to other rats. [Peptides are small organic molecules that link hundreds or even thousands of amino acid molecules together to form polypeptides].

(b) Changes in RNA in rats given a learning task found by Hyden's group in Sweden (Rosenfeld, 1972).

Hyden's group also found an increase in a brain-specific protein S-100 in rats trained to use their non-preferred paw. They then found that an antiserum to S-100 stopped this learning.

Subsequently much further work has been done to investigate the effects of inhibition of protein and RNA synthesis by antibiotics upon memory. One finding was that drugs that interfere with the uptake of amino acids by cells can selectively interfere with memory retrieval or formation.

Proteins are naturally occurring polypeptides.

Genes are nucleoproteins formed by combination of polypeptide and DNA (deoxyribonucleic acid) chains.

The process of cell reproduction or *mitosis* occurs when the two strands of the DNA double helix separate and manufacture protein and a new 'opposite' strand to form a new cell.

This process is assisted by RNA (ribonucleic acid).

If learning changes RNA then perhaps a process like the cell mutation that causes cancer (Weinberg, 1999) might also be responsible for human evolution, both physically (Selmes, 1974) and mentally (Darwin, 1999).

Cell mutation is the result of a DNA copying error. This may just be a statistical fluke, having a probability of one in a million or less.

A ground breaking case study of the mutation process was the *ras oncogene* found in a smoker with bladder cancer (Weinberg, 1999).

After 30 years of smoking, some of the many highly toxic carcinogens he had inhaled had not been detoxified in his liver and had passed into his urine.

The ras oncogene is 5000 DNA bases long but one base was incorrect where a sequence that should have been GCC GGC GGT was instead GCC GTC GGT with just one base incorrect, a T appearing instead of a G in the middle of this mutated 'string'.

The incorrect gene then governed the growth of this cell and its descendants, resulting in a cancer tumour years later.

It might be possible that, over time, gradual development of language 'enriched' our mental environment and produced lasting changes in human RNA and thence DNA that resulted in the evolution of our larger cerebral cortexes.

That we have a comparatively large brain size, therefore, might indeed be the evolutionary result of sometimes vicarious thinking over millennia, as often assumed.

ENRICHED ENVIRONMENTS

There have been many attempts to build better brains through breeding. Selective mating studies in the 1930s produced rats with better scores on maze tests, and at first these were assumed to be a result of genetic modification. It was then found that just putting rats in a complex environment for a few weeks produced similar effects (Lynch & Granger, 2008).

The classical rat environment experiment was that of Krech referred to in the last chapter (Packard, 1978).

According to Lynch and Granger (2008):

"Nutrition, hormones, blood circulation, and myriad other variables influence the activity of brain genes, and all are sensitive to genetic inheritance and to environmental variables."

INTELLIGENCE QUOTIENT (IQ)

Francis Galton (1822-1911), a cousin of Charles Darwin, proposed that human intelligence was inherited and developed a system of measurement based on physical attributes such as reaction time and skin sensitivity, but because it did not measure cognitive skills it was soon rejected (Craughwell, 2012).

Later, however, Galton became preoccupied with the importance of 'nature and nurture', a phrase he borrowed from Shakespeare's *The Tempest* (Mackintosh, 2011).

In France, asked by the French government to do so, Alfred Binet (1857-1911) and his colleague Theodore Simon developed the first IQ test using questions that tested a child's attention span, recall capability, and problem solving skills. In 1916, Stanford University psychologist Lewis Terman "tweaked" the Binet-Simon test to create the Stanford-Binet Intelligence Scale. In this, IQ is defined as a person's mental age score on an 'intelligence test' divided by their chronological age, the resulting fraction being multiplied by 100 to obtain the IQ score (Craughwell, 2012).

In the 1930s American psychologist, David Wechsler, developed three IQ tests: the Weschler Intelligence Scale for Children (WISC), the Weschler Preschool and Primary Scale of Intelligence (WPPSI), and the Weschler Adult Intelligence Scale (WAIS). These test results are compared to the results of other test takers in the same age group, and follow a Normal distribution with a median score of 100, with two-thirds of population scores being between 85 and 115, circa 5 percent above 125, and 5 percent below 75.

MULTIPLE IQ TESTS

Differential aptitude tests (DAT) for verbal, numerical and 'abstract/figural' IQ are preferable, the final IQ being an average of these. Figural tests might take the form of Raven's matrices which typically show 3 rows of 3 simple diagrams with the last diagram omitted, followed by several diagrams, one of which is the correct one to 'complete' the 3X3 matrix (Mackintosh, 2011).

IQ BUILDING

Measurable intelligence or IQ becomes meaningful by the age of four so that before that some effort should be made to 'build IQ' to give the child a head start.

The subject of IQ is sometimes controversial, particularly concerning differences in racial intelligence, but most experts consider that socioeconomic and cultural disadvantages are the main cause of any such differences.

Opinions also differ on what IQ tests really measure, some believing that they simply provide a measure of prior education. Binet, however, originally devised his classical test to measure the causes of learning retardation in public school pupils with a view to providing special classes for slow learners.

To help ensure that young children get a head start some conscious attempt should be made to 'build' their IQ at the age of three, if not before.

Most parents are well meaning and, at the outset at least, many imagine what prodigies their children perhaps are.

The very same parents, however, are those most likely to spoil the child with generosity and he or she may become a stubborn child and a less than good learner because of it.

It is for this reason that input from other parents, for example in play groups, and from professionals, for example in kindergartens, is important.

As for building IQ, the present authors believe one obvious step that can be taken is to note the questions in typical IQ tests, for example the Weschler Preschool and Primary Scale of Intelligence (WPPSI), example questions for which can easily be found on the Internet.

Then care can be taken to ensure that the child is taught the simple object identification and number and word recognition exercises it should be capable of at age three.

By way of example, here are a few examples of questions from Binet's intelligence test:

How old are you?
What are the names of these four colours?
Hand me five blocks from that pile.
What is the opposite of the word large?
Which one of these objects is different from the rest?
Point to your nose?

These are quite simple and the point is that a teacher can devise their own test and, as Binet set as a criterion, if on average students in the class can answer 75% of the questions, the test is representative of the norm for that age group.

Figure 6.1 shows an example Weschler Preschool and Primary Scale of Intelligence question. Again, this is quite simple.

Whether they measure learning or intelligence, or perhaps both, IQ test results generally correspond fairly well with the academic performance of children at school.

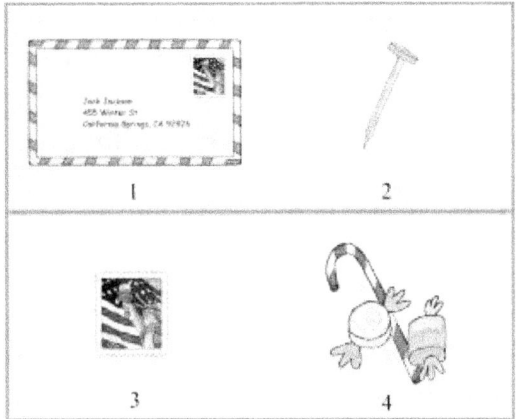

Figure 6.1. Pre-K to Kindergarten WPPSI question: *Which two pictures show the same thing?* [We have improved/simplified the original question. GAM]

Note too that separate IQ tests are available for verbal, spatial, and numerical ability and these tell more about an individual than just a single IQ score.

Therefore, any small learning difficulty identified by an early IQ test can probably be remedied quickly, avoiding much greater difficulties further down the educational track.

In addition, such tests provide an opportunity to observe other aspects of performance such as motivation, persistence or maladaptive behaviours.

Remember too the vivid example given in the last chapter of Krech's rats with an enriched environment being found to have developed larger cerebral cortexes, a result which strongly supports Weiss and Mann's view (1978):

> *Even if we assume that IQ tests measure something like intelligence, we have to recognize that, like*

many other variable traits, intelligence is very much influenced by the environment.

There is a strong incentive, therefore, for parents to ensure that a child has at least a modestly endowed personal learning centre.

EXAMPLE IQ TEST

In each question a missing number is to be deduced according to some logical arithmetic operation or sequence. In these example questions the answers are the numbers following a question mark and underlined (Mohr, 1995). The test the time allowed for these 10 questions would be circa 8 - 10 minutes.

Find the missing numbers:

[1] 6   7   9   13   21   ?<u>37</u>

[2] 447 (386)   254
     262 (?<u>518</u>) 521

[3] 4   7   9   11   14   15   19   ?<u>19</u>

[4] 2   10   6
     3   9   3
     1   3   ?<u>1</u>

[5]
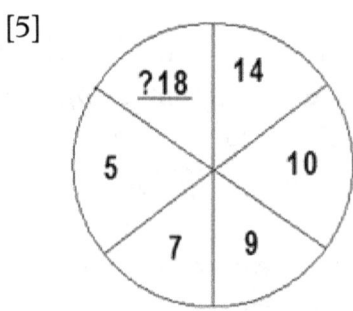

[6] 279   242   205   168   ?131
[7] 13   (78) 12
     11   (?55) 10
[8] 126   62   30   14   ?6
[9] 7   1   2
     5   4   1
     3   2   ?5
[10]

```
   ?152 | 2
  7 3   |   6
   34   | 15
```

KEYS TO ANSWERS:

[1] The increments double.
[2] Middle number is twice the difference of the others.
[3] Alternate sequences (+3, +2, +1, +0) and (+2, +3, +4).
[4] 3rd # in row = 2nd - 2 × 1st.
[5] Diagonally opposite number is double.
[6] Decrements of -37.
[7] Middle number is half the product of the others.
[8] Next # = half x last # -1
[9] Sum of rows = 10
[10] Going around next # = 2 x last + 2 (then + 3, + 4 etc.).

If the scoring system for Craughwell's 10 item tests is used then 16.5 points are given for each correct answer, ratings for various scores then being (Craughwell, 2012):

165 Genius
148-132 Gifted/superior intelligence
115 Higher than usual intelligence
99 Average intelligence
83 Low average intelligence
70 or below, very low intelligence

For more on IQ tests, for example the SAT test, and 'types' of intelligence (e.g. "Gardner's Eight Intelligences") see *In Search of the Human Mind* (Sternberg, 1998).

REAL IQ

Intelligence is part inherited and part developed thereafter by learning and experience, often referred to as 'nature and nurture'. It is claimed that IQ tests are "a standardized examination devised to measure human intelligence as distinct from attainments" (Carter, 2007), but many argue that they largely measure learning, not innate intelligence.

It is generally assumed that our IQ peaks at the age of 18, about when 'developmental' school education is finished in advanced countries. Studies then show that verbal IQ remains relatively stable thereafter, whereas 'performance IQ' (on puzzles and problems, sometimes with bonus marks for rapid answers) reduces considerably with aging (Mackintosh, 2011).

We contend that further education and study in later life should be able to increase IQ so we propose a *real IQ* calculated for those over 18 as

Real IQ = IQ(18) − a(disease/injuries)
+ b(years of learning since 18)
+ c(creativity) − d[(age −18) if over 18]

Here IQ(18) is that one develops, all going OK, by age 18 as a result of hereditary factors and education and 'a', 'b', 'c' and 'd' are constants.

These constants have the following roles:

(a) 'a' is a constant to calculate reduction in IQ resulting from any disease or injuries acquired later which affect the brain, including Alzheimer's disease and psychiatric conditions such as depression.[3]
(b) 'b' is a constant, perhaps circa 0.25, for the effect of learning after the age of 18.
(c) 'c' is a constant for creativity, perhaps circa 1 − 2 if creativity is measured on a scale of 1 to 10.
(d) 'd' is a constant for normal decline in intelligence with aging, perhaps about half the value of the constant 'b'.

In the terms involving the factors 'b' and 'd' the notion of 'use it or lose it' is considered, that is, learning doing intelligent things should help further increase one's intelligence, just as doing more exercise should help strengthen one's muscles.

---

[3] In contrast to depression, note that positive attitudes may improve real intelligence, an example being the 'teacher expectancy effect'.

Taking a hypothetical example, a top of the class student at 18 might have IQ = 140 at that age but one can increase this with further learning by studying, say, for 5 years, at which point the persons real IQ can be estimated as RIQ = 140 + 0.25(5) − 0.125(5) = 140.625.

This is only a small increase, but at least it is not the usual decline.

Then if this person goes into serious research, is careful with diet etc., as discussed in Chapter 5, then at age 48 the calculation becomes:

$$RIQ = 140 + 30(0.25) - 30(0.125) = 143.75$$

which is a modest but worthwhile improvement.

Creativity is obviously an important factor because if one has considerable ability, but no inclination to put it to tangible use, then one cannot be seen as having much real intelligence.

Whether creativity is, to any extent, in one's genes is debatable, but probably it is mostly a learnt trait, but one that relates to intelligence. In other words, without much ability to create, or intelligence, one is not likely to be very creative.

The foregoing simple equation should, indeed, encourage people to indulge in vicarious learning, surely the best kind because usually people are able to tackle subjects that genuinely interest them with more enthusiasm. In addition, being free to choose when and how one studies may improve results, of course, as this is far less painful than the all too many years spent listening to teachers regurgitate material from text books they have relatively little understanding of.

In our view, it also helps explain how people like Leonardo da Vinci and Isaac Newton, despite having only had very basic schooling, could achieve so much, namely because they did all the work themselves, whereas now most academics have research student slaves, effectively an apprenticeship historically (Mohr, 2012a), to work on often silly topics they dream up.

Finally, an example of the great 'plasticity' of the brain was a US woman, Michelle Mack, who was found when well into her twenties to have been born with nearly all the left side of her brain missing. Nevertheless, her brain having 'rewired' itself, she had "fairly normal language abilities" and only relatively minor difficulty in coping with abstract concepts and visual-spatial processing.

GENETIC FACTORS

Genetic defects can, of course affect coefficient a of the foregoing formula for Real IQ, for example Fragile X and Down's syndromes, and degrees of mental retardation can fall into four classes:

- Mild.
- Moderate.
- Severe.
- Profound.

Then there are external influences such as malnutrition, lead poisoning and foetal alcohol syndrome, to name just a few. Depressive illnesses, even being slave to a lousy, bullying boss could also be a factor.

What is needed for best results, whether in the home, school or workplace, is an 'enriched environment' and positive attitudes and encouragement to obtain better results, and rewards at least occasionally when better results are obtained.

Finally, as noted in Chapters 5 and 15, such substances as lecithin, magnesium fish oils, zinc, and vitamins A, B-group, C, D and E are helpful in improving brain function, especially in the very young and the very old (Holford & Colson, 2008).

☺☻☹☺☻☹☺☻☹☺☻☹☺☻☹

Chapter 7
PSYCHOLOGY AND PSYCHIATRY

Starting in the late 1950s and early '60s, the psychoanalysts set out to convince the public that we were 'all' walking wounded, normal neurotics, functioning psychotics ... and that Freud's teachings contained the secrets to eradicating inner strife and reaching our full potential.

Jeffrey A. Lieberman, *Shrinks,
The Untold Story of Psychiatry,*
Little, Brown & Co., NY (2015).

PSYCHIATRY

Sigmund Freud (1865 - 1939) developed what he called "the talking cure" or psychoanalysis which some regard as the first method of examining the human mind. He also proposed the division of the psyche into ego (our outer self), super ego (our conscience) and id (our inner self).

Modern psychiatry now assesses a wide range of mental disorders, several of which are discussed in following sections.

The field of psychiatry, however, has a disgraceful history. As late as 1815 the Bethlehem madhouse in England exhibited lunatics every Sunday and made a considerable amount of money in the process (Youngson and Schott, 1996).[4]

At the Bicêtre hospital in France attendants used whips to make the mad perform dances to provide traditional entertainment. At the Charenton asylum the infamous Marquis de Sade presided over theatrical performances by the inmates.

In the USSR dissidents were often confided to asylums for the insane, a policy no doubt practiced elsewhere.

The practice of lobotomy was particularly scandalous.

It can be traced back to Dr Gottlieb Burckhardt, the superintendent of a psychiatric hospital in Switzerland, who in 1890 drilled holes in the head of six severely agitated patients, thereby altering their behaviour.

Then in 1935 John Fulton at Yale University removed the frontal lobes from two chimpanzees, changing their behaviour greatly. Dr Walter Freeman, an American neurologist, was recovering from a nervous breakdown when in July 1935 he attended a seminar given by Fulton.

Egas Moniz, a celebrated Portuguese neurosurgeon also attended the seminar and two months later in Portugal he performed the first *leucotomy* by drilling a small hole in the skull and injecting alcohol into it to destroy the fibres in the frontal lobes of the patient.

The operation succeeded in making the patient less agitated and overtly paranoid but made her more apathetic and

---

[4]The word Bedlam is a corruption of "Bethlehem."

dull than Moniz had hoped. Nevertheless, further operations were performed and the procedure was refined by drilling six holes in the skull.

When he published he gave no hint of the downside of his procedure and Walter Freeman was bursting with enthusiasm to try it and he enlisted the aid of neurosurgeon James Watts to carry out his first leucotomy on 14 September 1936.

A week later the patient became incoherent and could not even recite the days of the week and when asked to write could only scribble nonsense. Her speech improved in following days and they operated on another five patients.

In November 1936 Freeman and Watts published a report in which they wrote:

> *In all our patients there was a ... common denominator of worry, apprehension, anxiety, insomnia and nervous tension, and in all of them these symptoms have been relieved to a greater or lesser extent.*

Freeman and Watts renamed the procedure *lobotomy* and made it more drastic by drilling only two holes in the side of the head and using a canula, the tubing from a six inch heavy-gauge hypodermic needle, to pave the way for a cutting tool to destroy targeted brain tissue.

Watts became so proficient that he could thread the canula through the brain from the small hole on one side of the head to that on the other. Though not qualified to do so, Freeman began to perform lobotomies on his own and became a celebrity in the process. He also simplified the procedure by using electroshock to subdue the patient and then plunging an ice pick into their head, usually producing a zombie-like person.

Often the procedure was repeated a second and third time and Freeman, a neurotic with severe depressive symptoms who needed 3 Nembutal to sleep at night, enthusiastically continued his crude procedure years after it had been discredited.

Such surgery had been performed on more than 40,000 people in the USA alone by 1955. Fortunately, lobotomy has fallen out of favour though it is probably still practiced occasionally.

The misinformation that allowed this brutal procedure to be performed for some 30 years, however, is all too typical of a world in which we are fed misinformation and brainwashed into accepting any new procedure or product no matter how dangerous.

Little better, however, is widely used electroconvulsive shock therapy (ECT) in which electrodes are placed on either side of the head and short bursts of high-frequency and high intensity electrical current passed through the brain. ECT can produce a strong amnesic effect, but it is not clear by what means this occurs (Atrens & Curthoys, 1982).

PSYCHOPATHS

This is the largest category of abnormal psychological types, involving the following behaviours such as (Davies, 1971):

[1] Assertiveness, aggression and bullying.
[2] Dishonesty and lying.
[3] Alcohol and drug addiction.
[4] Excessive sexual behaviours.

Psychopaths are usually 'bad mad' and usually have two or more of the above traits, but are not normally classified as mentally ill, in part perhaps because they are so common.

MANIA

Typical manic behaviour involves a period in which an expansive, elevated, or irritable mood, along with enhanced activity and reactivity persists abnormally. During this episode symptoms such as increased talkativeness and grandiosity, distractibility, decreased need for sleep, inflated self-esteem, and excessive involvement in pleasurable yet risky activities may be present.

Such symptoms occur during normal mood changes, but it is their magnitude and frequent recurrence that may indicate a psychiatric problem. The frenetic and driven behaviour of mania results in a non-functional individual who cannot work effectively (Atrens & Curthoys, 1982).

The neurochemical alterations in mania are less clearly understood, but it is well established that drugs effective in the treatment of mania are those that antagonize dopamine and serotonin. The mechanism responsible for the therapeutic efficacy of lithium for the treatment of mania is not yet clear. Although mood disorders have a familial background, the evidence for a genetic component is not convincing.

DEPRESSION

Depression is also very common, and it is normal to feel depressed from time to time. Severe depression, however, is characterized by despondency, diminished interest in most or all activities, weight fluctuation not due to dieting, disruption in sleep patterns, psychomotor agitation or retardation, feelings of worthlessness, excessive quiet, and recurrent thoughts of death or suicide.

A professional diagnosis of depression is made, however, when a person suffers frequent and/or prolonged bouts of depression of more than usual severity, perhaps associated with thoughts of self-harm or suicide.

Major depression is associated with decreased brain levels of the neurotransmitters norepinephrine and serotonin, and the most effective therapy consists of drugs that inhibit the breakdown of these compounds.

Much less common, manic depression, or bipolar disorder, involves both manic 'highs' of greater energy and activity, alternating with bouts of depression or 'lows'. Manic depression is often treated with lithium salts.

ANXIETY

It is normal to feel anxious about things ranging from minor issues such as getting behind with one's work or household chores, to worrying when a child is late coming home from a party. Many people have abnormal levels of anxiety, including phobias and fears, and tranquillizers such as Valium, which enhances the inhibitory actions of the neurotransmitter GABA, are used to relieve anxiety and relax muscles.

OBSESSIVE COMPULSIVE DISORDER

Obsessive Compulsive Disorder (OCD) is a form of anxiety which makes people worry about certain things and 'over-react' to their concerns, the two most common behaviours being washing and checking, for example some people wearing away skin on their hands by frequently washing them, others repeatedly checking such things as whether the door is locked when they leave home.

One OCD sufferer, for example, feels compelled to do many things four times, another to count to seven between each mouthful of food (Carter, 2000).

HYPOCHONDRIA

Hypochondria is an anxiety disorder in which people worry excessively about their health, for example just hearing someone mention a certain illness triggering fears that they might have that illness.

TOURETTE'S SYNDROME

Tourette's syndrome is also an anxiety disorder, and certainly sufferers do appear anxious and disturbed when they have a bout of Tourette's and stressfully utter a nonsensical word while some part of their body, usually the face, has a 'tic' or twitches.

ASPERGER'S SYNDROME

This is a psychiatric disorder usually noted during early school years and characterized by impaired social relations and by repetitive patterns of behaviour.

AUTISM

This an abnormal absorption with the self marked by communication disorders and short attention span and inability to deal with other people.

In 2016 a Finish study of 258 people found that religious people could be compared with those with autism because they didn't view the world realistically, many believing in such supernatural phenomena as demons, gods and inanimate objects being alive in some way.

ADHD

Attention Deficit Hyperactivity Disorder (ADHD) is normally associated with school children who have difficulty sitting through classes without feeling distracted and wishing to be elsewhere doing something else. They thus have trouble concentrating and their learning is affected adversely.

There is much current controversy about this condition, many feeling that it is diagnosed too freely with children needlessly being put on long-term medication that may do more harm than good.

DYSLEXIA

This is an impaired ability to comprehend written words usually associated with a neurological disorder. The cause of dyslexia is believed to involve both genetic environmental factors and it often occurs in people with ADHD and is associated with similar difficulties with numbers. It may begin in adulthood as the result of a traumatic brain injury, stoke or dementia. The underlying mechanisms of dyslexia are problems within the brain's language processing.

Dyslexia is diagnosed through a series of tests of memory, spelling, vision, and reading skills and should not be confused with reading difficulties caused by hearing or vision problems or insufficient teaching.

Treatment involves adjusting teaching methods to meet the person's needs which, while not curing the underlying problem, it may decrease the symptoms. Treatments targeting vision are ineffective.

Dyslexia is the most common learning disability and occurs all around the world. It affects 3–7% of the population but up to 20% may have some degree of symptoms. While dyslexia is more often diagnosed in men, it has been suggested that it affects men and women equally.

Dyslexia should not be confused with 'mirror writing', for which Leonardo da Vinci was famous, some believing that he wrote in this fashion deliberately as a sort of coding.

SCHIZOPHRENIA

Schizophrenia is a chronic neurological disease of distorted thoughts and perceptions which usually begins during adolescence or early adulthood (Sweeney, 2009) It has a strong genetic component, one which research shows may be largely physiological, and not a result of a "disturbed environment" Atrens & Curthoys (1982).

Schizoid people worry obsessively about being watched by others and being talked about, fearing that people know too much about them and have invaded their 'space'. When walking in the street, for example, they will worry that other people are watching them, in this way 'distorting' reality.

Schizophrenia is relatively common, occurring in about 1 percent of the general population worldwide. Because the incidence of schizophrenia among parents, children, and siblings of patients with the disease is increased to 15 percent, it is believed that heredity plays an important role in the genesis of the disease (Atrens & Curthoys, 1982). However, other studies suggest that non-genetic factors such as a "disturbed environment" are also influential.

In the last decade or two, for example, a correlation between excessive and prolonged marijuana use and the development of schizophrenia has been observed.

The biochemical basis of the disease may be an excess of the neurotransmitter substance dopamine, as high levels of dopamine and its metabolites, as well as increased dopamine receptors, are found in the brains of persons with schizophrenia. Further evidence for this hypothesis is that the drugs most effective in treating the disease are those that have a high capacity to block dopamine receptors.

PSYCHOSIS

Psychosis is any severe mental disorder in which contact with reality is lost or highly distorted, including severe schizophrenia. The drug chlorpromazine was developed and widely used to treat psychosis, by 1964 ten thousand peer-reviewed articles having been published on it. According to Lieberman (2015),

> *Like a bolt from the blue, here was a medication that could relieve the madness that disabled tens of millions of men and women - - the widespread adoption of chlorpromazine marked the beginning of the end for the asylums.*

The commercial success of this drug encouraged pharmaceutical companies to search for new antipsychotic drugs, leading to the massive pharmaceutical industry of today.

HYSTERIA

This is a neurotic disorder characterized by violent emotional outbreaks and disturbances of sensory and motor functions. The term hysteria comes from the Greek word *hustericos* meaning 'of the womb' because ancient Greeks associated such highly emotional and neurotic behaviour with childless women. This indicates that man has long had an interest in trying to understand human psychology and behaviour.

DEMENTIA

Dementia is simply mental deterioration usually associated with old age. Senile dementia of the Alzheimer type (SDAT) is a result of advanced Alzheimer's disease, a progressive form of pre-senile dementia that is similar to senile dementia except that it usually starts in the 40s or 50s, the first symptoms being impaired memory which is followed by impaired thought and speech and finally complete helplessness.

HOMOSEXUALITY

Homosexuality is on the increase. Once a trait one had to keep secret it is now rampantly displayed at gay Mardi Gras festivals, at gay bars in major cities, and in late night TV ads for homosexual dating services.

Some claim that homosexuality is inherited and a study of 113 people in 33 families in which at least two brothers were homosexual found a genetic marker on the X-chromosome (Xq28) that had a very high correlation with sexual orientation (Galton, 2001).

Genes may play a minor 'predispositionary' role but, largely, homosexuality is a learnt behaviour. Typically, for example, the normal heterosexual male has one or two homosexual experiences in adolescence (Robertson, 1981), and no doubt the same applies to women.

Those who become homosexuals, therefore, presumably do so as a result of imitative learning at an early age. There are, no doubt, also psychological factors involved, for example a lack of confidence in approaching the opposite sex coupled with the fact that there are earlier homosexual experiences to draw upon as an alternative behaviour model.

If alcoholism is to be regarded as a psychiatric illness, as it often is (Davies, 1971), then homosexuality is even more obviously a treatable psychiatric condition as well.

That said, most of our heterosexual behaviours are also learnt ones, many of them hardly natural or healthy, an example being 'tongue kissing', a truly revolting and very unhealthy practice like many other modern sexual practices.

POSTTRAUMATIC STRESS DISORDER (PTSD)

PTSD is caused by events of great stress and trauma in a person's life, perhaps the best-known example being that of Western Vietnam war veterans, whose vulnerability to symptoms of PTSD such as depression and suicidal thoughts was no doubt increased by feelings of isolation as a result of having fought in a war which many thought to be mistake in the first place, and which the West ultimately lost.

Losing one's job, or the death of a spouse or young child are also common causes of PTSD.

According to Cozolino (2002):

Someone suffering from PTSD is, in essence, in a continual loop of unconscious self-traumatization, coping and exhaustion. When these symptoms are experienced on a chronic basis, they can devastate every aspect of the victim's life, from physical well-being to the quality of relationships to the victim's experience of the world.

MADNESS, BULLYING AND GENIUS

A somewhat simplistic way of categorizing 'mad people' is to divide them into just three categories, in order of how commonly they occur these being:

1. Sad mad.
2. Bad mad.
3. Good mad.

The pathology of type 1 includes depression, anxiety, and OCD. That of type 2, the psychopaths, includes aggression, lying, bullying, cheating, 'backstabbing', fraud and other crimes.

A 2016 "anti-bullying conference" in Melbourne reported that "children as young as three are being identified as bullies amid concern many childcare centres and kindergartens aren't doing enough to stamp out the problem" (The Herald-Sun, 6/8/2016).

Recent research also shows that young bullies at school are likely to become anti-social adults, whilst a 2006 survey found bullying in the Victorian public sector to be "frequent", with almost 24% of staff saying they frequently thought of leaving the public sector. Similar findings have been made in Australian hospitals.

The third category refers to such people as 'mad scientists' whose discoveries are often of great benefit to mankind. Newton was no doubt an example, an accidental fire in 1692 in which he lost the records of 20 years of his work affecting him greatly (Egerton Eastwick, 1896), and perhaps contributed to him being remembered as somewhat eccentric:

> *He lived the life of a solitary, and like all men who are occupied with profound meditation, he acted strangely. Sometimes in getting out of bed, an idea would come to him, and he would sit on the edge of the bed, half dressed, for hours at a time.*
> Louis Figuier, *Vies de Savants* (tr. B.H. Clark, 1897).

Newton had two nervous breakdowns before retiring from Cambridge at age 42 to go into politics, saying: *Tis best to do a little well, and leave the rest to those that follow.*

No doubt these were a result of bullying, for example cartoons of him sitting under a tree and discovering his law of gravity with an apple falling on his head. In fact, this may also relate to him spending a period on his family farm, perhaps to recover from a breakdown.

Writers and artists, many of whom work in relative solitude, have also often been associated with depression, (Thomas & Hughes, 2006), Vincent van Gogh being a notable example (Sweeney, 2009).

TREATMENT OF PSYCHIATRIC DISORDERS

Psychiatrists and psychologists use interviewing techniques to diagnose mental illnesses, regular appointments being used in serious cases as part of their therapy. Drugs are, of course, the main means of treatment, and there is an increasingly wide variety of these available, ranging from simple lithium salts for manic depression to Valium for anxiety disorders.

Other 'natural' treatments include Cognitive Behavioural Therapy and mindfulness meditation.

CONCLUSION

A modern medical scandal is the way in which such drugs as Valium are prescribed for the long term to people. Such drugs are bound to be addictive and when patients forget to take their daily dose there will inevitably be withdrawal symptoms.

Such drugs, like the brain stimulant tobacco or the depressant and tranquilizer alcohol, alter pulse rate and blood pressure. Smoking two or three strong cigarettes in an hour, for example, will increase pulse rate significantly. The discomfort we feel when the next 'dose' of the drug is missed is known as 'withdrawal', in the case of alcohol overdose the symptoms being an increase in blood pressure and pulse rate.

Unless absolutely necessary, therefore, it seems madness to addict people to such drugs when they might only be briefly affected by some stressful event in their lives.

In an article entitled *Medication*, the *Weekend Australian* magazine of 10/9/2016 reported that: "Children are being over diagnosed as having ADHD – and now even 'daydreaming'." They are then put on drugs for the long-term and left feeling that they will suffer this really nonexistent disease for life, when in fact the problem will usually be one of poor study habits and motivation, often exacerbated by lack of a home environment that encourages good study habits and the much too long and drawn out education system.

All this is good for the 'pysch. professions' as they can provide parents and teachers with an answer for why children are not doing well scholastically. They can also much increase the size of the practice with the many visits the child will have to make for further prescriptions.

It is also good for the pharmaceutical industry which sometime rewards doctors financially or with holidays and other perks to encourage them to prescribe their drugs.

As for 'talk therapy', many people with depression, for example, suffer from social isolation, and simply dealing with this issue is a preferable course of action to the expensive one of psychotherapy.

It should also be noted that recent studies in which one group of depressed patients were given a healthy Mediterranean-style diet, and a second just regular 'consultations' with a counsellor, found that the healthier diet option significantly reduced levels of depression.

Notably, the 'Mediterranean diet' usually includes a couple of glasses of red wine daily for 'relaxational purposes', the procyanidins and other antioxidants in red wine being particularly helpful in reducing cardiovascular disease, and in this context it should be noted that brain function, and thence such ailments as Alzheimer's disease, are affected by poor diets that increase atherosclerosis. Thus 'natural therapies' involving healthy diet, including plenty of appropriate dietary vitamin and other supplements, and plenty of exercise, relaxation and sleep, improve both physical and mental health (Mohr, 2012b, 2013, 2015).

The authors therefore recommend improved diet and lifestyle, including occasional contact with supportive and helpful friends and neighbours, as a means of improving mental health, perhaps in conjunction with professional counselling if need be, though in most cases the latter should only be required for the short term, for example to help deal with a particular event such as a death in the family, divorce etcetera.

In choosing a counsellor one might, for example, be wary of those overly obsessed with sexual issues or dreams as being the root of many problems, as the authors believe Sigmund Freud and Carl Jung were.

When professional 'talk therapy' is used, however, the patient should take care to choose a counsellor intelligent enough to quickly work out what memories etc. are affecting them and suggest sensible and effective ideas to deal with any 'mental problems', and using pharmaceutical drugs only when clearly necessary, and then only for the short or medium term.

☺☹☻☺☹☻☺☹☻☺☹☻☺☹☻

Chapter 8
EDUCATION

Whereas a rattle is a suitable occupation for infant children, education serves as a rattle for young people when older.
                                Aristotle, Politics bk 8 (1340 BC).

Indeed one of the ultimate advantages of an education is simply coming to an end of it.
        B.F. Skinner, The Technology of Teaching (1968).

A BRIEF HISTORY OF EDUCATION

In Western Civilization our recorded history of education centres on the Greek and Roman civilizations. In the last stages of the classical Roman education system the Trivium (grammar, rhetoric, logic) and Quadrivium (music, astronomy, geometry, arithmetic) evolved and these were the basis of the medieval arts course in Europe centuries later (Niblett, 1969).

Elsewhere, before the medieval period academic pursuits were largely limited to clerical education in monasteries.

By the 12th century, however, a few cathedral schools were well established and these began to study law, albeit mainly clerical law.

Gradually small schools were established in most towns where basic education in reading and writing was given for a few years. Few families could afford to pay for such education, however, and much of the population was semiliterate at best.

The thirteenth century saw the development of the first Universities, in Paris and Oxford, and the 14th and 15th centuries saw many new Universities established in Europe. In these training was based on the three stages of membership of the craft-guilds: apprenticeship, journeymanship and mastership.

The ancient Trivium and Quadrivium, however, were still the framework of the arts course that all had to take before moving on to the higher courses of Theology, Medicine and Law.

A preliminary examination was required for entry to the first apprenticeship stage, one of study, at the end of which the student was examined for the bachelorship. The bachelor was then still under instruction but assigned certain courses of lectures. Then finally he was examined for his mastership, a licence to teach.

In the 14th century the Inns of Court were established in England to meet a growing demand for teaching common law

In 1368 the master-surgeons formed a guild and in 1540 the Company of Barber-Surgeons was set up with a monopoly of practice and teaching.

In both law and medicine, therefore, professions were raised in status and competence by initiatives of their members that were more responsive to the needs of society than academic institutions.

During the renaissance, as in biblical times, apprenticeship remained the main method of training.

The 17th century saw interest in science increase and new colleges began training in technologies such as mineralogy and glassblowing. By the end of the century most scientific work in England took place in laboratories in London, not in Cambridge and Oxford.

The 18th century saw many new academies established which spread higher education to a middle class of trade and industry.

In the 19th and 20th centuries the school curriculum grew to place more emphasis on science to educate students for an increasingly technological world.

Today, however, students in most Western countries spend at least 12 years at school and this is excessive. The early years of school are, as much as anything, simply conditioning for the routine for working life.

To add insult to this injury tertiary education courses have been introduced for a myriad of areas for which they were not required in the past.

Worse still, countless absurd postgraduate courses such as Sexology and Puppetry have been introduced, reducing the education system to long drawn out farce.

PRESCHOOL EDUCATION

Early brain development was discussed in Chapter Two. It is very important to take advantage of this capacity for early learning to provide infants with a stimulating environment which should include a 'personal learning centre' (PLC) that includes educational pictures and toys.

By the second year they should be involved in small learning groups supervised by a specialist teacher so that they can begin real learning (Packard, 1978). In the third year they should begin kindergarten for at least a couple of days a week and these learning efforts should continue. By now they have a modest vocabulary and are capable of *cognitive learning* which processes and stores *abstract* information.

At this stage deliberate effort should be made at 'IQ building', noting that IQ tests include questions testing verbal, spatial and numerical ability. If a child has a problem with numbers, for example, early detection and correction of this will prevent far greater problems later.

Then, given a head start, they should commence school at age four, rather than the usual five in most countries.

LEARNING CURVES

Suppose the degree to which a person or group has learnt something or been conditioned is given by the probability $p = 0$ to 1, and p depends on n, the number of repetitions of the learning process.

If we assume that the learning process is hyperbolic so that the degree of learning gradually increases towards 100% or the asymptote $p = a$ with a = 1, then this is represented by the hyperbola of Figure 8.1(a), the equation for which is $p = an/(b + n)$.

This equation can easily be rearranged to give

$$n/p = (b + n)/a$$

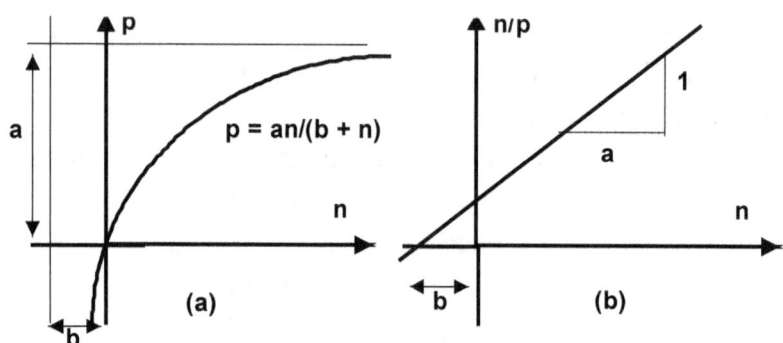

Figure 8.1. Mohr Plot for learning.

so that if we plot *n/p* against *n* the straight line of Figure 8.1(b) is obtained and the magnitude of the intercept with the *n* axis = *b* whilst, of more interest, the inverse slope of the line equals the horizontal asymptote *a* of the hyperbola.

In experimental situations this plot is useful in testing whether results are indeed hyperbolic and, if so, estimating the 'ceiling' value towards which some variable is converging.

Applied to the memory of a single person we set *a* =1 and a typical result might be *b* = 3, *n* = 3, giving *p* = 0.5, or 50% memory retention after three repetitions. Here *p* is either:

(a) How well an item is learnt. People's names might be a good example of this. Ourselves, we often think one needs about three repetitions of such things to remember them.

(b) How much of a 'block' of information is learnt. An example might be a list of names where, because of *interference*, words at the beginning (the *primacy effect*) and end (the *recency effect*) are remembered best.

For a slower learner, on the other hand, b might double to 6 so we need $n = 6$ to get $p = 0.5$ or 50% learning.

Applied to conditioning of the populace by advertising, p is the proportion of the population affected and larger values of the asymptote b which flatten the curve might occur when there are two or more competing advertisers in the market. In politics this highlights the advantage of dictatorship.

In education it perhaps highlights the importance of avoiding conflicting messages so that it is often best to learn one subject at a time.

THINKING

In education the four elements of thinking should be used carefully:

[1] **Images.** We often use *visual imagery* in thinking. For example, we often find it easier to describe the shape of something by sketching it or a physical operation by demonstrating it.

[2] **Symbols.** Language involves the spoken and written use of symbols. These symbols can be words, mathematical formulae, pictures (including diagrams, maps and graphs) or gestures that represent either *objects, operations, relationships* and *qualities*.

[3] **Concepts.** Concepts can be defined as categories that represent a class of objects, events or qualities wherein each item has a number of common features. A simple example are birds which 'mentally' are a concept and these have common properties such as two legs, wings and the ability to fly and lay eggs.

Such categorization is important for both efficient learning and memory storage and efficient recall and thence thinking.

Learning of concepts is made easier by *transfer* when they are similar to already familiar concepts.

When driving, for example, when you see a set of traffic lights (a concept) you note which colour is 'on' and quickly decide (a thinking process) what action to take.

[4] **Rules.** Rules involve connections between features of a concept and between different concepts.

In the example of traffic lights we should know the rules and have only to choose 'yes' or 'no' as to whether we follow the appropriate rule.

The rule for traffic lights might be represented as

(green = go) OR (amber = slow down) OR (red = stop)

and the rule for driving might be written

(accelerator = go) OR (no accelerator = slow)
OR (brake = stop)

so to stop at a red light we have to connect the two rules, a process probably carried out in short term memory.

CREATIVE THINKING

Creative thinking to obtain new ideas often involves *divergent thinking* (Morgan et al., 1979) and typically occurs in three stages:

(a) **Preparation:** define the problem and resources needed.
(b) **Incubation:** acquire information and think or dwell on the problem.
(c) **Assembly:** combine information to form the solution.

In a much too drawn out education system endless classes with a lecture format should occasionally be replaced by sessions with a seminar format. Sometimes these could involve *brainstorming* to solve a problem, for example devising an effective advertising campaign for a product.

Group brainstorming has been found effective because:

[1] People tend to have twice as many ideas in the group situation because of the more stimulating environment, 'cross fertilization' of ideas and arousal of competitive spirit.
[2] Alternation of individual and group thinking improves results.
[3] As more ideas are produced they tend to improve.
[4] Second sessions a few days later improve results because of the 'incubation' process so important in creative thinking.
[5] The group uses *critical thinking* to evaluate the ideas.

SHORTENING THE SCHOOL PROGRAM

No better example of *Parkinson's Law* exists than in education. Parkinson's Law is simply (Parkinson, 1980):

Work expands so as to fill the time available for its completion.

Leonardo da Vinci and Michelangelo were apprenticed at age 14 and Francis Bacon went to Cambridge University at age 12 and left at age 14.

The development of modern science from the 16th and 17th centuries is, perhaps, one of the reasons for the considerable growth in the number of years required at school.

According to a recent article by *The Australian's* national education correspondent on 16/9/2016:

Australian primary and secondary students chalk up significantly more classroom hours than any international peers but despite the grind their test results continue to flatline.

Clearly, our system of 12 years at school is far too drawn out and should be reduced to 10 years for the 'average' student, this involving six years at primary school and four at secondary school.

Here the curriculum for the last four secondary years could remain much as now so that reduction to 10 years would be achieved by condensation of the first eight years of the 12 year system to six.

This might simply involve

(a) Making preschool education compulsory and thus removing the need for at least the first year at school.
(b) Acceleration of the learning of the three R's in the first few years and elimination of most unnecessary material.

The result should be better educated and brighter children who will be better prepared for life and the faster pace of tertiary courses.

LESS FRAGMENTATION

Classes at both school and University are usually scheduled in a somewhat haphazard fashion so that hours of subjects A, B and C appear as A, B, C, A, B, C and so on. This results in a 'parade of clowns' effect that does more to confuse students than anything else.

The present author has always found it better to, for example, give two lectures consecutively, rather than at almost random times in the week a day or more apart.

This has the advantages of:

[1] It saves students and/or staff a considerable amount of inconvenience.
[2] It results in better learning because more *proactive interference* and less *retroactive interference* occurs (Morgan et al., 1979).
[3] A break of about 10 or 15 minutes is allowed in the middle and this provides a good opportunity for questions and discussion.
[4] The result is a more mature and friendly seminar approach and more motivated, inquiring and effective students.

Similarly, in the first years of school it might be better to tackle the 12 times tables, for example, by devoting a few weeks to it, rather than spreading it over years.

Then if the learning task is returned to a week or two later it should be found that *latent learning* has occurred and good progress has been made.

Indeed, it might be a good idea in later school years to fit classes into four days to allow students a fifth week day to do homework. If unnecessary activities were removed as far as possible then, for example, just half an hour more of formal classes per day might allow all the required class work to be fitted into four days.

Application of this less fragmentary approach is possible at University when students might have four or five subjects with one day of the week dedicated to each, rather than having them randomly spread throughout the week in bits and pieces.

UNIVERSITY COURSES

There has been excessive proliferation in new University courses. My father, also an academic, used to joke about there being degrees in bee keeping in the USA. At the more reputable Universities there this may not, in fact, be the case. In Australia, however, this has come to pass with degrees where none were needed before, examples being journalism, marketing, nursing and viticulture.

There has also been a plethora of new postgraduate certificates and diplomas and Masters Degrees. Some of these, such as courses in Sexology, Puppetry or Citizenship studies are either lightweight, absurd or both, and any material that is worthwhile should have been included in undergraduate courses.

Some so-called postgraduate courses, on the other hand, introduce an entirely new vocational area. If these are all that is required in these areas then these courses should be offered as relatively short undergraduate certificate or diploma courses.

That we have masters "courses" at all is questionable. Mastership in Universities took its meaning from the Master status conferred by the craft-guilds of 500 or more years ago and was given after a relatively short period of teaching experience. Consequently, Cambridge and Oxford award Masters Degrees on completion of undergraduate courses.

Why then do 'latter day' Universities enslave their students for a couple of further years in usually redundant, if not frivolous Masters Degrees?

The answer undoubtedly comes in two parts:

(a) The education bureaucrats are ignorant.
(b) Simply money. The longer the education process, the more "products" and the more money to be made.

Research degrees may also be questionable. As just noted, Masters degrees as separate and additional courses are redundant. As for PhDs, historically these were awarded for further self-study, usually by academics. This has no connotation of teaching so that it is absurd that graduates are now able to be enrolled as "students" and then used as slave labour at the whim of supervisors for often useless research topics.

TAFE

TAFE, an acronym for Technical and Further Education that originated in the UK, is an important alternative to University for school leavers. Here students are trained for the *real* occupations in the basic industries essential to human life, that is, food, clothing and shelter.

In contrast, and increasingly so, University courses are, strictly speaking, unnecessary. In other words we can usually live without a doctor or lawyer, house builders can usually do without an architect or engineer if need be. People used to run businesses without business degrees and we certainly don't need degrees in Sexology and Puppetry.

Many TAFE courses are part-time ones for apprentices. Unfortunately, many apprenticeships are unreasonably long and bordering on exploitation of a cheap labour source. An example are hairdressing apprenticeships which we believe take up to 6 years in Australia, certainly too long when most us would think a couple of weeks training would suffice.

Another looming problem is the slow introduction of diploma and degree courses in business to TAFE institutes when absurd numbers of people already do these in the Universities. Even MBA courses, let alone undergraduate business courses, are lightweight material that should be taught at school.

PROBLEMS IN EDUCATION

There are many problems in the education sector today, including:

[1] Children being incarcerated in long-day-care centres which, cruelly, do little more than expensive babysitting almost from birth. This is an inhuman practice that reduces children to toys that amuse parents after work, a sick situation that must do more harm than good.

[2] As the discussion of brain development in infants in Chapter Two points out, the early years are a critical time that should not be lost. Weiss and Mann (1978), for example, refer to a project in Milwaukee that found that children given more attention by the

mother or a specially trained teacher, showed markedly higher IQ.

This is no doubt the reason that only children tend to have higher IQ and that, in families with more than one child, the eldest child has a slightly higher IQ on average (Vernon, 1960).

The youngest child in larger families, on the other hand, does not do too badly compared to those 'sandwiched' in the middle and perhaps most deprived of attention.

[3] As noted earlier, 12 years at school is too long and 10 years would be a more sensible norm.

[4] There is far too much rote learning at school.

[5] Poor teacher training. Sykes (1995) reports widespread disillusionment with modern teacher training, much of which is a hotchpotch of psychology, sociology and history that cannot develop real expertise in any of these areas.

He cites several examples of recent doctorates in education being granted for dissertations with such titles as:

"The use of goal setting and positive self-modelling to enhance self-efficiency and performance for the basketball free-throw shot" for a PhD at the University of Maryland.

After such largely useless studies, Sykes laments, 'educrats' move into educational administration and oversee a decline in standards over the whole spectrum of education comparable to that evidenced by their largely irrelevant doctoral studies.

[6] Declining academic standards. A survey of 24,000 students in twelve countries by the Educational Testing Service in Princeton found that, compared to 40% of US students scoring at the 500 level in a standard test, the results were 78% for Korea, 73% for Quebec and 69% for British Columbia (Sykes, 1995). A similar decline in standards has occurred in Australia.

[7] In the USA outcome based education (OBE) has gone a long way towards disallowing fail grades, instead allowing students to retake tests until they pass. The idea of this is to avoid attaching negative labels to students, and much effort is also made to avoid attaching positive labels to the brightest students as well. OBE also eschews 'tracking' to permit accelerated learning for gifted students, despite conclusive evidence of its positive results, in this way ensuring that the overall standard of education is lowered further.

[8] In the USA new 'soft' approaches to teaching and grading reading and maths have led to a dramatic decline in literacy and numeracy skills.

[9] Drugs for school-age children. The overlong school education system should bore anyone with half a brain. To make matters worse increasing numbers of 'unruly' children are diagnosed with such doubtful disorders as Attention Deficit Hyperactivity Disorder (ADHD) and prescribed drugs such as Ritalin to sedate them.

In the USA and Australia in turn, increasingly large numbers of children suffer this fate. Reports of up to 15% or more children in some areas being on such drugs have not brought action to curb this disturbing trend as yet, but visions of a future society in which both parents and children have to be drugged to cope are unacceptable.

[10] Overgrown educational bureaucracy. In the US in 1960 one third of education employees were not classroom teachers. By 1991 46.7% were non-teaching staff and the teaching staff's share of the total payroll had shrunk from 54% to 41%. Much the same has occurred in England and Australia both in school and tertiary education.

[11] Growing up faster. Today's young, thanks to better nutrition grow faster than in the past. Da Vinci observed that children were half their ultimate height at age three. Now that figure is about 55%. Along with that, in part because of the ubiquitous media today, in many ways they mature faster than ever before. Many children by their mid-teens, therefore, are becoming bored with school and drop out. Robertson (1981), for example, reported that 100,000 assaults against teachers occur in US schools each year. Doubtless this is one of several factors that contribute to the increasing discipline problem in schools.

[12] There are far too many assignments, tests etc. at school and University. When the first author was an undergraduate and teaching in Universities in Australasia there were 8 subjects in second year engineering, yet in Engineering Maths students were given sheets full of problems each week. It should be all about showing

how to do things and giving *answers*, not asking endless questions.

At Auckland University these maths problem sheets often involved 2 or 3 different areas lectured by different people, an absurd situation. Including the secretary who typed them, up to four morons helped fill their week redoing these sheets each year, a fine example of Parkinson's Law for all involved.

Needless to say:
(a) The staff were simply a pathetic, mindless bunch of no-hopers who had never, and never will, achieve anything.
(b) The students were somewhat demoralized. Eight Uni. subjects in a year is too much, let alone being asked to spend up to several hours on the worse than useless homework for just one of them.

[13] Many University courses overlap with school. At Auckland University, for example, top school leavers were exempted from the first year of the course. Q: Why on earth, therefore, was that year needed at all? A: To employ a few more dumb academics.

[14] Excessive growth in tertiary courses. The ridiculous University courses like those in sexology were mentioned earlier in the chapter. MBAs etc. are not much better and are now so common that with an MBA one might now only be able to gain employment as a salesperson, if that.

[15] Once upon a time correspondence courses were poorly regarded. We are such slaves to fashion, and

thence brainwashing, that the morons in Universities are happy to run courses by *distance education* over the Internet.

[16] There is insufficient emphasis on developing inquiring minds capable of finding answers to their own questions, rather than zombies so used to endless rote learning and tests that they have become too tired and bored to care about anything but going through the motions of life as perpetual consumers and slaves to big businesses that produce and sell mass marketed consumer products.

PERSONAL EXPERIENCES

The first author in the mid-1990s wrote an entire MBA course involving 14 subjects ranging from business finance, economics, maths and OR, IT and numerical methods, to the more lightweight areas of BP (business policy), business law, HRM and advertising.

The concise lecture notes came to about 400 somewhat cramped pages and he tried to publish this course without luck, but was pleased that an editor at Heinemann agreed with his proposition that, a lucrative Harvard invention, MBA courses could now be found *"on every street corner,"* yet another example of how the USA has debased the education system.

CONCLUSIONS

IQ in the UK diminished by 1.5% between 1920 and 1950 (Vernon, 1960) and two decades ago it was claimed that the average American IQ was diminishing (Fancher, 1985), some claiming that it is now dropping by about 1 point per generation. Judging by the international survey results quoted earlier this has, indeed, happened and the country is deep into reverse evolution.

Australia is probably the most Americanized country in the world and our education system, particularly in the Universities, has certainly become farcical. There it is no longer a matter of education but one of highly paid 'educrats' who have never done anything significant overseeing invention of increasingly ludicrous courses to advertise to increase the size of the University.

From birth to death it is all corporate stuff at the day care centre, school and University and with the invention of more silly courses students are expected to study longer and longer.

During the first author's undergraduate student days a lecturer explained that, owing to the *time value of money*, we would not in our lifetimes make as much money as a plumber who had started work at 15, even if we were paid substantially more. Plumbers make far more money now than they did way back then!

Thus, a recent article by *The Australian's* national education correspondent on 16/9/2016 noted that: *Australians pay more, get less back from degrees.*

If your parents spent a lot of money on a private school education the comparison is even worse. Unless they were rich they should have spent just a little of that money to give you the edge at a government school. The rest they should have invested at a good interest rate to buy you a shop in which to start up a lucrative business. Then you might not need to go to University to study Accountancy, Architecture, Engineering,

Dentistry, Law, or Medicine, businesses in which it really is best if you start up your own practice and that may be in a shop front office anyway.

As for dragging school out for too long, when the first author was doing BE + the new and stupid MEngSc in Melbourne (half lectures unfunded then by the Uni – and WE gave the lectures in the FEM subject to help out the ignorant professor for that subject) – the BE took 4 years, and on average one might take the best part of 2 more for the MEngSc.

Compare this with Oxbridge then – BE was 3 years and one was given a Masters degree *automatically* one year after graduation. Not only that, in Cambridge back then one studied all branches of engineering as a single degree, greatly widening a graduate's later career options. Now that is civilized, as was the Dean of Engineering saying:

> *Decide what you want to do*
> *and see if you can get anybody interested*

when the first author arrived in Cambridge to do his PhD there, presumably being given such latitude because he was already a college lecturer in Melbourne.

In contrast, in Melbourne his Masters Degree research topic had been 'given' to him – he had no say in it at all. This was because somebody had modest funding for the topic and, as usual, he was just yet another graduate student slave.

☺☻☹☺☻☹☺☻☹☺☻☹☺☻☹

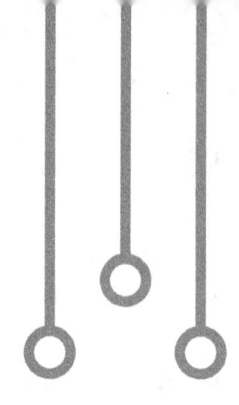

Chapter 9
LEARNING LIFE SKILLS

*Wise men learn by other men's mistakes,
fools by their own.*
H. G. Bohn, *Handbook of Proverbs*,
quoted in *Cassell's Book of
Humorous Quotations* (1969).

*All inequality that has no special utility
to justify it is injustice.*
Jeremy Bentham, British jurist and
philosopher (1748 - 1832).
Writings (W Stark ed.), 1952.

A NEW GENERAL STUDIES SUBJECT

We need to teach children more about real life at school rather than simply spin out the Three Rs and little more over year after boring year. Thus students should have been taught a little about life skills such as diet, exercise, hygiene, and sex in primary school.

In secondary school a good argument can be had for a new 'general studies' subject which might briefly embrace such real-life topics as:

[1] **Psychology:** emotion, motivation, attitudes, thinking.
[2] **Sociology:** cultures, social learning (of habits), social inequality.
[3] **Business and economics:** interest rates and the 'time value' of money, marketing and consumer issues.

Psychology topics that should prove useful both in their studies and throughout life include those of human thinking processes, problem solving and decision making and these important topics are discussed in following sections.

There should also be courses in 'life management' dealing with such issues as workplace bullying and consumerism so that they do not get into trouble in such areas.

CAREER PLANNING

We should have a society in which children develop a vocational idea relatively early in life, and are then helped to achieve it, rather than a lottery process based on a few marks 'either way' in just one set of exams. At school, therefore, there is a need for students to have a great deal more information on different career possibilities given to them well before their final year at school. This should be 'hard' information that gives a realistic idea of remuneration (discounted to allow for the years of training required) and working conditions in different occupations.

To help assure that student career ideas are realistic some counselling should be given. It might also be worthwhile to conduct fairly simple examinations aimed at determining vocational aptitude perhaps one or two years before the final year at school.

In this or some other way, however, it is desirable that a student would have had his or her sights set on a certain career for at least a couple of years before they finish school, giving plenty of time for second thoughts if necessary.

Then, in the final years at school, every effort should be made to ensure that, for example, a small marks shortfall in a subject not essential to the career plan might be ignored. In other words, every effort should be made to help a student reach their career goal.

CRITICAL THINKING

Critical thinking is needed to examine alternative solutions to determine which is the best solution and typically involves such steps as:

[1] Define the problem and the criteria that a solution must meet.
[2] Compare alternative solutions to these criteria.
[3] Evaluate which solution best satisfies the criteria.
[4] Revue this decision.

Decision trees are sometimes a useful way of depicting business strategies. A simple example is that of a manufacturer asked by a supermarket chain to make a 'home brand' version of its product, a decision tree for which is shown in Figure 9.1.

As another example Figure 9.2 considers the problem of deciding whether to launch a rocket at a certain time or

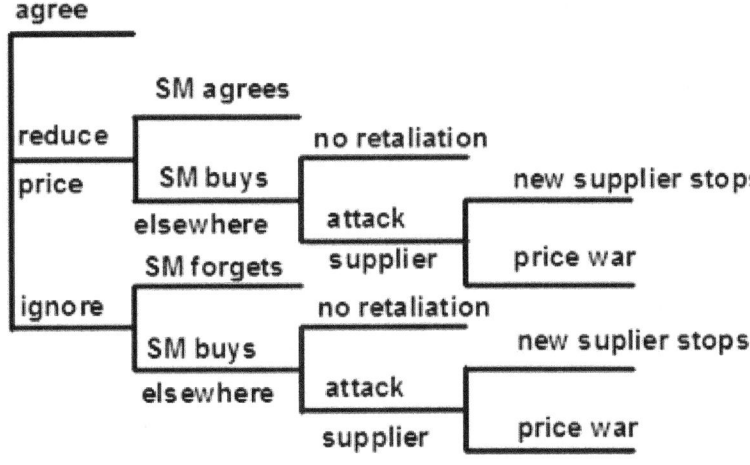

Figure 9.1. Example of a decision tree.

not, attaching probabilities and profit figures to the decision tree.

Then the *expected monetary value* (EMV) of a launch is $0.3(5.5) - 0.7(3.5) = -\$0.8M$ so we should decide to hold.

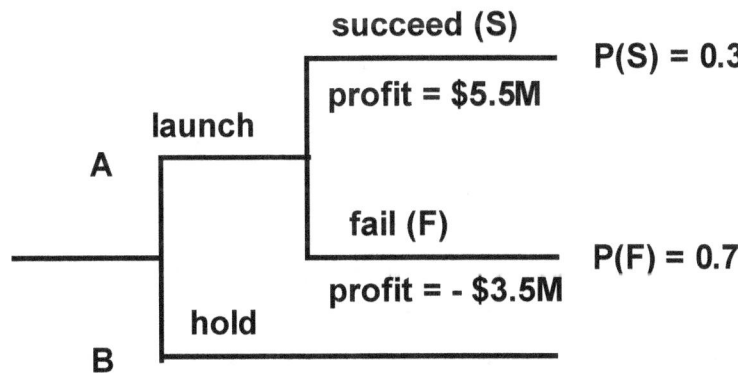

Figure 9.2. Decision tree with probabilities & financial outcomes.

With more optimistic figures, for example $P(S) = 0.7$ and $P(F) = 0.3$, the EMV of **A** is \$2.85M and the launch decision is much more favourable, though perhaps still not certain.

LATERAL THINKING

Edward de Bono (de Bono, 1982) proposed lateral thinking as an alternative to logical or *vertical* thinking. Some of the features of lateral thinking are:

Steps can be jumped (and 'filled' later).

Steps need not be 'correct' so long as the conclusion is correct and may be made in order to *generate* a new direction or branch.

Interpretation of task criteria and alternative solution properties can be changed and the process is not *finite,* that is it need not reach a conclusion in any given time.

It is *probabilistic* so that less obvious solutions are considered so that the best solution is obtained (if a valid solution exists).

Lateral thinking is not quick to say no to less obvious solutions and, rather than stop at obstacles to a solution, one should *go around* them by such means as those summarized above.

Selecting the best candidate for a job is a good example and if this is done with lateral thinking:

[1] Some criteria might be ignored or downgraded in importance so that more candidates will be considered.
[2] Those who do not satisfy some criteria might remain under consideration.
[3] Candidates not at the top of the list are re-evaluated.

PROBLEM SOLVING

Problems can be attacked in three stages:

[1] Defining the problem

At first this might involve realizing that a problem exists.

Then we need to determine:
- (a) What is the initial situation, i.e., what is known about the problem?
- (b) What is the goal?
- (c) What are the restrictions or *constraints*?
- (d) What moves or *operations* are required to reach the goal?

[2] Generating possible solutions

Solutions to a problem can be obtained by such *strategies* as:
- (a) In the case of mathematics problems, for example, algorithms can be used to try large numbers of solutions on a computer.
- (b) Use an existing heuristic rule or 'rule of thumb.'
- (c) Redefine the problem, for example by breaking it down into stages and seeking a 'solution' for each stage. Such means-end analysis is sometimes more successful if the problem is examined by working backwards through these stages.
- (d) Use a new arrangement of existing techniques or materials.
- (e) Invent new techniques or materials, i.e., use insight learning.

This requires *creative thinking* which often involves *incubation* periods.

Creative thinking can be inhibited by:
(i) *Functional fixedness,* the difficulty of imagining new uses for materials or devices.
(ii) Mental set, the difficulty in finding new strategies for approaching a problem. Set can be induced by recent experiences or old habits.

[3] Testing and evaluating the solutions
Alternative solutions are tested to see how well they work in relation to predetermined criteria.

Sometimes problems can be solved by *trial and error* so that trial solutions are repetitively adjusted until satisfactory.

Selection of the best solution from a number of alternatives should be done with a quantitative basis, preferably using a process of summing *weighted attributes.*

A good example is the task of selecting the 'best' of three candidates. Tom, Dick and Harry, for a job using the *decision table* of Table 9.1.

Table 9.1 Job candidate selection using weighted attribute scores.

Attribute	Weight	Score			Weighted score		
		Tom	Dick	Harry	Tom	Dick	Harry
Qualifications	2	8	5	3	16	10	6
Experience	3	5	7	6	15	21	18
Age	1	5	5	8	5	5	8
Interview	2	3	5	8	6	10	16
Referees	1	5	5	5	5	5	5
Total					46	41	43

Here five attributes: qualifications, experience (relevant), age (or total experience), impression made at interview and strength of recommendations made by referees, are used and each of these is given a weight in the second column.

Then the three candidates are given a score out of ten for each attribute by each member of the selection panel and the results averaged (to the nearest round number for simplicity here), giving the results shown in columns 3,4,5.

Finally, these scores are multiplied by the weights, giving the results of columns 6,7,8, and these figures summed to give the totals shown.

The final result indicates Tom as the best candidate.

In practice, however, it is best to include other considerations such as:

[1] Who top scored in the most important attributes?
[2] If the candidate is an existing employee (in another position) has there been any bias?

In this sort of analysis the choice of attributes is crucial, as is their weighting, so that such factors should also be reviewed before making a final decision.

HIERARCHICAL ORGANIZATIONS

Figure 9.3 shows a small hierarchical network modelled as a DC network using the simple BASIC program given in Chapter 3. At node 1 we have the pyramid building and lunatic 'boss' and a current 'load' of 100 is input. Then zero datum voltage is specified at nodes 4-7 and unit resistance is given to all 6 elements so that the result will be voltage 75 at node 1, 25 at nodes 2 &3, and zero at nodes 4 to 7,

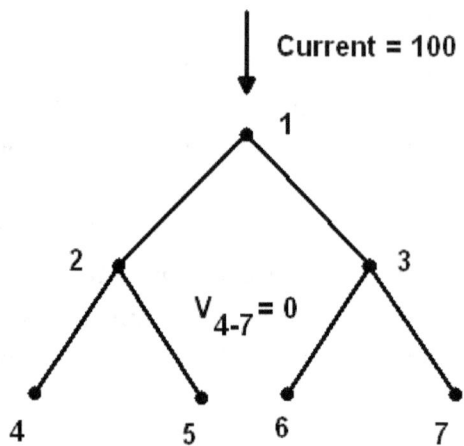

Figure 9.3. Hierarchical network.

giving rise to currents 50 in the top two elements and 25 in the rest.

This illustrates what the 'econobabble' calls 'the trickle-down effect', that is, the boss of this very small hierarchy has 3 times the voltage (or power, money and status) as his subordinates (the front line managers) one rung below. The workers at the bottom have no status at all.

If we add a further bottom row of 8 nodes in Figure 9.3 then now the 'voltage hierarchy' is 87.5, 37.5, 12.5, 0 so that the boss now does 7 times as well as the 'front line managers' on the row above the bottom row.

Then if we add a further fifth row of 16 nodes the voltage hierarchy is 93.75, 43.75, 18.75, 6.25, 0 and the boss does 15 times as well as the front line managers and infinitely better than the workers at the bottom.

This is the fundamental principle of modern management and capitalism, leading to Mohr's Law of Hierarchies:

In hierarchical organizations the amount of real material-producing work people do is inversely proportionalto their rank or level in the organization.

The amount of compensation they receive, however, is proportional to their level, sometimes to an exponential degree.

This, of course, is not fair at all and posters that were so common in the USSR decades ago which pictured the workers as heroic perhaps made some sense. Then, of course, the hammer and sickle on their flag was also symbolic of the importance of the workers.

A FAIRER SOCIETY

In industrialized societies workers are stressed as the result of the preaching of such people as F. W. Taylor. An engineering graduate, he wrote a pioneering book on operations management which suggested that piece rates were the best means of achieving greater productivity (Taylor, 1911).

That same principle has been put into great use in factories in China to employ thousands of young girls to work ridiculously hard to increase profits and thence the huge salaries and bonuses of executives of US clothing companies. The result of such 'offshore manufacturing' has been the large scale destruction of manufacturing industries in such countries as the US, UK and Australia.

So the bottom line is that we have to create fairer societies which have *real democracy,* not the oligarchies that Aristotle commented about:

> *A democracy exits whenever those who are free*
> *and are not well-off, being in the majority,*
> *are in sovereign control of government,*
> *an oligarchy when control lies with the rich and better born.*
>   Aristotle, *The Politics* (343 BC).

Worse still, however, is the increasing level of violence on TV and at the movies. Inevitably the result is 'copy cat' behaviour in the society made audience to these movies (Cipolla, 1974):

> *It is disturbing to see that still today, even in the most advanced countries, in large sections of human society, aggressiveness is praised as a virtue - or at least as a valuable asset - and it is constantly advertised in the motion pictures and on television. We need - more than anything else - to educate people to tolerance and gentility.*

SOCIAL AND EMOTIONAL INTELLIGENCE

'Social intelligence' and 'emotional intelligence' are closely related, and tests of social intelligence include questions about how people would feel in certain social situations, and questions about the emotions shown in pictures of people smiling or frowning.

Some EI tests use self-report questionnaires, and according to Mackintosh (2011): - *a distinction needs to be drawn between self-report questionnaires, which seem to be a largely measures of well-established aspects of personality, and more objective measures which may more reasonably be called measures of intelligence.*

Performance on the Mayer-Salovey-Caruso Emotional Intelligence Test (MSCEIT), for example, improves with age, and females usually do better than males. Assessments of social behaviour by teachers, friends and managers, however, sometimes show negative correlations with EI test scores (Mackintosh, 2011).

CONCLUSION

The first author was going on 14 when he finished Grade Eight after a long drawn out process of daily imprisonment that was largely child minding. As said in the last chapter, 12 years at school is far too long and condensing this to 8, or at most 10 years, would give better results, particularly if important life skills such as how to deal with the consumer society and bullies and bad bosses were included in the curriculum.

As for hierarchies, which some feel a natural and inevitable part of human societies, noted chimpanzee scholar Joan Goodall was reported in the Weekend Australian of 30/8/2008 as saying: *I have observed chimpanzees for many years, and it's clear that we share many traits. I'm very conscious now of things like body language and people's eyes, and it does become easier to predict how somebody might behave.*

She also observed that chimp alpha males behaved much like chief executives, concluding that the most successful chimp groups had a leader who was not aggressive, saying:

The best ones are .... self-confident, smart and have alliances. And as soon as you lose an alpha male, you have absolute chaos.

Noting that circa 50% of personality may be genetic (Galton, 2001), 'Mohr's Morphology' postulates three personality types based on a scale of aggressiveness:

(a) Placid (the meek).
(b) Neutral (the OK guys).
(c) Aggressive/assertive (the bossy types).

The meek do not inherit the earth, as The Bible has it, for the bossy little Hitler types usually end up as boss. These bossy types typically have type A behaviour associated with assertiveness, ambition, impatience and dishonesty.

Worse still, Australian research reported in October 2016 found that about half of all people will be victims of workplace bullying, a disturbing finding.

Other research has found that, contrary to popular belief enshrined in such terms as "executive stress," being boss involves less work stress and thus it is the slaves, of course, that really are stressed, and perhaps never much more so than in today's high-paced consumer society.

Human history might not have been so catastrophic, in fact, had quieter, less aggressive, more intelligent, more honest, and harder working people been leading us.

We believe, however, that the aggressives often have few friends, the 'neutrals' tend to get on with one another, whilst the placids tend to keep to themselves, Thus, on average, you should only expect to get on OK with one out of every two people, the point being don't be too upset when you are frustrated by people that you can't get on with. Instead, try using *'stroking'* on them, John Dean in his book *Blind Ambition* describing how this was used to 'butter up' people in the Nixon administration in order to get them to do what you wanted.

It also helps to be able to read *body language*, as well as facial expressions, to gauge people's attitudes to you. One should also note that people that only talk to you in 'one-liners' are likely to be enemies to some degree, so communicating with those who you do 'get on' with can be crucial to getting on in life, particularly if those friends are in the right places.

Chapter 10
THE MASS MEDIA

The idea that the media is there to educate us, or to inform us, is ridiculous because that's about tenth or eleventh on their list. The first purpose of the media is to sell us shit.
Abbie Hoffman, speech at U South Carolina (September 16, 1987)

THE PRINT MEDIA

The *Acta Diurna* of the Romans contained daily official reports, and the Chinese claim to have had a similar journal of much greater antiquity (Egerton Eastwick, 1896).

The earliest regular newspaper is thought to have been the *Notizie Scritte* published in Venice around the middle of the 16th century. The paper could be seen at various places in the city for the price of a small coin, the *gazeta*, from which came the term Gazette.

Around the end of the 16th century casual publications of various professions, parties and other special interest groups had limited circulation in England. In 1622 the one-page *Certaine News of the Present Week* was first printed and followed by many other one-page weeklies.

Later, two-page newspapers circulated twice a week appeared, eventually being printed daily. In 1785 a newspaper renamed *The Times* three years later was established and by 1829 it was eight pages. During the Crimean war the first war-correspondent letters appeared and the circulation rose to over 50,000. The era of the modern newspaper had begun.

Today's major newspapers are larger than ever and many have large weekend supplements devoted to such things as additional news commentary and the arts.

Articles in major newspapers tend to become a routine mix of such topics as major local and international events, local and international politics and crime, traffic other accidents, business news and sporting news

In most of these areas outcomes or results will be reported, along with editorial comment and discussion of coming events.

The many local and regional newspapers naturally focus more on events in their area so that, for example, plans for alterations to a local park might be a main article.

There are also many magazines which focus on news in special interest areas such as business, cars and computers.

For all newspapers and magazines advertisements are a major source of revenue. There are also a few newspapers and magazines devoted to advertising second hand goods for sale or to advertising products such as cars and computers.

As ever, editorial comment in the major newspapers is usually very guarded so that a rare hint of dissent with government policy is barely noticeable.

Ways in which editorial policy can influence politics, however, include:

> By simply giving less coverage to one party than another.
> By giving heavy coverage to a mistake or embarrassing incident involving a member of one party.

Over time, therefore, newspapers can have a considerable political effect and always have, so much so that they have often been subjected to government censorship.

Newspapers also play a cultural role, most obviously in discussing local arts and sporting events. The quotation that commences the next chapter is an excellent example of this role and the way in which advertisers can use newspapers to brainwash the young into becoming lifelong consumers of their products.

RADIO

Radio has been one of the great advances in human life. It allows international communication of news, embraces the people of most cities and towns, and plays an important role in ambulance, police and other essential services.

Radio has evolved from a novelty in its early days to a habit of modern life. The first author recalls the first 24 hour broadcasting by a radio station in Melbourne taking place in the early 1960s. Since then radio has evolved in major cities to provide a wide variety of 24 hour AM and FM stations such as:

- 24 hour news.
- Classical music.
- Popular music.
- 'Old time' music.
- Talk-back.
- Sports.
- 'Traditional' radio: a mix of news, sport, music etc.

Most of these are supported by a good deal of advertising and it is often claimed that many people spend more time listening to radio than they do watching TV and that, therefore, radio ads are more effective.

Radio stations have much smaller audiences than prime time TV, however, though in Australia the government owned ABC radio sometimes has a good sized audience. No doubt, therefore, it will eventually be privatized!

Some of the talk-back stations cater for the sick, deranged, drunk and lonely in the later evening and throughout the early hours of the morning.

Whether radio has much effect politically is doubtful, TV playing a much greater role in this area.

Culturally, however, radio has great influence. The latest styles of pop music are played to the young and this has always had an effect on their behaviour.

Before the 1950s popular recording artists sang in a semi-classical style or were 'crooners' like Bing Crosby who only older people could identify with.

In the mid 1950s the young Elvis Presley was viewed as a potentially bad influence on the young. He was endorsed by such well-known TV personalities as Ed Sullivan, however, and that seemed to overcome early prejudice from the older generation, or at least guarantee the approval of the younger generation.

There is no doubt, however, that rock and roll music has had a bad effect on the young as its performers were often doubtful characters afflicted with all the vices. Inevitably a whole generation was influenced by such behaviour and began themselves to behave less politely and become a little more immoral. If the lyrics of a popular song talked about 'having it off' in the back seat of a car, then young people of that generation would do just that.

Currently we still have stylized singers who 'croon' a song and dress according to some current fashion. We also have bee-bop and other pop music styles that have become more and more 'in your face'. These sorts of songs are accompanied by music clips with scenes of dark and desolate alleys in the poor parts of major cities that project an image of loutish behaviour and crime that seems to rub off on young males in particular.

Popular music has occasionally had positive effects, for example through songs protesting war, and there are those that claim that the 'hippie' and 'flower power' movement in the USA of the late 1960s and early 1970s had through a few large pop concerts played an important role in galvanizing public opinion against the Vietnam war and bringing it to an end.

Evidence of the power of pop music is seen in the emergence of radio stations run by religious organizations that play 'nice' pop music for the young with only occasional interviews or ads concerning religious opinions and events.

Finally, some evidence of the power of radio is exemplified by Radio Vatican in Rome which can be heard globally on the Internet. This, no doubt, plays an integral part in the Vatican's ongoing task of propagating Catholic propaganda.

The 'brainwashing' role of radio, however, became relatively limited with the advent of TV because this became a far more potent medium for political and other propaganda.

TELEVISION

TV has an enormous impact on modern life and people typically watch TV for at least 3 or 4 hours on most days.

The wide variety of shows on TV includes news, current affairs, interviews, panel discussions, documentaries, movies, sitcoms, children's programs, live sport, sporting panels, quizzes, cooking, home renovation and reality shows.

Most of these types of shows play a cultural role and in Australia they are a mixture of US, British and local products, exactly in line with our traditional alliances.

Many documentary shows, particularly those about past wars and other events in history, tend to reinforce those alliances. A notable example are the almost weekly documentary shows concerning Adolph Hitler which seem designed to keep us 'conditioned' for the concept of justified war and the next 'villain' around the corner that our allies the US or UK want to denigrate as a lead-up to yet another war.

As with newspapers, TV news has editorial controls rarely allowing much criticism of the status quo. The many interviews on current affairs shows allow politicians and others to express a view, but only in short 'grabs' which have little impact.

Occasional panel discussion shows allow groups to express their views but again only in short grabs, a sequence of views contradicting each other having little influence on an audience.

As with any media, however, by judicious choice of material shown the public can be brainwashed most effectively.

In Australia, for example, recent Prime Ministers seem to have had a media team that even Hitler might have envied, one that has them seen on TV almost every day saying a few mindless words on some topic or engaged in some public event to identify themselves with the public. As a result, a typically unlikely politician becomes highly successful.

Children's shows on TV play a positive role. Early morning and afternoon shows help keep very young children occupied and entertained and also have some educational content. In the later afternoon shows which sometimes include quizzes help entertain older children and sometimes have significant educational content.

AN EXAMPLE OF TV BRAINWASHING OF THE PUBLIC

A fine example of TV brainwashing of the public in Western nations occurred before the 2003 invasion of Iraq when for months pictures of Sadam Hussein holding a rifle were shown almost daily, accompanied by misguided speculation on whether he possessed Weapons of Mass Destruction (WMDs).

This charade was so persistent as to make many viewers want to scream the next time they heard the term WMD. The purpose of this orchestrated litany of lies and deceit was clearly to 'condition' people into acceptance of the forthcoming military invasion of Iraq by the US and the few of its allies willing to assist it.

In fact, Iraq had been so severely weakened by the 1991 invasion and subsequent sanctions and continuous bombing in the broad 'no-fly' zone placed through it that is was incapable of anything but minimal resistance.

The whole shabby and gutless affair was possibly at the behest of the Saudis, with whom the Bush family had strong connections, perhaps still regarding Sadam as a long-term irritation in the region.

Just as Osama Bin Laden wanted, however, the Iraq invasion damaged an already sick American economy even further and removed Sadam from power, opening the way for eventual fundamentalist Islamic control of the country. Indeed, another possibility is that al Qa'ida themselves may have fed the long-incompetent CIA misinformation about Iraq possessing WMDs to suck them into invasion.

RELIGION AND MORALITY ON TV

Religious shows on TV mainly appear in the early hours of Sunday morning. These are bible bashing US shows which cannot be watched and taken seriously by many.

In Australia, however, there is an interview show that concerns itself with religion around midnight during the middle of the week and the government run ABC runs a program on Sunday evenings which shows documentaries on religious topics.

These few shows with a religious basis, however, cannot have much influence on an increasingly immoral society. In fact many of the banal sitcoms and movies now involve high levels of foul language, violence and sex which should not be seen by anyone, let alone children.

Panel shows also involve plenty of poor language, somewhat stupid and loutish behaviour and too much joking about sexual matters.

Some of the ridiculous and voyeuristic reality shows are also completely tasteless. *Big Brother* was filled with bad language, silly behaviour and obscene talk on such absurd topics as farts. *Survivor* seems bent on reducing groups of people to a more nearly primeval state, exactly mirroring the reverse evolution taking place in our society which is so much encouraged by ever lower moral standards in TV.

To top it all off there are those ads shortly after midnight for sex shops and 'sex' chat lines for 'straight' and homosexual people which are a sad reflection on a sick society.

Worse still, however, is the increasing level of violence on TV and at the movies. Inevitably the result is 'copy cat' behaviour in the society made audience to these movies (Cipolla, 1974):

> *It is disturbing to see that still today, even in the most advanced countries, in large sections of human society, aggressiveness is praised as a virtue - or at least as a valuable asset - and it is constantly advertised in the motion pictures and on television. We need - more than anything else - to educate people to tolerance and gentility.*

Only a few days ago there was yet more news of a gang of youths in Melbourne beating up two lone people at separate locations in Melbourne late at night. Melbourne used to be considered a quiet, if not dull city, and now it is developing a history of crime reminiscent of Chicago.

The mass media, particularly the many movies that glorify crime and violence play a large role in desensitizing people to violence to the point at which is comes almost naturally to them.

The final insult is not only the violence, but to find oneself in a city half covered in graffiti painted by mindless louts who enjoy other irresponsible and dangerous practices such as throwing rocks and bottles at the windows of cars, trams and trains.

We need to draw a firm line quickly regarding mass media that encourages this sort of behaviour before life in this society becomes intolerable for decent people.

TV ADVERTISING

TV advertising has moved from the simple situation of a presenter reading a script while holding the product in question up in front of the camera to ads that have various styles such as:

- 'Basic' ads that mention the product and concentrate on telling you its name and where to get it. Sometimes these have no presenter and only text messages.
- Sophisticated ads that show the product in 'classy' surroundings.
- "Laid back' ads were the presenter extols the virtue of the product.

- ➢ Semi-humorous ads which sometimes use cartoon characters to present their message.
- ➢ Ads where the reader just about screams at you not to miss some bargain sale or to go to some cheap store.
- ➢ Ads targeting children which involve cuddly characters and fantasy scenes and the like.

More than other forms of advertising, TV advertising is sometimes very psychological. Many ads aimed at children, for example, are tested on young children who are asked whether they feel persuaded by them to pester their parents into buying the product.

Most important, however, is that ads only have to persuade a few children to try a product and they will spread the idea to their friends by the powerful pyramid effect of social learning which, unfortunately, is the main way in which children pick up bad habits like smoking and drugs.

MOVIES

An example of the Christian church using movies for brainwashing is a set of 5 movies of about 40 minutes duration and involving the following leading characters and languages:

1. Dini – Indonesian.
2. Khalil – Arabic.
3. Ali – Turkish.
4. Khosrow – Tarsi.
5. Mohammad – Hausa.

#3 is about a bossy, bad-tempered, alcoholic Muslim husband who beats his wife. He has a vision that leads him to

Saudi Arabia and en route he has a vision of Jesus. Telling others it, his wife is doubtful, whilst his friends deride him. He hears the voice of Jesus again, however, and converts to Christianity, his wife doing the same, feeling it has saved them.

#5 is about a young African boy who while herding has a vision of Jesus, moving him to go to Saudi Arabia where he stays 18 months and learns Arabic. Returning home, his father pesters him about beginning to acquire wives but he has another vision, this of Jesus saving a man from attack by black-hooded men. He tells his father who sends him to a medicine man where he is given a potion without result. Another medicine man is tried before the boy has visions on six successive nights of Jesus defending him from the devil. A 7th dream promotes the Bible and the boy converts to Christianity. This upsets his father who calls him an "infidel" and the boy leaves home. Two years later, hearing his father to be ill, he returns to visit him, when his father forgives him, dying 3 hours later.

THE INTERNET

The Internet has provided a new form of mass media which combines all the other mass media. Thus the now ubiquitous PC is linked by modem to the Internet and thence to web sites that link to newspapers, radio and TV, as well as to countless other information and advertising sites.

Through e-mail the Internet also provides an important new means of communication for both social and business purposes.

For business it also provides an alternative medium for both marketing and sales, as well as for other transactions such as bank account transactions and bill payments.

For children seeking information for school projects, for example, the Internet is often useful.

The widespread use of the Internet to present University courses, on the other hand, is deplorable and debases these greatly. Such a practice also tends to encourage lightweight courses like the absurd postgraduate courses in Sexology and Puppetry introduced at two Australian 'latter-day' Universities.

In recent years increasing numbers of people are becoming addicted to various 'social sites' such as Facebook and spend up to hours a day sharing mindless and useless gossip on them.

Undoubtedly the worst result of the Internet is the many sites devoted to sexual matters. Some of these involve the sex chat lines and dating services advertised in newspapers and on TV. Others involve pornography, including illegal child pornography, yet another indication of an increasingly sick society perhaps.

CONCLUSION

The mass media play a great part in our lives. They 'condition' us to accept our culture and the attitudes of our government and society.

TV is perhaps the most potent of the mass media as it is the centrepiece of the modern home and often some of its bedrooms as well. The Internet provides social, educational and business access via telephone links and also links to the other mass media. TV programs and advertising, however, provide the most powerful means of brainwashing people politically and behaviourally, and advertising is the subject of the next chapter.

The major newspapers, however, have considerable political influence by way of frequent poll results and editorial comment, particularly in the weeks leading up to an election.

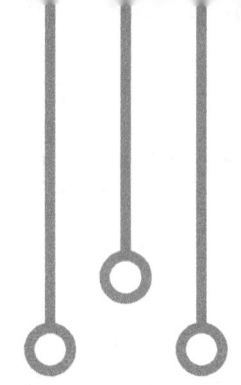

Chapter 11
THE PSYCHOLOGY OF ADVERTISING

*The chief customers of the public house today are the elderly and middle-aged men. Unless you can attract the younger generation to take the place of the older men, there is no doubt that we shall have to face a steadily falling consumption .....
if we begin advertising in the press we shall see that the continuance of our advertising is contingent upon the fact that we get educational support as well in the same papers. In that way it is wonderful how you can educate public opinion, generally, without making it too obvious that there is a public campaign behind it all ...*

Sir Edgar Saunders,
Director of the Brewers' Society,
Birmingham, 1930 (Sargent, 1979).

THE PURPOSE OF ADVERTISING

Nowadays, of course, there are massive media and advertising industries devoted to turning us into consumer zombies.

The main objectives of ads, in approximate order of priority, are to:

1. Make the brand name familiar.
2. To give the brand a distinct image.
3. Attribute at least one key attribute to that brand name.
4. Associate the product with certain usages.
5. To convince us that this brand is the best (for us).
6. To persuade us that we should buy the product.

To meet these objectives ads will involve: slogans, demonstrations, comparisons, testimonials, and repetition.

Comparisons, of course, are usually of price, but sometimes also some sort of semi-official rating, for example safety ratings for cars.

By way of style ad types include basic facts, 'mood', feel-good, social setting, slice-of-life, humour, fantasy, hard-sell, and anxiety/danger/risk or 'fear' ads.

An example of fear type ads are those for household insect sprays, and the TV program *More Hidden Killers Of The Victorian Home* reminds us that fear ads have been around for a long time, ads in the Victorian era selling such products as poisonous Borax (sodium borate) as a household cleanser, the "new science of germs and microbes" helping promote a fear of myriad household 'bugs'.

To make ads more appealing attractive female models, smooth talkers, or sports and movie stars are often used to promote products.

To give ads more authority statements by experts or organizations may be used to convince us of the merits of a product.

To make purchase more imperative ads will scream of huge price reductions for a limited time, huge bargains for as little as two days only, and buy on the never-never deals with no interest for a year or two.

In their efforts to get you in ads will go to ends which range from boring to extremely irritating, from dull and routine to the heights of excess and absurdity, from mere suggestion to downright pleading, and from slight desperation to screaming at us to buy the product.

More subtle are 'advertorials' of bought space in newspapers, conspicuous 'product placement' in movies, or internet sites. For maximum tedium there are half-hour infomercials on afternoon or late night TV which sometimes repeat night after night, week after week, and year after year. In these and most other types of ads there are often trial offers, bonus products for quick purchase etc.

In economics we equate aggregate demand and aggregate supply to obtain $MV = PQ$ where M is the amount of money in circulation, V is its velocity of circulation (in transactions per year), P is the price of goods in circulation, and Q is the quantity of goods in circulation per year.

Then if, for example, we increase Q we should advertise to ensure a corresponding increase in V or turnover. As the first author puts it, Mohr's First Law of Advertising is that we *'increase the velocity of bullshit in order to increase turnover.'*

One way of maintaining higher levels of production is through planned obsolescence of which there are three types (Packard, 1963):

[1] **Quality:** the product wears out in some planned manner.
[2] **Function:** a new product performs the function better.
[3] **Desirability:** the product is 'restyled', making the old version seem obsolete.

In case [1] we would hardly advertise product deficiencies. On the contrary we would do everything we could to prevent bad publicity and would always advertise claiming quality and reliability or at least ignoring these points. Cases [2] and [3] would be advertised as 'new, improved' and 'the new - - - ."

THE PSYCHOLOGY OF ATTITUDES

Attitude can be defined as 'psychological *tendency* expressed by *evaluating* a particular entity with some degree of favour or disfavour.'

Figure 11.1 illustrates the three types of response involved in attitudinal psychology. These are:

1. *Cognitive response.* This response is that of recognition of, for example, a name, a picture or other stimulus.
2. *Affective response.* This is a hypothetical construct and a latent variable. Here the sympathetic nervous system responds to (1) with feelings or emotions.

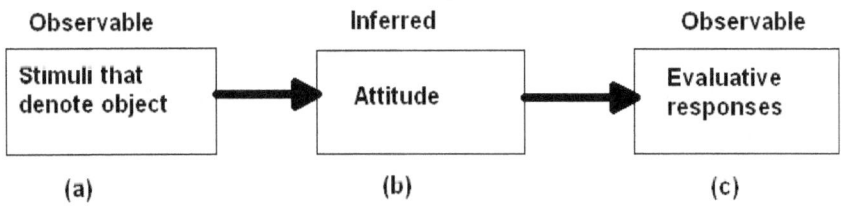

Figure 11.1. Psychological responses

3. *Behavioural response.* This is the outward expression of (2) and may be a positive, neutral or negative response of some degree or intensity involving some observable action.

In this context conservatism, environmentalism or racism are objects. Then when we label a person a conservative, environmentalist or racist we infer an attitudinal position. Such attitudes are evidenced and also developed by the 'CAB' mechanism illustrated in Figure 11.1.

Schemas are cognitive structures that represent a person's past experience in a stimulus domain by a higher order or abstract cognitive structure. Then attitude is a subset of such a schema.

Schemas have a selective effect on the remembering of information so that people have a better remembrance of stimuli that 'fit' their schemas and also for those that 'oppose.' This same selectivity applies to the 'output' of information as well as its input.

Figure 11.2 illustrates the reception-yielding model of attitude formation (Eagly and Chaiken, 1993). Here 'reception' refers to comprehending a 'message', for example an advertisement. This model postulates that the probability of attitude change is given by

$$P(C) = P(R) \times P(Y)$$

so that a maximum change is obtained where the reception and yielding curves intersect, as shown in Figure 11.2.

One application of this idea is to 'get them young' so that advertising companies target the young and naive before they have the maturity or 'consumer intelligence' to develop

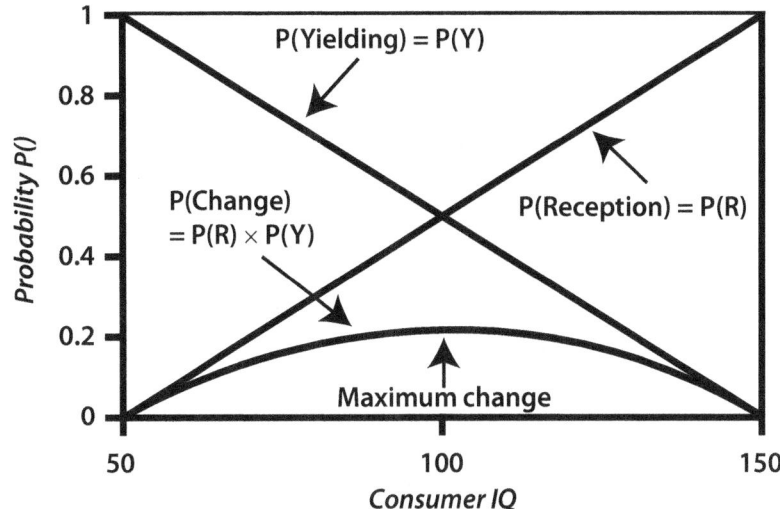

Figure 11.2. Probability of reception, yielding and attitude change.

resistance. Indeed, it is for this reason that the horizontal axis in Fig. 11.2 is labelled Consumer IQ.

The quotation that opens this chapter is an excellent example. Once an idea like 'beer is for men' is buried in a boy's brain he may become a beer drinker for life, the habit occasionally reinforced by ads that make the habit look completely appropriate.

The basic mechanism of persuasion, therefore, is to 'get them young' (and naive or 'less intelligent consumers') as Figure 11.2 suggests. To do this ads need only persuade/ brainwash some of the target audience and then imitative or 'social' learning ensures that many of the rest follow them.

Advertisements having achieved this, regular advertising reminds the audience of a product. Then in Figure 11.1 the

'C' response will be one of recognition of your brand, the 'A' response will be one of approval of it, and the 'B' response will be to make a mental note to buy it.

Learning curves were discussed in Chapter 8 and in advertising it is important to have sufficient repetitions of an ad to ensure adequate average learning by the audience. The forgetting curves of Figure 11.3 also have important application in developing long-term marketing plans. Here curves A and B are for two messages and curve B★ is the result after the second message is repeated.

Then, when time has elapsed after an advertisement its 'residual' effect depends upon both the *primacy* (strength) of the ad compared to others and its *recency*.

In Figure 11.3, after two weeks ad B★ has greater recency than ad A, but less primacy so that they have nearly equal effect.

Such repetition of ads will ensure long-term potentiation of the remembered message, an important objective

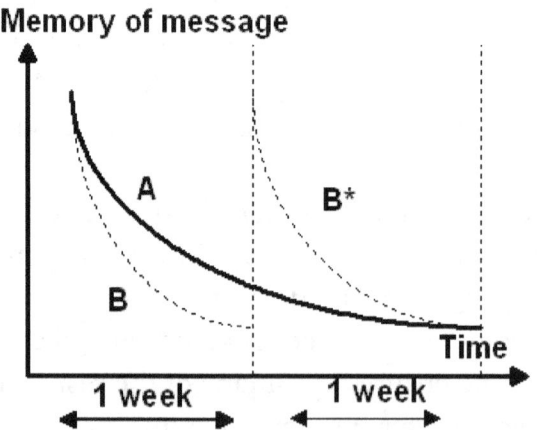

Figure 11.3. Forgetting curves.

(Vander et al., 1994). Correlation between retention and persuasion, however, is by no means guaranteed and ads can be tailored to these two ends.

TARGETING ADVERTISING

Maslow defined two kinds of needs (Lindzey at all, 1978):

(a) *Basic needs* such as hunger, thirst, sex and security.
(b) *Metaneeds* such as achievement, beauty, goodness, justice, order and unity.

Maslow defines achievement as a basic need but the present authors prefer to classify it as a 'higher' or more human metaneed.

First, we must meet our basic or 'animal' needs. That done we can turn our attention to the higher 'human' metaneeds and thence Maslow's 'meaning of life' goal of 'self-actualization' as a human being.

These needs provide *primary goals* that may motivate us towards *secondary goals* such as money in order to achieve them.

Most of our basic needs are *intrinsic motivations* whereas most of our metaneeds are *learned goals*.

Advertising usually targets the metaneeds of your *ego*. A Coke ad, for example, is not designed to remind you that you may be thirsty. If so, you might rush to the fridge and grab whatever drink you can find to satisfy that thirst. No, a Coke ad makes it look 'cool' to drink Coke with your friends and being 'cool' is a metaneed! So next day a young boy will want to be 'cool' when hanging out with his friends so they will all drink Coke and act foolishly, just like the actors in the Coke ads.

Here again we see the down side of advertising, namely that increasingly ambitious executives will stop at nothing to sell their product, even if it has to brainwash the young into acquiring both bad behaviour and bad teeth.

In marketing to children, of course, familiar cuddly looking cartoon figures are often displayed on packaging and used to speak the lines of TV ads. Here, however, ads usually target the *Id,* the basic 'animal' personality that has basic needs like hunger. Young children tend to eat in smaller doses and often so that almost any time they are awake is a good one to put a picture of confectionery in front of them.

One of the best examples of brainwashing, however, is the use of *consumer panels* of children in marketing research. The children are often asked what they will say and do to persuade parents to buy them the product.

Finally, the extent to which children are exposed to advertising is incredible:

> - - *"it is estimated that children between two and 11 years old may see over 20,000 advertisements in a year,"*
>
> (O'Guinn et al., 2006).

Advertising, therefore, will brainwash someone in your family, even if it doesn't brainwash you!

In marketing to adults well known sporting identities are often used to market such things as golf clubs, household appliances and cars and houses. Indeed, this was the basis of Mark McCormack's very successful IMG (McCormack, 1986) and one of his earliest clients was Greg Norman who, marketed as 'The Shark', was made out to be a much better golfer than he was and made an awful lot of money from TV ads.

ADDICTION

There is no doubt that advertising has the effect of conditioning people. Just as Pavlov's dogs were conditioned to associate a bell with the appearance of food so that they then salivated when only given the stimulus of the bell, so too will a psychological 'trigger' be thrown in our minds when the 'CAB' responses to an ad are invoked.

In the same way advertising seeks to develop *habits*. Habits can be quickly formed and very hard to break. It only takes as little as one or two first exposures to learn something. Then only a few repetitions are needed for the memory to become *long-term potentiated* (Vander et al, 1994) and more easily recalled than most other memories in your brain.

In young children the result of confectionery advertising is often a virtual addiction to sugar. In teenagers this continues but junk food and Coke are added to their habits, soon followed by bourbon and Coke and then beer for the boys and perhaps some of the new vodka based mixed drinks for the girls.

Booze ads often *associate* booze with celebration so that at 'rave' parties for young people primeval music seems to go hand in hand with drugs and booze.

The psychology of this sort of behaviour is doubtless based on imitative learning from adults. In other words, as long as adults are stupid enough to drink booze children will too.

Since cigarettes are now discouraged in the media teenagers will smoke marijuana, arguing that it is not as harmful. This is not only an intoxicating drug but a hallucinogenic one as well. So, why not harder drugs like a little cocaine after that?

Then addiction quickly becomes likely. From booze to most other drugs, poisons have two problems:

(a) They don't really taste nice unless diluted enough by other things such as water and sugar in the case of booze.

(b) They alter the metabolic rate, resulting in changes in pulse rate and blood pressure, and contraction or dilation of blood vessels in the brain and elsewhere. Thus every fair sized dose of most drugs gives you withdrawal symptoms, whether you realize it or not. If you have an overdose you will realize it and you might want some 'hair of the dog' (that bit you) as alcoholics call a dose of booze early in the day to help overcome a hangover.

Celebration is not the only excuse for booze. Wine goes well with food, it is said, so that is another. The reality is that, because alcohol is a poison, wine will tend to eat at your stomach so it is best to line your stomach with a little food to ease the discomfort that you should be able to feel after a few glasses of wine.

This somewhat corrosive property of alcohol is the reason why it causes stomach ulcers and cancer of the oesophagus and stomach. It is also the reason why, as noted in Chapter 7, it was used to dissolve the connective tissue in the frontal lobes of the brain in the first lobotomy operations.

One way or the other, booze is inculcated as a daily habit, whether that be granny's tot of fortified wine, a bottle or two of wine with dinner, or a six pack while watching TV in the evening.

In other words *advertising* does reduce us to brainwashed zombies who will enjoy drinking poison if told to. We will leap about to primitive music like savages if told to. Many of us still smoke because ads used to tell us to.

All too many of us take drugs like marijuana, heroin and cocaine. All these addictions are practices that supposedly more civilized European explorers learnt from primitive societies and took back to Europe with them!

PUSH AND PULL MARKETING

Some marketing campaigns use *push strategies* which concentrate on the availability of products. In this case the ads are 'basic' and concentrate on telling you the product name and where to get it. Examples of such ads on TV are

- ➢ A presenter reads a script while holding the product in question up in front of the camera.
- ➢ Ads with only text messages and a voice-over.
- ➢ Semi-humorous ads which sometimes use cartoon characters to present their message.
- ➢ Ads targeting children which involve cuddly characters and fantasy scenes and the like.
- ➢ Ads for junk food which play on having a high 'reward/effort' ratio (Govoni et al., 1988). That 50 million people a day eat McDonald's stuff is testament enough to the success of their advertising.
- ➢ Ads where the reader just about screams at you not to miss some bargain sale or to go to some cheap store.

Advertisements for 'basic' food, junk food, confectionery, clothing and home appliances are usually of the 'push' type.

Marketing campaigns often use *pull strategies* which promote the product in order to attract buyers. In this case the ads concentrate on 'image' to attract the audience to the product and the product name is secondary and *associated* with the imagery. Examples of this sort of ad on TV are:

- ➢ Sophisticated ads that show the product in 'classy' surroundings with actors dressed stylishly.
- ➢ "Laid back' ads were the presenter extols the virtue of the product with, for example, an island resort as a backdrop.
- ➢ Ads that use glamorous people such as movie stars as actors.

This type of advertising is usually used for higher priced or more 'up market' products, including fashion clothing, cosmetics, expensive furniture, luxury cars and overseas holidays.

One of the most important 'levers' in advertising, undoubtedly, is *keeping up with the Jones's*. This is exploited heavily in marketing cars and new gadgets of which the mobile phone is the supreme example at present.

Another powerful inducement is selling on the 'never-never', for example with no repayments for a year.

UBIQUITOUS ADVERTISING

Today advertising is literally everywhere. On TV in Australia there used to be regulations limiting the amount of advertisements per hour to something bearable. Now there seem like 20 minutes or more of ads per hour at times. Worse still, owing to the increasing cost of TV advertising time a truly bewildering string of ads appears in each ad break, sometimes up to about a dozen.

It is almost as bad on radio where there are sometimes as many as half a dozen ads at once on the higher rating commercial stations.

Junk mail from supermarkets and other retail chains has reached epidemic proportions. Other 'direct marketing' is done by phone and is increasingly irritating, often involving requests to complete lengthy market research surveys over the phone.

In addition, free local papers almost totally full of advertisements are also stuffed into millions of letterboxes in major cities.

Trams, trains and buses carry plenty of ads, as do train stations and tram and bus stops. Taxis and trucks all carry signage, as do many vehicles belonging to small businesses.

Shopping strips are becoming more and more cluttered with advertising signs above the shops, and sandwich boards and often products on the footpath.

Shopping malls are filled with advertising and more and more stalls with spruikers have appeared in them.

Sporting grounds carry more and more advertising and sporting teams now carry prominent advertising on their clothing.

Casual clothing often comes complete with the brand name writ large upon it.

The Internet is full of advertising, of course, some of it of a lurid nature.

Then there is the despicable practice of placing confectionery and soft drinks near the checkouts at supermarkets, resulting in many a tantrum as young children taken shopping throw a tantrum to get another dose of perhaps the first 'drug' of addiction, sugar.

Perhaps the most predatory advertiser of all, Coca Cola, has its vending machines just about everywhere, including pubs and clubs, office buildings, stations and heaven knows where else (they are probably there too!).

USING RELIGION

In the West Christianity has been heavily exploited in marketing for example by

- The use of religious symbols such as stylized crosses in the jewellery business.
- The confectionery industry makes heavy use of Easter to sell chocolate. Bakeries join in by selling Easter buns and industries such as the entertainment and travel industries rely heavily on the Easter holiday period.
- Christmas, of course, is a bonanza for business and has become almost completely devoid of its original meaning. Indeed, the image of Santa is actually from a 19th century cartoon of a rich robber baron with some of *his* toys which he certainly isn't going to give away (Solomon, 1992).
- Not too distantly related to this are Mother's Day and Father's Day which are also exploited by, and were probably created by, big business.

Religion also makes increasing use of TV and radio programs for promotion and in the US some religious sects have also spent large sums of money to employ advertising companies to run PR campaigns to promote themselves.

A notable new religion is Mohronism which is proposed in the recent book *World Religions* (Mohr & Fear, 2015).

Mohronism has 10 laws, the ninth of which is that the prophet of Mohronism is Murphy, whose law sums up mankind's disastrous history very well. The tenth is that nothing is quite so simple as 'black and white', or 'good and bad', and everything should be judged on the Mohr Scale of 1 – 9, zero being disallowed (in the case of health it would = dead) while 10 or perfection is deemed impossible.

Like all religions, Mohronism appeals to morons and doubtless countless millions will adopt it eventually.

NEW TRENDS IN MARKETING

Some of the many new trends of late include:

1. Healthy foods, for example low fat products.
2. Recycling.
3. Pollution free and environmentally friendly products.
4. Diets and weight watching.
5. Alternative therapies. Of these the list grows daily:
   a. Aromatherapy.
   b. Herbal remedies.
   c. Acupuncture and Chinese medicine.
   d. Group therapy.
   e. Exercise therapy, for example Yoga and Pilates.
   f. Transcendental meditation.
   g. Reflexology - and so on.

In many large cities where house prices have tended to become unaffordable to new entrants to the market there is a growing 'live for today' approach to consumer spending and this is seen in:

1. The growing fast food industry, including take-away food and packaged 'heat only' meals sold in grocery stores.
2. Increasing diversity in consumption of alcohol.
3. Increasing use of drugs which may perhaps be encouraged by the legalization of marijuana.
4. Increasing use of leisure industries such as gambling.
5. Increasing use of restaurants by young childless workers (who may remain childless).
6. Greater spending by young and independent working women on cosmetics, clothes, jewellery and other beauty and fashion products including hair dressing and magazines.
7. Greater spending on magazines, videos, books, computer games, music and other home entertainment products.
8. Greater spending on cars, holidays and other major items by young childless couples or unattached persons.

In these and many other areas there seems to be a growing market which advertisers are busy exploiting. In some communities, however, one or two of the foregoing examples may be on the wane.

THE DISASTROUS SOCIOLOGICAL RESULTS

The extent to which advertising has reduced us to *consumer zombies* strolling around in uncomfortable jeans and carrying a mobile phone in one hand and a bottle of drink in the other is mind boggling.

An article in *The Australian* newspaper on 23 May 2005 reported that psychologists had found that regular use of text messaging on mobile phones could reduce IQ by as much as 10 points, a staggering outcome.

More important, advertising corrupts young minds by showing young people behaving irresponsibly, for example a recent Pepsi Cola ad showing a few youths riding a large wheeled garbage container down a steep street and into a harbour.

In the early 1960s a US Department of Justice official expressed alarm at the "startling" pace at which youthful lawlessness was increasing and concluded that by 1962 a million American teenagers would be arrested each year.

The same official remarked (Packard, 1963):

> *We seem to have misplaced the sense of values which made this a great nation. Self-indulgence and the principle of pleasure before duty on a vast and growing scale have become a phenomenon of the adult world. These are warning symptoms of the decadence disease which has contributed to the decay of so many civilizations throughout history.*

The role that advertising has played in promoting decadent movies, music and behaviour has resulted in a more violent, lawless, indebted, miserable and brainwashed society.

Propaganda has always painted socialism as communism which permits little freedom. How free are we when we are all brainwashed to dress and behave in the same, often stupid way?

Advertising contributes heavily to the increasing debt levels carried by families in the West. Many people have half a dozen credit cards and get way above their heads in debt, often leading to family disunity and break-ups.

THE DISASTROUS ENVIRONMENTAL RESULTS

Closely related to advertising is the slick packaging of many products, an example being the easy to use 'heat in the tray' packaging of frozen pizza and lasagne. The economic cost of such packaging is enormous and the environmental consequences drastic.

Another example of this are the thin plastic supermarket bags used in Australian supermarkets. Unbelievable numbers of these are used each year and many of them end up littering streets and parks and clogging creeks and storm water drainage systems.

Atmospheric pollution has reached serious levels in many large industrialized cities and global warming has already been significant not long after the term was first coined.

Parkinson's well known law *work expands so as to fill the time available for its completion* was mentioned in Chapter 10 where it is highly appropriate. The present authors prefer to generalize this to Mohr's Universal Law:

Junk fills the time and space available.

This covers a wide range of the problems of mankind including:

- Bureaucratic inefficiency, as in Parkinson's Law that work expands to fill the time available, when people are the junk.
- The Peter Principle problem of the most incompetent people being those that rise in hierarchies. Here those rising are the junk (Peter & Hull, 1969).
- The problems of pollution.
- The problems of resource depletion as a result of excessive consumption of 'junk products' which are unnecessary, extravagant and wasteful, and have planned obsolescence built into them.

Four wheel drives and other cars with massive engines are a good example. The Club or Rome Report (Meadows et al., 1974) pointed out that we were then running out of chromium, once so heavily used by ostentatious American cars. That we are now running out of oil promises to be a major catastrophe because we have built our major cities around the car.

All this has occurred because we have long been brainwashed into becoming mindless zombies consuming not for our own benefit, but for the benefit of insanely greedy and highly overpaid executives whose motivation is an even bigger multimillion dollar bonus.

Though the world was already becoming overpopulated by then, "adman-columnist" E.B. Weiss commented in the 1950s (Packard, 1963):

> *Ever since I've been regaled with the current multitude of wonderful forecasts of a population future sparked by a remarkable growth of our population I have wondered about the magical powers of a large population automatically to assure eternal prosperity - at successively higher peaks . . . The most populous regions of this mortal coil tend to be the most poverty-stricken.*

In other words, capitalist industry has been happy to brainwash us into mindless consumption and has even been happy to count on excessive population growth to help boost profits even further, all the while ignoring the finite nature of the world's resources and its finite capacity to absorb the waste products and pollution arising from extravagant consumption.

A reader's letter in *The Age* newspaper on Friday 29 July, 2016, sums up another key issue:

> *Congratulations to - - on realizing that selling off state assets leaves us, the public, out of pocket. Let's hope the scales will now fall from the eyes of other masters in relation to tax evasion dressed up as tax avoidance.*

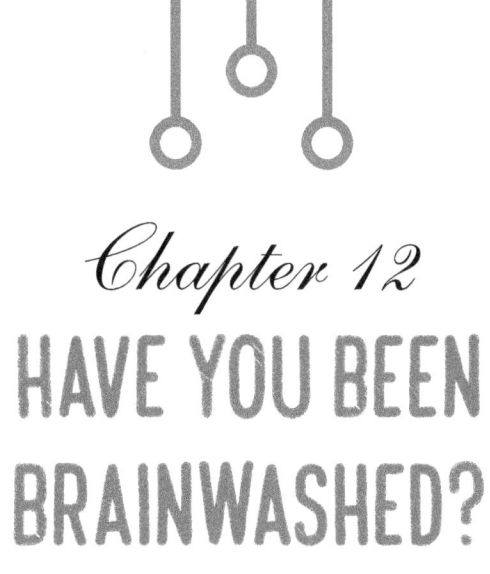

Chapter 12
HAVE YOU BEEN BRAINWASHED?

"For your own good" is a persuasive argument that will eventually make a man agree to his own destruction.
Janet Frame, *Faces in the Water* (1961).

FEW, IF ANY, ESCAPE FOR LONG

Few of us get wise to the fact that we have been brainwashed almost from birth so that by the age of 20 or 30 or so we end up zombies more defined by the products and habits we have been brainwashed into than anything else. This is illustrated beautifully on the cover of a book on consumer behaviour (Solomon, 1992) which shows people in a city street dressed according to some product they indulge, for example a man 'dressed' in a Coke can.

If you, dear reader, have already realized what a brainwashed mess you have become then you are one of the few people coming to their senses. You might, for example, have given up smoking, then realizing what a sucker you were in the first place to fall for whatever bullshit that brainwashed you into taking up such a disgusting and unhealthy habit.

You may not be the typical brainwashed zombie with mobile phone in one hand, drink bottle or cigarette in the other, jeans, baseball hat and perhaps a 4WD if you are old enough and affluent enough to waste that much money on a heap of gas-guzzling metallic junk.

Chances are, however, that you still have other behaviours that are the result of brainwashing earlier in life and which you would be better off without.

HOW WE ARE BRAINWASHED

We are brought up and educated, of course, with a good deal of conditioning in which various kinds of rewards and punishments, most of them verbal, are dished out along the way.

As part of that education, moral, religious, ethical and legal arguments will be brought to our notice to influence and control our behaviour.

On top of all that, of course, modern people spend a large part of their lives absorbing TV and other media bullshit half full of repetitive advertising and, consequently, they also spend a lot of time at sporting venues or in pubs and clubs where they are indulging some brand or other, whether it be a sporting team or a brand of beer.

At work, as at school, we are likely to be at the bottom end of a hierarchical system of 'top-down one-way' (TDOW) communication which treats us no better than slaves or lab rats.

The result is that our behaviour at times can often be likened to that of animals in conditioning experiments, for example:

(a) Rats in a Skinner box pushing a lever to receive food pellets [c.f. working in a production line to receive pay and thence food].
(b) Pigs using their snouts to push the right spot on a PC screen to receive a food reward [c.f. poker machines = Skinner boxes].
(c) Rats in 'running wheels' etc. [c.f. humans with their myriad of usually ridiculous sports].
(d) Pavlov's dogs salivating at the sight of food [c.f. humans doing likewise over food or wine].

Humans at times, however, are far more ridiculous than animals could ever be, for example how we carry on and 'perv' over sex and now have our media littered with it. We have no doubt that a good deal of *social learning* that is very equatable with conditioning is associated with that sort of behaviour.

Social learning and *imitative learning* (IL) are much the same thing but we associate IL more with infants who at the outset imitate their parents with whom they have *imprinted*. People of all ages, however, imprint a group of friends or role models whose behaviours they imitate.

HOW BRAINWASHED A CONSUMER ARE YOU?

The simple test of Table 12.1 uses Likert scaling (much used in market research) to rate your consumption habits.

Table 12.1. Survey of consumption habits.

#	Item	Score
1	Soft drinks, confectionery and snack 'foods'.	
2	Fast food	
3	Booze	
4	Smoking	
5	Drugs - illegal or unnecessary prescription drugs	
6	Jeans, baseball hat or other originally foreign clothes	
7	Cosmetics	
8	The fitness industry: gyms and fitness equipment	
9	Do you indulge in insane activities like skate boarding, rollerblading, bowls or golf?	
10	How much attention do you pay to TV ads?	
11	Do you buy the latest pop music?	
12	Do you go to restaurants and pubs?	
13	Do you go to the movies?	
14	Do you gamble (pokies, horses etc.)?	
15	Do you pay to attend commercialized sporting events?	
16	How much do you use your mobile phone?	
17	Do you have a 4WD or other 'fashionable' car?	
18	Do you have domestic pets?	
19	Do you take holiday trips?	
20	Do you buy things just because they are 'on special' and supposedly a bargain?	
	Total	

Give scores to each item (RH column) according to whether you consume/indulge the particular item to the following levels:

1 = Not at all or minimally
2 = To some extent/a little
3 = Moderately
4 = Quite a lot/a bit too much
5 = Much too much

If your total score (/100) is greater than 20 you are fairly badly brainwashed. If your total score exceeds 30 you are a hopeless case!

[The first author's score at an earlier age would have been about 20].

Of course countless other questions could have been included in Table 12.1, for example:

(a) Do you give regular allegiance to a particular political party?
(b) Do you 'consume' sex products, that is, prostitution, pornography, sex chat lines etc.?

DO YOU REALLY BELIEVE THE BULLSHIT?

The foregoing crude quantitative test is of consumption habits. At a more qualitative level the following subjects are areas in which your views may have resulted from brainwashing, that is, mere acceptance of the bullshit given on the topic in the media.

➢ US propaganda incorrectly calls socialism communism.

- How free are we when we are all brainwashed to dress and behave in the same, often stupid way?
- How free are we in schools, Universities, workplaces and hospitals increasingly operated like assembly lines and in which our roles are reduced to those of mere automatons?
- How free are we when increasing numbers of us spend time in jail or psychiatric institutions, millions school children are doped to help them bear a far too long 12 years at school, massive numbers of us take to booze and other drugs, and increasing numbers of us commit suicide or drop out of society?
- How secure are we when 50% of marriages end in divorce, we have to work longer and longer hours, and women have to work as well when once they didn't?
- How free are we when there is less and less job security and the idea of one career or occupation for life has vanished? Now you are expected to be prepared to change career three or more times which cannot be a reasonable or economically efficient way of life.
- Do you really believe in God or that Jesus Christ did the definitively impossible and rose from the dead? Do you really think it is right that religious sects throughout history have kept on killing each other, as they still are right now in many parts of the world?
- Do you really believe that Coke or booze, or whatever junk is pushed at you by advertising, is a smart and healthy thing to consume?
- Do you really believe locking infants up in day care is right?

- ➢ Do you really believe 12 years at school is necessary when Francis Bacon left Cambridge at age 14 and Michelangelo and da Vinci were apprenticed at that age?
- ➢ Do you believe that increasingly corporatized Universities should be able to con people with crap courses like postgraduate courses in Sexology and Puppetry?
- ➢ Do you really believe it is sensible that Australian Unis increased their output of PhDs by 85% between 1996 and 2006 (the increase in the USA was only 15% in that time)?
- ➢ Do you really believe the Westminster 'revolving door' two-party system is anything like halfway democratic?
- ➢ Do you really believe that 'she'll be right' and the politicians and other leaders who have always led us into wars or profited from them will fix everything when we have just about bred ourselves out of existence and ruined and depleted the planet beyond repair?

JUST WHAT THEN IS SENSIBLE?

If one wishes to avoid being a sucker for advertising and other bullshit one should do almost nothing. There are, however, a few necessities of life such as:

- ➢ **Food:** obviously one should try and develop a healthy diet which has minimal fat and sugar, plenty of complex carbohydrate, and sufficient protein, fibre and essential nutrients. To that end, therefore, junk food,

fatty snack foods and confectionery should be largely avoided.
- **Clothing:** Neat, well fitting and practical clothing at modest prices should be sufficient for all but those with too much money. Other money spent on appearances should be minimal, for example women should not have to spend heaps on cosmetics and hairdressing.

In the old days, of course, women did their own hair. Now we have to have people do this, mow the lawn, wash the dog and, before long, wipe our bums. Now there's my business idea for the day:

JIM'S BUM WIPING SERVICE - WE COME TO YOU.
- **Shelter:** Modest, practical and not too cramped housing should be all that we need. Indeed, with our collapsing standards of living and everybody but the children needing to work at often menial jobs most young families can barely afford that or pay at least double or triple in the long run to a greedy bank.
- **A partner:** It is difficult to do or achieve much in life alone. A writer such as I, for example, needs above all else a publisher, and preferably an agent also to get publishers interested in the first place.
- **A job:** As did the hunter-gatherers, society needs people to produce food, clothing, shelter and a myriad of other things, production of these involving countless 'service' occupations such as selling products. Whether one needs the money or not, however, some sort of occupation is necessary to pass the time so that,

for example, geriatrics are given OT or *occupational therapy.*
- ➢ **Exercise:** Most of us have relatively sedentary occupations so that we need healthy exercise such as walking, running, callisthenics and weights training.
- ➢ **Relaxation and sleep:** Rest and sleep are, of course, absolutely necessary and for good health one must make sure of getting enough of both.
- ➢ **Pastimes and entertainment:** After the foregoing essential activities have been done one normally still has spare time each day as well as days off from work. To fill the gaps we need 'pastimes' which for most people include watching TV, listening to music, interacting with immediate family, or going out to dinner or the movies.

In most of the foregoing there is considerable scope for excess. In the last, for example, it is possible to spend a fortune on restaurants, pubs, gambling and going on holidays over a lifetime.

If we consider needless habits such as smoking, booze and expensive clothes and cosmetics, however, then even the average married couple can spend the price of a halfway decent house (two if they were still fairly priced!) on such habits over a lifetime.

CONCLUSIONS

An article in *The Age* on 8/8/2016 was headed:

> *Today's consumer buying the fridge rather than what should fill it up.*

The main point of the article was that today consumers are focusing mainly on 'big ticket' items such as cars rather than the essential basics such as food and clothing.

Most of we consumers, therefore, can greatly improve our lives by being careful and economical in our consumption practices and habits, in turn improving the prospects of the planet as a whole. Not least of these, of course, is making every effort not to have more than a couple of children, if that. In addition, we should not waste precious time and resources on keeping unhygienic household pets and it would be a great deal saner to instead spend a few dollars supporting a starving child in Africa, or better still, supporting population reduction programs in such countries.

We can also make a difference by actively supporting ethical and sustainable business practices, perhaps by joining organizations that push for sustainable practices and conservation.

Most of all, however, people should push for 'real democracy' that might limit wasteful global marketing and reduce the greed and influence of ruthless transnational companies (Mohr, 2012c).

The bottom line, therefore, is that both at a personal and public level we should do what we can to reverse the power and influence of the 'brainwashers'.

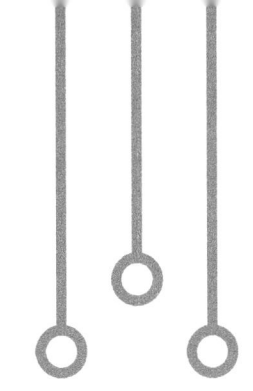

Chapter 13
THE PSYCHOLOGY OF HABITS

How use doth breed a habit in a man.
William Shakespeare,
The Two Gentlemen of Verona, act 5, sc. 4, 1.1.

Television has spread the habit of instant reaction
and has stimulated the hope of instant results.
Arthur Schlesinger Jr, In Newsweek, 6 July 1970.

A habit cannot be tossed out the window, it must
be coaxed down the stairs one step at a time.
Mark Twain, attributed.

ACCOMMODATION
Piaget used the 'term' accommodation to describe how infants come to terms with their environment of a cot,

etcetera, and also become familiar with the small group of faces that they regularly see often smiling at the infant so that, of course, ere long the infant copies this behaviour and smiles back.

TEACHING

A great deal of what a child learns, of course, is taught by parents, other relatives, and teachers in a relatively formal didactic manner. Indeed, modern societies rely almost totally upon teaching at schools, colleges and Universities to train children and young adults for a vocation that in many cases will occupy them for most of their life.

Indeed, for many people learning becomes a habit, and they continue to learn throughout life by reading and studying subjects related to their jobs, or subjects that simply interest them, such interests often having been 'adopted' from parents and other life role models.

IMITATIVE LEARNING

Young children learn many behaviours by imitating or 'modelling' those of their parents, siblings, teachers and friends etcetera. Such imitation ranges from manner of speech to eating and recreational habits. Thus many children take up the same sports as their parents, whilst others may learn swear words and such bad habits as smoking from friends at school.

SOCIAL LEARNING

Social learning is simply imitative learning that takes place on the larger context of society, rather than the confines of home or the classroom. It includes social groups such as friends, religious groups, and sporting and other clubs that a person might belong to.

It is by a combination of imitation of parents and social learning from a small group of friends that children may acquire an interest in beer and/or wine, for example, or worse still and far more dangerous to their health in the long run, illegal drug habits usually begin with social learning, for example at teen dances and parties etcetera.

Studies have also found that children with only one parent are more likely to smoke or drink by the age of 11.

RELIGION

Throughout history religion has played a major role in instructing adherents in how to behave according to guidelines established by each religion. An example of this, a Pope in the 1960s said something along the lines of: *Give me a child before the age of five and I will make him a Catholic for life.*

The current plague of Islamic conflict and terrorism that afflicts much of the world at present, of course, is in part a result of Islamic teachings based on the Koran's frequent advocacy of jihad against "unbelievers" in order to establish caliphates for a particular Muslim leader.

An example of the satanic Muslim religion, in one "barbaric" episode in Mosul IS captured a group of fleeing women and children and burned them alive. Thus we hope that all Islamic jihadists sooner rather than later burn in the fires of Hell.

POLITICAL PROPAGANDA

In like fashion to that of religion, political propaganda has played a major role in human history, usually with disastrous results as often clearly insane and greedy leaders seek power over more and more people and territory, often using religion as a pretext for their aims at greater self-glorification.

Hitler was perhaps one of the best examples, the Nazis doing an excellent job of 'brainwashing' the German people with a constant hail of propaganda to support them. The Nazis also provided their troops with massive amounts of amphetamines to 'energize' their military efforts, whilst Hitler became addicted to a cocktail of drugs including cocaine during WW2, perhaps contributing to increasing depression as the war turned bad for his forces, and ultimately contributing to his suicide.

Two factors in his hate of the Jews were

(a) The centuries old European prejudice against them for, because they had trouble being employed by Christians, they would go into such businesses as running pawn shops and banking, thereby getting rich, the 1964 US movie *The Pawnbroker,* and starring Rod Steiger, being about a pawn shop owner – no doubt Rod was Jewish, whilst the movie biz then in US was largely run by Jews in LA at least.

(b) Rumour had it, and we tend to believe it, that he had contracted syphilis from a Jewish prostitute during WW1. Syphilis not being curable in the long run back in those days, there being no antibiotics to have early on etcetera, the later stages of it no doubt added to his madness gradually as the years rolled by.

A globally widespread example of propaganda of sorts is the use of the terms 'right' and 'left' to compare capitalist sympathetic political parties and parties with more socialist policies, the term 'right', of course, being intended to sound 'right' in the sense of 'correct' or the 'right thing to do'. Here then is a major example of how the mass media in the West promulgates its bias towards the capitalist system that runs it.

THE MASS MEDIA AND ADVERTISING

As discussed at modest length in Chapters 10 and 11, the mass media and advertising are the main means by which modern society is fed information, whether to 'sell' a particular religion or political party, or a household or other product.

The persuasiveness and effectiveness of advertising is, of course, sometimes remarkable, the Reception-Yielding Model of Figure 11.2 illustrating quite well why advertising is so successful in appealing to more 'gullible' consumers.

Indeed, modern advertising involving such subtleties as the somewhat subliminal effect of 'product placement' in movie scenes is often colloquially called 'brainwashing', and for that reason Chapter 12 puts the question: *Have You Been Brainwashed?*

Recognition and *approval* are important factors in how 'consumer zombies' are brainwashed into lifelong habits of consumption, as emphasized by the 'CAB' model of Figure 11.1 in which cognitive, attitudinal and behavioural responses follow exposure to a stimulus such as that of an advertisement. Then, positive attitude or 'approval' is likely to lead to consumption of a product, and perhaps habitual consumption of it.

Indeed we are creatures of habit, much of our lives being spent in the company of just a few friends or family, consuming certain products we have come to like, and spending our spare time in certain adopted pursuits, for example going to the same pub or restaurant and following a particular sporting team regularly.

PSYCHOPATHIC BEHAVIOURS

As noted in Chapter 7, this is the largest category of abnormal psychological types, the pathology of which may involve such traits as:

[1] Assertiveness, aggression and bullying.
[2] Dishonesty and lying.
[3] Alcohol and drug addiction.
[4] Excessive sexual behaviours.

Psychopaths usually have two or more of the above traits, but are not normally classified as mentally ill, in part perhaps because such behaviours are so common.

Bullying may be learnt by an eldest brother or sister, and the first author knew examples of both cases both within his own 'nuclear family', his extended (by his own marriage) family, and people with whom he was friendly for a while. Evidently the eldest is able to boss younger siblings around from an early age, and often stays bossy with both these siblings, and perhaps others, if not most, people throughout most of the rest of their life until too old and feeble to be bossy anymore.

Bullying usually involves a 'superior' or boss, or somebody with psychopathic aggressive tendencies based on feelings of superiority, 'bad mouthing' the victim to their face with brief but hurtful and disturbing insults. These insults are repeated regularly to both the victim, often a 'loner' in an isolated situation, and to the bully's small group of friends and supporters who then repeat the same insults to the victim, increasing his or her feelings of isolation and helplessness.

In the schoolyard, for example, the bully is often bigger and stronger than the victim, who may be of the 'nerd' type. Indeed, the bully is often better at sport, but jealous of the victim getting better marks in class and perhaps occasional praise from teachers and others.

In the workplace the reasons for bullying by bosses or 'superiors' in the workplace hierarchy are often less clear, but often, for example, involve male bosses abusing women with 'sexual insults' that they are ugly, or that women in general are in some way inferior.

ADDICTION

Addiction to legal substances such as nicotine, a brain stimulant, of alcohol, a vasodilator and thus subtle tranquilizer, are, of course, very common.

Alcohol abuse can lead to problems in the workplace, home or social venues. Heavy drinkers suffer unusual brain shrinkage of both white and grey matter, reduction of the latter giving rise to the widespread belief that alcohol kills neurons (Sweeney, 2009).

Western governments have taken several measures to limit smoking, particularly limitation if not prohibition of advertising of cigarettes, in part to reduce the huge impact that the long-term health effects of smoking have upon public health system budgets.

Similarly, measures such as tougher drink-driving laws, earlier closing of some late night clubs and bars, and tougher penalties for family violence, have been put on place to limit some of the harmful consequences of drinking to excess.

As for quitting smoking and moderating booze consumption, the first author devoted a chapter to this subject in three books (Mohr, 2012b; Mohr, 2013; Mohr, 2015).

Increasingly, addiction to pharmaceutical drugs such as Valium prescribed for anxiety, or the raft of drugs prescribed for relatively newly 'invented' conditions such as ADHD and OCD is commonplace and, indeed, something of a modern medical scandal comparable to that of the practice of lobotomy and leucotomy 50+ years ago.

The global illegal drug industry is now, unfortunately, along with the global arms industry, one of the world's largest. Some of the most widely used illegal drugs include:

[1] Cocaine and its derivates, including morphine, are highly addictive and have been widely used for more than a century. High quality cocaine, however, is very expensive, so that users often turn to crime to 'feed' their habit.

[2] Heroin, a narcotic that is considered a 'hard drug', is a highly addictive morphine derivative, intravenous injection providing the fastest and most intense 'rush'.

[3] LSD became quite popular in the 1960s but is rarely used now. It binds to serotonin receptors, only very small amounts having profound effects, including altered states of consciousness and hallucinations. In some cases LSD has been associated with psychosis,

particularly when taken by a person with an existing mental disorder (Sweeney, 2009).

[4] Marijuana grew greatly in popularity from the 1970s, and is still widely in use, being easily able to be grown on country farms, and in suburban backyard and sheds.

Marijuana's active ingredient delta-9-tetrahydrocanniabinal (THC) inhibits release of the glutamate and GABA neurotransmitters, reducing cognitive function. Caffeine has the opposite effect of increasing neuronal release of glutamate and GABA, thereby slightly increasing cognition.

As noted in Chapter 7, marijuana use has been found to correlate with the incidence of schizophrenia.

[5] Methamphetamines, particularly crystal meth or 'ice', have become widely used in the last two decade, and are easily able to be manufactured with quite small and simple chemistry apparatuses in suburban houses and garages.

CONCLUSIONS

Behaviours and habits are learnt from the outset by accommodation, modelling and imitative and social learning, as well, of course, by formal learning whether this be in the home or at school.

Such often lifelong habits as interests in and perhaps participation in music, reading, movies, and certain sports are acquired by both imitative and social learning, as well as teaching in many cases.

The mass media and advertising, of course, play a key role in modern society, informing us of current events, and also persuading us to adopt a particular religion, support a particular political party, or buy an advertised produce.

Indeed, the extent to which we in today's consumer society are 'brainwashed' led the first author to coin the term *consumer zombie* (Mohr, 2012a; Mohr & Fear, 2016).

Chapter 14
HUMAN CONICT

*Mankind must put an end to war or war
will put an end to mankind.*
John F. Kennedy,
speech to the UN 25th Sept. 1961.

*If we cannot now end our differences, at least we
can help make the world safe for diversity.*
John F. Kennedy, address, American University,
Washington D.C. (June 10, 1963).

The first author: *Is the problem of the
human race anthropology?*
Answer: *Of course!*
J.H. Argyris, private communication (1998).

INTRODUCTION

Sadly, conflict has dominated man's history. This is, no doubt, because we are, when all is said and done, just animals with an enlarged cerebral cortex for the semantic memory needed for our advanced languages. Many other animal species, including our close relatives gorillas, have dominant and aggressive alpha males who take charge of groups.

In humans we call this type A personality, a set of traits including ambition, competitiveness, impatience and hostility. Such people are often sociopathic psychopaths, the pathology of their condition also including lying and general delinquency (Davies, 1971), and in man's history many leaders have exhibited these characteristics.

Group conflict, whether tribal or imperialist, seems also to have become a habit in human societies. The Agricultural Revolution saw us establish not only towns and farms, but also armies to defend or to take new territory for growing populations.

Now with the exponentiating human population greatly excessive, and with resources, including arable land, being rapidly depleted, the prospects of conflict are increasing (Mohr, 2012c).

In the last century we had two world wars, the second involving circa 60 million dead. We also invented nuclear weapons and a range of potent biological ones, giving every reason to fear that future wars may be far more devastating than any previous.

AN ATTITUDINAL MODEL OF CONFLICT

Equation 14.1 is a 'first approximation' formula proposed by Mohr (2014b) for assessing the potential for conflict between a person or group assessed and another person or group:

$$A^* = A + xB + yC + zD \qquad (14.1)$$

where
  A^* = current 'overall' attitude,
  A = initial or 'basic' attitude (based on 'known history'),
  B = attitudes towards behaviours of the second party,
  C = contact history between the two parties,
  D = degree of difference between the parties considered,

and x, y, z are scaling factors that indicate the relative importance of the terms and here these will be assumed unity for simplicity.

Equation 14.1 can, of course, be used to assess the attitude of both parties involved in the assessment.

Here attitude is assessed in the same way as attitude is measured by the information integration model of attitudinal psychology (Eagly & Chaiken, 1993), but for simplicity only scale values (but not weights) will be given to a small set of items in measuring A.

Similarly, only scale values are used in assessing B, C and D. These extra terms add a great deal to the 'basic' A assessment to give a 'picture' of the 'overall' attitude.

EXAMPLE APPLICATION

As an example of application of the Equation 14.1 the attitude of a typical individual towards a hypothetical terrorist organization 'HTO' is assessed in Table 14.1.

The assessment uses five simple questions for the initial attitude, behavioural, contact and difference terms in Equation 14.1. 'Scoring' is similar to that used for the 'five-factor' model of personality (Larsen & Buss, 2002) and uses five possible scores:

Table 14.1. Person's hypothetical attitude towards 'HTO'.

SCORE:	-2	-1	0	1	2
A, initial/basic attitude		*Dislike/Like*			
The people			0		
Their government(s)		-1			
How they look		-1			
What they say	-2				
What they do	-2				
B, group behaviour		*Dislike/Like*			
Sectarian conflict		-1			
Negative rhetoric		-1			
'Pushing' their religion	-2				
Threats	-2				
Terrorism	-2				
C, contact history		*Uncomfortable/Comfortable*			
See on TV			0		
See on street			0		
Close to		-1			
Talk to		-1			
Socialize	-2				
D, differences		*Different/Similar*			
Language		-1			
Economic				1	
Culture		-1			
Religion	-2				
History		-1			
TOTAL SCORE, *A**:			-22		

+2 = strongly like/very similar etc.
+1 = like/similar etc.
0 = neutral
-1 = dislike/different etc.
-2 = strongly dislike/very different etc.

Table 14.1 gives an example assessment for a 'typical' individual. Here total scores less than -30 are 'very negative', -10 to -20 'negative', -10 to +10 are moderate, +10 to +20 'positive', and more than +20 'very positive'.

Thus the results of Table 13.1 are 'negative', the total of -22 indicating a considerable degree of disapproval. It is only very negative scores of less than -30 that might be a cause for concern if they were obtained for a significant percentage of a population.

Weighting factors can be assigned to items in Table 14.1 to reflect differing importance associated with them, for example the 9th and 10th items might have weights >1.

EFFECT OF SOCIETAL VIEWS

The effect of the views of society on individuals and groups can be included in Equation 14.1 by adding an extra term comparable to the inclusion of 'social norms' in the Theory of Reasoned Action (Eagly & Chaiken, 1993):

$$A^{**} = A^{*} + fS = A + xB + yC + zD + fS$$

where *f is a scaling factor* here assumed = 1 for simplicity, and the factors x, y, z are also assumed =1 so that:

$$A^{**} = A + B + C + D + S \qquad (14.2)$$

Table 14.2. Person's assessment of society's attitude.

SCORE:	-2	-1	0	1	2
S, perceived society view	\multicolumn{5}{c}{Negative/Positive}				
TV/radio/papers		-1			
Politicians			0		
Religious leaders		-1			
The public		-1			
Friends & family		-1			
TOTAL SCORE:	\multicolumn{5}{c}{-4}				

and S is the person or group's assessment of the attitude or 'position' of society, society here including the media, politicians, religious leaders, the public, friends and family.

Then measurement of S is done in the same way as for A, B, C and D in Table 14.1.

For the views of a 'typical' person regarding society's attitude towards 'HTO' the result might be that shown in Table 14.2. Adding this result to that of Table 14.1 the aggregate score is -26, a 'negative' overall result.

A 'very negative' score would be less than -30, so the combined result of Tables 14.1 and 14.2 (i.e. -26) for an individual or a group is not of concern but worth taking some notice of.

RESPONSES TO CONFLICT

When the group, attitudes towards which are sought, is in some form of dispute or conflict, whether this be economic

Table 14.3. Attitudes towards measures against group.

SCORE:	0	1	2	3	4
		Level of support for action			
Government condemns					4
Cut diplomatic ties				3	
Trade embargo			2		
Public demonstrations				3	
UN sanctions		1			
War	0				-
TOTAL SCORE:			13		

or armed conflict on any scale, the attitudes concerning what 'negative' measures should be taken *against* the group can also be measured in like fashion to Table 14.1.

Table 14.3 shows an example assessment for a hypothetical individual concerning his or her views towards HTO's terrorism around the world. The total score is $R_N = 13$ out of a possible 24, perhaps a 'fail' mark by way of assessment of the group in question, but not an extremely bad score. Total scores of close to 20, on the other hand, would indicate very strong feelings of which, perhaps, considerable notice should be taken should they be found to apply to a significant number of people.

The results of Tables 14.1 – 14.3 can be combined as:

$$A^{\star\star\star} = A + B + C + D + S - (R_N - 12)$$

with the last term adjusted to allow for its different scale of measurement, giving $A^{\star\star\star} = -27$ for the present example

Table 14.4. Attitudes towards measures to reduce conflict.

SCORE:	0	1	2	3	4
		Level of support for action			
Point out grievances					4
Peace negotiations			2		
Diplomatic visits			2		
Trade talks		1			
Financial aid	0				
Formal apologies	0				-
TOTAL SCORE:			9		

case. When the results of Table 13.3 are included, those of Table 13.4 should also be added for 'balance.'

If faced with conflict, in preference to the negative responses of Table 14.3, we should consider the more positive responses of Table 14.4.

Table 14.4 shows an example of an assessment for a hypothetical individual concerning his or her views towards some external group currently in conflict with the individual's group or an ally thereof. The total score is a modest $R_P = 9$, or moderately supportive of negotiation etc., and this should be compared to the total obtained in Table 14.3.

The results of Tables 14.1 – 14.4 can be combined as:

$$A^{***} = A + B + C + D + S - (R_N - 12) + (R_P - 12)$$

where R_N is the score from Table 14.3, R_P is the score from table 14.4, and the last two terms are adjusted to allow for their different scale of measurement.

PSYCHOPATHIC LEADERS

Table 14.5 shows Cattell's personality factor scales, the letters being named, like vitamins, in the order in which he became convinced of their existence. Where a letter is missing, for example D, this is because the factor in question was eventually found to be unimportant. There are four 'Q' factors because these were thought to be factors often found in self-report questionnaires (Larsen & Buss, 2002).

Table 14.5. The 16 Personality factor scales.

	Factor	Trait
1	A	Interpersonal warmth: easy to get along with
2	B	Intelligence: information processing efficiency
3	C	Emotional stability: tolerates stress well
4	E	Dominance: assertive, aggressive etc.
5	F	Impulsivity: doing without much aforethought
6	G	Conformity: follows group standards
7	H	Boldness: adventurous, not shy
8	I	Sensitivity: artistic, insecure
9	L	Suspiciousness: critical, irritable, paranoid
10	M	Imagination: creative, a thinker
11	N	Shrewdness: thinks things through first
12	O	Insecurity: worrier, moody
13	Q1	Radicalism: against tradition, likes the new
14	Q2	Self-sufficiency: loners, like working alone
15	Q3	Self-discipline: controlled, organized
16	Q4	Tension: anxious, frustrated, hard to calm

Factors A, B, C, M, N and Q3 are the factors that we should like our leaders to have.

History is long, however, whereas leaders come and go, often quickly in the case of elected leaders, Italy being perhaps the best example over the last 50 years, having had 50 leaders in that time.

All too often, therefore, our leaders exhibit factors E, F, H, and L, and perhaps could be likened to the psychopathically competitive, dominant, and hostile alpha males in the animal kingdom. This, of course, corresponds to type A personality syndrome, a cluster of traits including ambition, impatience, competitiveness, and hostility (Larsen & Buss, 2002).

Such people are more likely to have been bullies in the classroom, also being somewhere near the bottom of the class, the 'nerds' at the top being those they might have bullied and also those more likely to make an important scientific breakthrough later in life.

The Gaussian distribution of intelligence spreads wider for men than for women (Mohr, 2012d), those at the lower IQ end often being the criminals in society when they grow up, here criminal including lying and war-mongering leaders.

Then, as discussed in Chapter 9, hierarchical organizations empower those who rise up in them and then, as all history shows, 'power corrupts'. Indeed, it seems that something comparable to the behavioural changes of Transactional Analysis (TA) occurs (Campos & McCormick, 1974).

In TA it is postulated that we can switch, according to circumstances, from behaving in child, adult and parent modes. When someone is made boss they change into 'boss' mode, comparable to TA's parent mode, whilst the lowliest workers or slaves must remain in child mode, at least while they are at work. When they get home perhaps they can switch to parent or 'boss' mode if they have children.

Thus, those who rise high in hierarchies are, of course, ambitious and competitive, but hostility may only be added to their behaviour when they become leader. Then they are able to delegate the dirty deeds of conflict and war when it is never they who are said to be at war, but the royal 'we are at war', really meaning the slaves in the army who do the actual fighting.

Thus, as US sportswriter Grantland Rice summed it up so well: *All wars are planned by old men in council chambers far apart.*

As this statement suggests, however, it would be a better outcome if the leaders engaged directly in conflict, whether in a council chamber or duelling at a rifle range where they could each play the role of target at opposite ends of the range.

OTHER FACTORS AFFECTING ATTITUDES & CONFLICT

[1] Hierarchical influences.

These include the influence of strongly hierarchical organizations that have very great influence on society and its individual people, some of these being:

(a) Governments of any type, whether they be monarchies or dictatorships, have considerable influence on the populace by way of propaganda and enforceable laws, for example those of conscription.

(b) Political parties. Even when they are not in government, supporters of political parties are often considerably influenced by their views.

(c) Religions. These, of course, have had great influence throughout history but have less influence in the West now, whilst in contrast Muslim sects still have great influence on many of the world's 1.5 billion Muslims.

(d) TV, radio and print media also tend to come from 'on high' and also have considerable influence.

[2] Social norms.

Social norms have a great influence on the thinking of individuals and groups within any society, for example the wearing of scarves, veils and burkas by Muslim women is still very widely practiced.

The structure of society has also been an important factor. Fairly soon after the Agricultural Revolution and the formation of man's first permanent towns and farms the first small armies would have been formed to defend them, at first only temporarily.

Indeed, with the diversification of occupations that the Agricultural Revolution brought, permanent armies were one eventual result, notably in Rome and its empire, for example. Then, of course, given the availability of armies, there has always been a tendency to use them sooner or later, most obviously as the 'external police force' to deal with external problems, albeit a very large force all too often in history.

[3] Economic factors.

Economic considerations have often been the cause of human conflict, for example competition for resources, a good historical example being the Spanish Empire's enthusiastic search for gold in the Americas.

Man has always been inventing new tools and weapons, particularly since the Industrial Revolution. Now the arms industries have become massive and are able to considerably influence government policy in many countries whose economies have suffered a steep decline in their manufacturing industries in recent decades (Sampson, 1977; Thomas, 2006).

An example of the absurdity of it all, the CIA knew that chemical weapons were pouring into Iraq from Chile and South Africa in the 1980s. Cardoen industries in Santiago, for example, sent its chemical weapons, and the German-made artillery 'cups' or shells to contain them, to Iraq (Ben-Menashe, 1992). Then, the US later condemned Iraq for using these weapons on the Kurds and used this as an excuse for their first invasion of Iraq early in 1991.

In recent decades, of course, economic sanctions have often been used against various countries for political, economic and humanitarian reasons. In recent times China's emergence as an economic superpower has caused much resentment in some Western nations, particularly the USA which has seen its manufacturing industries decimated. As the first author has written, however, this is in part because ignorant Western economist still:

(a) Use the law of supply and demand in its original form that applies largely to commodities, and not manufactured goods (Mohr, 2012a & 2012c).

(b) Believe, against all common sense, that increasing interest rates reduces inflation, whereas the simple equations of the 'liquid money supply' and 'interest sensitive demand' curves show that the opposite is the case (Mohr, 2012a & 2012c).

China's hybrid system with a centralized socialist government and capitalist business system, however, keeps wages low and pegs its exchange rate to keep its manufacturing exports relatively cheap. As a result the US is essentially 'owned' by China who holds much of its growing national debt. It is not unlikely, therefore, that conflict between China and the US could erupt eventually, perhaps with China's modest territorial claims in the South China Sea as an excuse.

[4] Growing populations.

Even as far back as early man's troglodyte days it is not hard to imagine an extended family group growing to the point at which a second cave was needed.

Similarly, when man had towns and then cities these too grew in size, needing ever more space and, more importantly, resources, particularly food.

This, coupled with man's habit of exploration, which no doubt dates back to his hunter-gatherer days and thence the hunt for food, has led man to engage in conflict with neighbouring populations.

Conflicts may have arisen simply out of the suspicion that the sight of strangers aroused when they suddenly appeared. Perhaps, for example, a spear might be thrown to scare them away. Then, of course, there might be retaliation and thus conflict.

As man's population continued to increase, of course, the tendency for migration and thence conflict must have increased, for example people leaving crowded and disease-ridden cities in Europe to colonize the 'New World' from the 16th to 19th centuries.

[5] Proximity.

For tribal man, as with his chimpanzee relatives, proximity was a key factor in regular tribal conflicts.

Indeed, until only about two thousand years ago, human conflicts were only between neighbouring cities, regions, or countries. With the building of ships capable of sailing hundreds of miles, however, came the ability to explore more widely, and human conflict began to occur over greater distances and on a greater scale. Eventually ships travelled even greater distances and great empires were built, notably the Roman Empire and the Spanish and British Empires.

Proximity also affects people's attitudes as does contact which, of course, is facilitated by proximity, the more 'negative' the contact the more negative the attitude formed.

[6] Competitiveness.

In the Roman Empire, for example, there was a competitiveness in its governments, an obvious drive that made it wish to become 'bigger and grander' and go out and conquer other lands to achieve that end.

This obsession with competition runs all through the history and cultures of Homo sapiens, an example being our obsession with sport, or any kind of competition even if it is called a 'game.' It seems fundamentally related to the alpha-male behaviour of several other animal species.

Man, however, takes the alpha-male issue to absurd lengths, for example the original Olympic Games in Ancient Greece being conducted in the nude and, indeed, it seems to be returning slowly towards that situation now.

Equally, man has often indulged in war without good reason, usually because some loony leader and his acolytes want to 'beat' some other foe.

[7] Intelligence bungles.

Modern warfare involves intelligence services heavily, but all too often these are corrupt and/or incompetent, resulting in massive mistakes. Recent examples include the perhaps deliberate WMD's misinformation that led to the US invading Iraq again after 9/11. Similarly, the US has made a mess of things in Libya and Syria, in the latter supporting terrorists allied with al-Qa'ida, reminding us of how the US supported Osama Bin Laden in Afghanistan in trying to combat the Taliban.

Similarly, it is very doubtful whether Churchill's enthusiasm for war justified England declaring war on Germany after it invaded Poland, when perhaps alternative measures such as trade sanctions should have been considered.

In contrast, after Germany invaded Russia early in WW2 an organization of Soviet Jews code-named MAX fed misinformation to the Nazis that Russian forces were weak, freezing, and on the point of collapse. This encouraged them to persist, the turning point of the war being German Panzer divisions running low on food and ammunition and freezing encamped outside Stalingrad, and ultimately being defeated, this being the turning point of the war.

[8] Religion.
Religion has, perhaps, been the most frequent 'excuse' for human conflict, the spate of Islamic jihad in recent decades that is termed *World War 3* in the book of that title (Mohr et al., 2014) being perhaps the best example in all history.

An article by Robert Manne in the *Weekend Australian* of October 22-23, 2016, headed *Growing Zeal of Jihadist Battalions,* summarized how the brutal ideology of the Islamic State jihadist movement was encouraged not only by the Koran, but also by a succession of Islamists, including:

(1) Egyptian Muslim Brother Sayid Quth, whose prison writings, especially his 1964 book *Milestones* published shortly before he was executed, were one of the major seeds of today's Islamic State movement.

(2) Egyptian Abd al-Salam Faraj whose followers assassinated Egyptian president Anwar Sadat.

(3) Palestinian Islamic scholar Abdullah Azzam who encouraged the Afghan and Arab mujaheddin to drive Soviet forces out of Afghanistan.

(4) Osama Bin Laden, a rich Saudi who had worked with Azzam, and who established al-Qa'ida in 1988, and in 1998 issued a fatwa for the mujaheddin to kill Americans and Jews.

(5) Ayman al-Zawahiri, an Egyptian Qutbist revolutionary who was a signatory to this fatwa, and who joined al-Qa'ida in 2001 and is now its leader.

(6) Jordanian revolutionary jihadist Abu Musab al-Zarqawi who was one of the leaders of the Sunni resistance to the US-led invasion and occupation of Iraq in 2003. He was "largely responsible for provoking a Sunni-Shia civil war in occupied Iraq and for adding several new elements to the political ideology", one of those elements being the re-establishment of the "Islamic caliphate that had been dissolved in 1924".

(7) Abu Omar al-Baghdadi who led Islamic State in Iraq in 2011 when US forces were withdrawing, IS then overtaking much of Iraq and moving into Syria under the name Jabhat al-Nusra or al-Nusra front.

(8) Abu Bakr al-Baghdadi who was announced as the first 'caliph' of the restored Islamic caliphate after IS captured Mosul in June 2014.

By early 2017 Iraqi government forces and their US and other allies were had retaken most of Mosul, but as Manne concluded in his article:

> *No matter what the outcome of the battle of Mosul those two branches of Salafi jihadism – the Zawahiri [al-Qa'ida] version and the Zarqawi [IS] version – will continue to influence the shape of Middle Eastern and international politics for many decades into the future.*
>
> *It is easier to defeat an army than an ideology. As so often in history, ideas matter, ideas kill.*

CONCLUSIONS

Equation 14.1 combines the measurement techniques of attitudinal psychology with the concepts of the contact hypothesis to assess the attitudes of individuals and groups of people to other groups of people. The point of this exercise is that, when the attitude of one group to another is very negative, then conflict between the groups is, of course, more likely.

The attitudes of leaders are of particular importance, as it is these that may lead to conflict and war. The attitudes of leaders will, of course, be influenced by many of the same factors and stimuli that affect the public.

There are many other factors that affect modern human conflict. For example, particularly in modern times, alliances between nations have played a part in many wars, World War 1 and World War 2 being notable examples.

One difficulty is that, if two groups of 4 nations are allied, then a single nation attacking some part of another may quickly result in 8 nations being at war. In other words, the larger the parties involved, the bigger the conflict.

One fear for the future, therefore, is the increasing power of such populous nations as China and India, and also of the 1.5 billion Muslims around the world, so many of whom indulge in jihad and terrorism. The numbers involved here are an order of magnitude greater than those involved in the two world wars of the last century.

Indeed, the present authors in the recent book *World War 3* point out that we are now embroiled in a world war one major 'seed' of which was the creation of the state if Israel in the UN-mandated British protectorate of Palestine in 1948, and which now involves high levels of conflict around most of the world instigated by such Islamist jihadist organizations as ISIS, al-Qa'ida, Boko Haram etcetera.

Chapter 15
REVERSE EVOLUTION

An asylum for the sane would be empty in America.
George Bernard Shaw, attributed.

REVERSE EVOLUTION IN MANKIND?

Chapters 2 and 3 discussed brainwashing or *coercive persuasion* and gave a brief account of the evolution of mankind and its leadership.

Chapters 8 to 12 discussed how we are brainwashed by unscrupulous or incompetent leaders in every walk of life.

The first author's book *The Doomsday Calculation*, (Mohr, 2012c), discussed the disastrous global consequences that now threaten the survival of many species, including man.

The book *World War 3* discusses ongoing Muslim conflict since circa 700, concluding that it can be hoped that, as in WW2, Russia + USA and their allies can finally at least curb Muslim terrorism enough to give a bit more peace in the world (Mohr, Fear and Sinclair, 2015). The reality is, however, that the evil and Satanic religion of Islam with all its jihad etcetera, is far too primitive and should be banned from as many countries as possible.

To be fair on this point, however, the book *World Religions* (Mohr & Fear, 2015) makes it clear that all religions, to various degrees are BS invented by people seeking power, influence, sex and concubines, little boys for sex, etcetera.

Chapters 18 and 19 of the book *The Brainwashed* (Mohr & Fear, 2016) discuss Islamism and the now global scourge of jihad afflicting the world today.

The present chapter discusses a consequence of man's excessive breeding, that of *reverse evolution*, the following two sections discussing experiments with rats showing that:

(a) 'Enriched' environment improves their brain size and intelligence.
(b) Learning in rats changes their RNA.

Case (a) involves the *nurture* component of intelligence and case (b) the *nature* or genetic component of intelligence.

Findings (a) + (b) demonstrate how greater intelligence can develop and be passed on genetically in a species.

Leading biologists and anthropologists believe that we are evolving 100 times faster than our hunter gatherer ancestors were (Callaghan et al., 2008), but is this rapid evolution for the better or for the worse?

The thesis of this chapter is that our increasingly overpopulated, capitalist and greedy consumer societies have become unethical and are beginning to regress, resulting in lower physical and psychological standards, in turn resulting in reduced intelligence and *reverse evolution*.

MAN'S DETERIORATING ENVIRONMENT

If some of Krech's rats discussed in Chapter 5 got smarter because of an 'enriched' environment then it would appear that in the more affluent West we are now going through the opposite process as our living standards decline.

Now more and more of us live in bloated and crowded megacities where even houses in the outer suburbs are becoming unaffordable and they also involve the downside of large numbers of hours spent commuting on crowded freeways or increasingly strained and packed public transport systems.

To cut commuting times many live in high rise apartment buildings that can only be likened to filing cabinets for forgotten and soulless people that have once again reverted to being troglodytes.

At the same time big business has bought out so many farms that many rural communities and towns have shrunk to a less than viable size.

Back in the 'big smoke' big business grows still further while job conditions and security have decreased drastically, for example most retail businesses now working seven days a week, often with extended hours, and often without compensating employees for these ludicrously unnecessary 'rat race' hours.

To make matters worse, these slaves are brainwashed zombies hooked on increasingly junky, if not frivolous, products.

In other words, most have become like Krech's deprived rats and, just as our lives become duller, so too do we and our children. When we start to talk about economics, however, the picture becomes even bleaker.

ECONOMIC INFLUENCES

According to Lynn and Vanhaven (2002), the world average IQ is 90, understandable bearing in mind that IQ tests originated in more advanced Europe and the USA. Only one in five countries have average IQ near the British average of 100, half have IQ < 90, and Africa rates bottom with average IQ of only 70.

They find that the GDP of nations correlates halfway well (to 0.7) with national IQ, the next most important factor being whether the country has a socialist or market economy, the third most important factor being it's natural resources.

They argue that more progressive and freer countries have greater inventiveness or IQ, in turn improving GDP, pointing to Japan's progress in the 20th century and China's current progress as examples.

In other words, some countries in Asia have undergone industrial revolution somewhat later than those in Europe and North America.

In the once most affluent countries, however, things are now doing downhill.

Thanks to wrongful marketing practices, government taxes and childishly crude economic modelling and management house prices in many countries have grown absurdly high.

At the same time governments in the more affluent countries have run up increasing national debts while their politicians electioneer with bullshit that we've never had it so good and that they have a budget surplus, that is, they have increased national debt only marginally less than their deliberately high forecast figure.

Meanwhile big biz continues to go offshore to use cheap labour so that, for example, most of our clothes and household goods now come from China or thereabouts.

Ourselves, we have increasing job insecurity and are expected to be prepared to retrain two or three times in our life, this despite being expected to study for increasingly long periods before beginning work in the first place. To add insult to injury more and more of the courses of study are ridiculous, ranging from postgraduate courses in sexology and puppetry to MBAs that are largely, if not totally, high school level.

Young students today, therefore, run up increasingly large higher education debts, study longer and thus spend less time in the work force, and yet face retraining further down the track along with ludicrous house prices. The result is that they can't afford to get married, let alone have children or buy a house, and are worse off than primitive man was.

LOWER STANDARDS

Standards are falling more generally than just economically, however. Big biz is increasingly unethical with tunnel vision for the bottom line so that CEOs make absurd amounts for sitting on their backsides and coming up with lousy ideas while the increasingly insecure workers suffer increasingly and are little better off than Roman slaves were.

These modern slaves live increasingly miserable lives of brainwashed consumerism to the limited extent they can afford it, and the result can only be a decline in intelligence.

To make matters worse, according to the Peter Principle that 'the sour cream rises' in human hierarchies (Peter & Hull, 1969), the rich brainwashers are even more stupid in most respects except for the something akin to animal cunning and viciousness with which they accumulate personal wealth.

Meanwhile, we see a 'reverse Keynes δG effect' of massive injection of capital by transnational companies setting up in China and India to find cheap labour [the original 'Keynes δG effect' was the notion that increasing government spending G has a snowball effect that increases GNP].

Now, therefore, the economies of these countries are growing rapidly and their peoples, at least to some extent, now see themselves as the smart ones.

In India, for example, their education sector has been turning out engineers in droves for decades. As noted in Chapter 8, however, in the West we have dumbed the education system down to the point at which:

(1) Teachers are sometimes not allowed to fail students.
(2) Up to half of primary students in the USA are given drugs for the recently 'invented' (by nut cases in the 'psycho' professions) ADHD.
(3) Almost from infancy children are locked up in long day care instead of being given the sort of specialist attention that would increase their intelligence.
(4) Apprenticeship to be a hairdresser takes up to 6 years.
(5) School remains an excessively drawn out 12 years.
(6) A high proportion of courses at so-called Universities are quite simply ridiculous, for example courses in sexology and puppetry, whilst others like MBAs are so low-level and commonplace that they are almost worthless like the latter-day institutions that run them

simply because they are popular and therefore good money spinners.

(7) Only 40% of US school students score at the level that 80% of students in some other countries achieve (Sykes, 1995). A similar decline has occurred in Australia and like countries.

Speaking of education, however, where else but the USA could it happen? That is, there are more people in jail that at University. This in the 'land of the free' and all that bullshit.

This dumbing down has extended throughout our society. Long ago noted psychologist Hans Eysenck aroused public condemnation for saying the black people were less intelligent though in Africa to this day that does prove to be the case.

Recently a (male) president of Harvard University was heavily criticized for saying that women had somewhat different abilities to men.

The bottom line now, therefore, is that we must all be equally stupid and nobody is allowed to be otherwise.

BRAINWASHED ZOMBIES

It is pitiful to see how many of us are brainwashed into carrying a drink bottle or cigarette in one hand and a mobile phone in the other, wearing stiff denim jeans and choking ourselves with ties that derive from the scarves that Roman soldiers carried to bind sword wounds.

We morons must also have the latest fashion in cars, houses and other possessions. Never mind that the cars are often gas guzzling 4WDs with aircon and the houses 'McMansions' way beyond the needs of shrinking modern families and which consume massive amounts of energy, much of it for air conditioning that is usually unnecessary.

Then there are the lifetime habits, or should we say addictions, like smoking and booze, the quotation opening Chapter 11 being an excellent example of how the beer barons bring such public addictions about.

The startling reality is that a great many of the things we do we don't really like anyway. Few, for example, like smoking or beer at first try but like fools we persist and condition ourselves and especially our brains to bear each new and ludicrous habit.

The same goes for dry white wines such as Chardonnay which tend to eat away at the oesophagus and stomach like acid, a reminder that alcohol tends to cause cancer all the way through the digestive path.

As for food, the list of ludicrous and downright nasty things we eat and claim to enjoy is endless, including tripe, offal, frog's legs, snails and so forth.

Often, of course, we acquire such ridiculous habits by imitative learning, that so many of us must have dogs as pets being an excellent example, this simple being a comparatively modern 'fashion' that caught on and is copied by one generation after another.

Usually, however, we are encouraged a good deal, if not a lot, by the skilful brainwashing of attention demanding and repetitive advertising. Arguably, in fact, the way in which humans are affected by advertising is directly comparable to lab experiments on conditioning of animals.

No better example can be found in the mindless poker machines that seem to hypnotize countless people for hours and hours on end. Such suckers are very comparable to rats in a Skinner box except that they seem dumber than the rats because, far from being rewarded, they are punished by being 'milked' of a great deal of money.

As for mass BW, the bullshit about Saddam Hussein having 'WMDs' that the US administration used to justify their invasion of Iraq is one of the better BW examples in history. Like Vietnam, Iraq has been a disaster for the US army as is sadly highlighted by the statistic that at present 17 US war veterans commit suicide a day, this toll each year far exceeding the total toll of US soldiers in the mistaken Iraq campaign over five years.

EVER WORSENING DIET

Nowhere is evidence of our reverse evolution greater than in our deteriorating diet. Now, more and more of the global population fill up on fast junk food, salty and fatty snacks such as potato crisps, biscuits, cake, sugary soft-drinks and, of course, the demon booze.

Indeed the medical profession in the West at large considers the modern diet problem as something of a crisis because obesity has reached epidemic proportions as a result of excessive consumption of fatty and sugary foods.

Still probably a billion or so of us smoke, which we like to consider part of the 'total diet' because we believe substituting food for cigarettes, and especially chewing gum, is helpful in quitting smoking. Indeed the first author found this approach helpful in finally quitting.

Then, of course, there is the growing problem of drugs in society. As a result we have to have regular drug testing in sport and elsewhere, we would suggest in parliament judging by the raving performances one sees there which, everybody knows, may well be fuelled by generous doses of booze with lunch and long dinners in favourite restaurants.

Just a couple of days ago we saw an elderly man on crutches who had lost the lower third of his right leg. Interested in atherosclerosis, which we have researched a good deal, we asked him what had caused his loss of much of a lower limb. He told us that the cause had been a twenty-something male drunk driver, a hoon who had had a blood alcohol reading in excess of 0.20 and was also loaded up with illicit drugs.

Having moved to one of Melbourne's much cheaper, less affluent, Western suburbs from a suburb on its Mornington Peninsula of late, the first author noticed that more people smoke and/or are obese. This, he believes, relates to the Reception-Yielding model of Fig. 11.2. That is, as he prefers to term it, people here have lower 'consumer IQ.'

Himself, the first author's diet has often tended to be below healthy par, even thinking it a joke in his Auckland days. In childhood his friends and he indulged as much as they could afford from their 'pocket money' on lollies, chocolate and cakes, washing them down with soft-drink or 'milk-shakes' or 'malted milks' which Milk Bars did a good trade in the 1950s and 1960s, in those days always using full cream milk. Now we know, of course, that it is wiser to drink low fat or skim milk to help avoid excessive consumption of saturated fat, a key villain in atherosclerosis.

The first author's well meaning parents gave him plenty of food but breakfast eggs and bacon were cooked with fat laden and carcinogenic re-used dripping. They bought plenty of cake at the local Herbert Adams shop and tons of (full cream) milk was consumed. At dinner or Sunday lunch (a roast) he well recalls being exhorted to eat the fat on the meat, another no-no given our dietary science knowledge of today.

Then, of course, he was fool enough to take up smoking for keeps from age 15, eventually becoming a very heavy smoker.

His disastrous marriage made his diet hit rock bottom on a permanent basis. A wife who produced food with stubbornly bad grace in sluggardly and slack manner gave him what he thought of as his (one plate) dog's dinner each night, in his Auckland days one of two braised steak and rice dishes that he had heard of, but not tried, in his undergraduate days. These were cooked terribly and unappetizingly to say the least.

He drank gallons of coffee at work (2 or 3 litres) and gallons of tea at home, each mug had with a cigarette or two. If awoken at night by his wife's terrible snoring he'd make yet another pot of tea, drinking 2 or 3 mugs of it, each with a cigarette, before trying to get back to sleep.

He doesn't remember what he ate for breakfast at any stage of the marriage except the very beginning when, one day at least, he remembers being given some cereal with bad grace. He does remember always having a pot of tea for breakfast, always with about 3 'fags', of course.

For lunch in his Auckland days he would just get a single sandwich or local crumbed sausage on a stick oddity, and wash this down with 2 mugs of coffee, one taken back to his office to keep working (he often worked through lunch times during his all too short University career).

Finally, unable to afford wine, like the local men he had 3 'long neck' bottles of low quality local beer to drown his bullied at home and work sorrows.

MONKEY BUSINESS

Much of our so-called education of young children should be called monkey business because they are encouraged to act like monkeys on climbing frames and in often senseless ball games, some of which, like football, are positively dangerous and reduce some players to paraplegics.

Then there are the ludicrous crazes we fall for. When the first author was a child there was a mindless yo-yo craze. More recent were skateboard and roller blades crazes.

As for dangerous activities, roller blades and skate boards are bad enough but those concrete slopes built for kids to do bike tricks on are highly insane.

The list of insane human activities here is endless, including sky diving, climbing up vertical rock faces, skiing, and so on.

As for racing, it seems that we will race just about anything that can be made to move ranging from dogs to camels.

Most of these activities have become spectator sports, some of them viewed by massive audiences brainwashed by hype and heavy media publicity into taking childish games played by overpaid adults seriously.

The complete insanity of this is that worrying oneself greatly over who wins a silly ball game is supposed to be recreational, that is, entertaining and relaxing. That riots often occur both off and on the field, however, are anything but relaxing.

Worrying too are the increasingly animalistic celebrations that accompany scoring and victory in most sports.

In addition, that many people enjoy watching brutal sports such as boxing and kick boxing doesn't say much good about the human race and only suggests that it is somewhat sick.

When you think about it, in fact, most of our ridiculous sport and recreational activities make us look like Krech's 'environment enriched' rats on their running wheels and slides.

The bottom line is that, as they used to say, *small things amuse small minds*, in other words we sure as hell are not getting any smarter.

SOCIOLOGICAL DEVOLUTION

Not only is our environment in polluted and unsightly megacities unpleasant, but as noted in Chapter 14, our societies are becoming meaner, nastier and more violent at an alarming rate. Violence is on the increase everywhere to the point that many older people and women don't feel safe on the streets at night and, of course, there is no shortage of street crime during the day as well.

Experiments with rats show that when they are housed beyond a certain population density they begin to fight each other. Evidently humans do the same and we are now accustomed to associating crime and violence with big cities like Chicago and New York.

Increasing numbers of us are addicted to booze, illegal so-called 'party drugs,' as well as prescription drugs like Valium for anxiety, Ritalin for ADHD, and lithium for bipolar disorder (formerly called manic depression).

With divorce rates around 50% we are living less safely in this respect at least than our Neanderthal ancestors did. Childhood is miserable enough at times under the best of circumstances and family break-ups often make it much more so for far too many children.

Women loose tolerance of the fact that men, especially when younger, can drink far more booze than they. They also fear violence from men though are more often than not at least, the instigators by way of a foul, hysterical, bossy, and bullying tongue. Try that on the footy field and, predictably, you can 'get an opponent in' so that they take a shot at you and risk being 'rubbed out' for a few weeks by the umpires.

In marriage, as well as in courtship, there is little or no meaningful communication. If you eavesdrop on a couple that has been married for a decade or two, you will find the dialogue at all times entirely trivial, for example "do we need milk?," in modern times this being said as often as not over a mobile phone while one partner is in the supermarket.

To complicate matters further, in the fast declining West women are taking over to some extent. Only about 100 years ago women were not to be seen in Cambridge University. Now far more women than men go to University in Australia.

Women also have a lower unemployment rate, already having the advantage that, merely by lying on their backs and having children they have a job for life as motherhood was certainly construed to be in the '[good] old days.'

One billion Muslims are more old-fashioned and tolerate the man being the boss still and, indeed, with the West in decay, it may well be that they have same sort of potentially winning advantage in this regard.

The ghastly music that young and not so young listen to and gyrate all night too mindlessly boozed and/or drugged in discos is another indicator of social decay. The manic pop groups of today dress and sing atrociously and leap about like primitive loonies.

The bottom line is that you can see the writing on the walls, that is, the graffiti that covers much of our miserable megacities, a sure sign that we are regressing back to grunting cave men once again.

SEXUAL PROLIFERATION AND DEVIANCE

Amongst the most disturbing indications of the corruption and decadence in our society are the all too frequent reports of sexual abuse of children by priests, teachers and others. It seems therefore that even the once most trusted people in our society can't be trusted any longer.

Sex, of course, is ubiquitous in our increasingly depraved society. Brothels were once illegal back street affairs. Now they and all manner of sexual products are widely advertised on late night TV, a pathetic attempt to shield children from it, and also in free local newspapers which children of all ages collect from the letterbox after coming home from school.

A fundamental change is that homosexuality is on the increase. Once a trait one had to keep secret it is now rampantly displayed at gay Mardi Gras festivals, at gay bars in major cities, and in late night TV ads for homosexual dating services.

Some claim that homosexuality is inherited and a study of 113 people in 33 families in which at least two brothers were homosexual found a genetic marker on the X-chromosome (Xq28) that had a very high correlation with sexual orientation (Galton, 2001).

Genes may play a minor 'predispositionary' role but, largely, homosexuality is a learnt behaviour. Typically, for example, the normal heterosexual male has one or two homosexual experiences in adolescence (Robertson, 1981), and no doubt the same applies to women.

Those who become homosexuals, therefore, presumably do so as a result of imitative learning at an early age. There are, no doubt, also psychological factors involved, for example a lack of confidence in approaching the opposite sex coupled with the fact that there are earlier homosexual experiences to draw upon as an alternative behaviour model.

If alcoholism is to be regarded as a psychiatric illness, as it often is (Davies, 1971), then in my view homosexuality is even more obviously a treatable psychiatric condition as well.

That said, most of our heterosexual behaviours are also learnt ones, many of them hardly natural or healthy. A seemingly innocent example might be what was called 'French kissing' in my youth, that is what can be described as 'tongue kissing', a truly revolting and very unhealthy practice like many other modern sexual practices.

The bottom line on sex, though, might well be that if we were aiming to get any smarter and wiser then abstinence might be the wiser course, especially as a sound exercise regime is clearly a healthier option. Obviously, however, quite the opposite is happening, all part of our *reverse evolution*.

DECLINE AND FALL OF EMPIRES

Modern civilization is based on our learning from the Greek, Roman and also Middle Eastern civilizations of 2-5 thousand years ago.

From these civilizations we learnt sophisticated art, music, architecture, mathematics and philosophy.

These civilizations became great empires but declined and fell ultimately, suggesting that, in the long run at least, the basic need of humans to live on a more 'local' basis is paramount. That is, our priority is, and should be the wellbeing of ourselves, our family, and our immediate community, not grand visions of empire achieved by violent war, or grand visions of a global economy motivated by greed.

Thus, in the last few hundred years, the British, Dutch, French, Germans, Portuguese, Spanish and Turks have built empires and then lost them.

The British Empire dominated much of the world but finally collapsed after WWII, in part because of the massive debts, much of them to the USA, incurred by that war. As a result, in the words of Dwight Eisenhower: "This conjunction of an immense military establishment and a large arms industry is new in the American experience."

As always, the devastatingly accurate Peter Principle applies, and corruption and stupidity cause society at large to lose out, an example being that between 1978 and 1998 the US Air Force requested only 5 C-130 transport aircraft but funding for 256 was approved. An example of why came later when the four biggest arms manufacturers gave more than $11M in campaign donations for the 2000 election.

Then, in 2002, the proposed increase in the US military budget was $48B, more than the entire UK budget, bringing the US total budget to $396B, more than the combined total of the next 15 big military spenders, including Russia and China.

Long before that, however, the US had 'liberalized' its economy, cutting the top tax rate from 70% to 50%, and eventually to 28% and reducing controls on banks.

The result? During Reagan's 8-year Presidential tenure the total deficit grew from $900B to $3,000B (note that $1B = 10^9$) and in the 1980s more than 650 Savings & Loan companies collapsed as a result of widespread fraud.

During that period the average American's leisure time per week was reduced to 16.6 hours from the 26.2 it had been in 1973 while, of course, the rich got richer than ever as a result of increasing slavery.

Since then, of course, we have seen the spectacular demise of Enron and the 2008 GFC in which major US banks collapsed and others, along with GM and Chrysler, had to be bailed out at great expense, along with increased government expenditure to prop up the economy, further drowning the US in debt.

Yet another example of economic mismanagement, banks have been getting into trouble in the USA and Europe, in particular, because statutory reserve deposit (SRD) and liquidity guarantee ratios have been reduced to ridiculously low values, as little as 2%. Traditionally the very basis of the banking system was SRD circa 10% (it was 7% in Australia in 1985).

In 2011 the US raised its debt limit yet again, after a long drawn-out battle in congress, and it looks certain that the days of the US being the "world's only superpower" are numbered.

To add insult to injury, the last century having been referred to by some as "The American Century," we are now hearing this new century being referred to as "The Asian Century."

Perhaps the bottom line on the USA was the headline **GLOBAL JOKE,** followed by "We are witnessing the decline of a civilization", for an article in the *Weekend Australian* of October 15-16, 2016, the article being inspired by the US presidential contest between Donald Trump and Hillary Clinton.

With Europe now in economic crisis as well, a total reversal of fortunes seems to be happening on a grand scale as China, India and other countries undergo their own, belated, industrial revolutions which, given their massive populations, are bound to have still further transformative effects on the world economy at the expense of the USA and Europe.

Globally, however, the problems of overpopulation, resource depletion, global warming, and desertification are likely to limit the prospects of future prosperity for all but the richest people in the world.

If the world's population reaches 10 or even 12 billion by the middle of the century, however, it seems certain that the long-term prospects for the human race are poor, this the subject of the recent book *The Doomsday Calculation* (Mohr, 2012c).

CULTURAL CRAP

Even the most intelligent of us, however, are likely to pick up a few mindless habits. Most of the intelligentsia laugh at modern pop music which certainly is crap, but many of them get dressed up as though they were going to a funeral to go to the opera, which is equally farcical. Opera singing at the best of times is somewhat ridiculous, involving both fat men and fat ladies making a ludicrous and comical racket. In the pop sphere 'rock' concerts and so-called 'musicals' are equally absurd.

Any form of dancing is animal stuff but ballet, with loonies in tights and ladies in very short skirts, is simply for closet perverts.

Even grandiose symphonies perhaps make little sense if one considers that music really should be for relaxation and thus should only require few instruments and fairly quiet scores.

The intelligentsia, however, is more concerned about snob value than intelligent culture so they still like stage plays. Whether Shakespearean or modern, plays are rather childish to say the least.

Many people regard choosing wine as an exercise in intelligence and 'wank' themselves into old age over the virtue of this or that 'red'. This too is pretty mindless stuff when, truth be told, most wines are really not as nice as some modern fruit juice mixtures and just an acquired taste.

When it comes to snob value, of course, flash cars and big houses are key items but these are expensive and not necessarily affordable to the intelligentsia, some of whom are happier to 'slum it' and, indeed, look like down and outs. This only indicates how stupid they really are, however, another symptom of our *reverse evolution*.

FALLING IQ

Vernon (1960) and Lynn and Vanhaven (2002) point out that we have dysgenic fertility trends so that the least intelligent people have the most children. Burt (1957) found that average IQ in the UK had dropped by 1.5% between the years 1920 and 1950 for this reason and he predicted a further 2.5% drop by the year 2000.

Vernon (1960) also points out that a Royal Commission on Mental Deficiency in the UK discovered a "big increase" in the numbers of defectives between the years 1907 and 1929.

It has also been suggested that IQ in the USA is in decline (Fancher, 1985), some claiming that the rate of decrease is 1 point per generation.

Remarkably, Internet search for 'declining human intelligence' yields over 3 million results, for example:

(a) Norwegian conscripts were found to have scored lower in IQ numerical subtests after the mid 1990s.
(b) Danish men assessed for military service in 2003/4 dropped in IQ by almost two points compared to those in 1998 (Teasdale and Owen, 2005, 2008).

The picture is far worse from a global point of view. As noted earlier, average IQ in Africa is only 70 and, of course, it is in such places that population has exploded in the last century while population growth in more advanced countries has ground to a halt.

The bottom line, therefore, is that, on average, the human race has become a good deal dumber simply as a result of demographic reasons. Considering that even the most intelligent of us in the most advanced countries, however, have been also reduced to brainwashed idiots in part, at least, the overall situation is grim to say the least.

The implications of declining average intelligence are far reaching. It has been shown, for example, that a drop of just 3 points in average IQ results in increasing numbers of:

(a) Men in jail - 13%.
(b) High school dropouts (permanent) - 15%.
(c) Women chronically dependent on welfare - 15%.

No doubt declining IQs have also produced even more 'low IQ/high cunning' people trying to brainwash the rest of us into 'believe anything/buy anything' consumer oblivion.

INTERBREEDING AMONGST MUSLIMS

An article posted recently by Cairns News entitled *Muslims suffer insanity, low IQ, recessive disorders from 1400 years of inbreeding* said that "the massive inbreeding in Muslim culture may well have done virtually irreversible damage to the Muslim gene pool, including extensive damage to its intelligence, sanity, and health."

According to Danish psychologist Nikilai Sennels, close to half of all Muslims in the world are inbred, and in Pakistan the numbers approach 70%, whilst they are 67% in Saudi Arabia, 64% in Jordan and Kuwait, 63% in Sudan, 60% in Iraq, and 54% in the United Arab Emirates and Qatar. As a result British Pakistani families are 13 times more likely to have children with recessive genetic disorders.

According to Sennels, research shows that children of consanguineous marriages lose 10-16 points off their IQ and that social abilities develop much slower in inbred babies. The risk of having an IQ lower than 70, the official demarcation for being classified as "retarded", increases by an astonishing 400% among children of cousin marriages. He concluded: *There is no doubt that the wide spread tradition of first cousin marriages among Muslims has harmed the gene pool of Muslims.*

The article concluded:

Bottom line: Islam is not simply a benign and morally equivalent alternative to the Judeo-Christian tradition. As Sennels points out, the first and biggest victims are Muslims.

Simple Judeo-Christian compassion for Muslims and a common-sense desire to protect Western civilization from the ravages of Islam dictate a vigorous opposition to the spread of this dark and dangerous ideology.

These stark realities must be taken into account when we establish public policies dealing with immigration from Muslim countries and the building of Mosques.

PHYSICALLY PAST OPTIMUM

Let's face it, take our clothes off and have a look at homo sapiens sapiens. We look damn stupid, like an evolutionary mistake or Martians on this damned planet: like we don't belong.

We are, in fact, less evolved physically than chimpanzees.

Quite simply, we are pathetic, for example:

- Male baldness appears to be on the increase.
- In contrast, we have hair too long in places and have to cut and shave our hair off frequently, a ridiculous situation.
- Somewhat anachronistically we have evolved with men designed for hunter-gathering and women for child bearing.
- Since that time mankind got smaller, the average European male being only 165 cm tall in Shakespeare's time. Thanks to improved diet our height has returned to that of the hunter gatherers (178 cm average for men) but we have lost a good deal of muscle tissue (Callaghan, 2008), no doubt why it has been found that Negroes have a genetic factor that makes them better sprinters.
- The disturbing obesity epidemic sweeping more affluent countries where, of course, people are most brainwashed by advertising. The result has been that, although not a great deal taller, women weigh on average 20% more than they did in 1926 (Callaghan, 2008).
- Poor diet caused generations of us immense amounts of tooth decay and type II diabetes is now 5 times more prevalent.
- We seem increasingly susceptible to new viruses like HIV and VRE which already pose a very serious threat.
- The incidence of most types of cancer has increased dramatically, often as a result of defective genes (Weinberg, 1999).

- Even amongst children blood pressures are significantly higher.
- A French TV documentary *Men in Danger* (Cuthbertson, 2008) notes that pollution is causing significant changes in humans:
  (a) Decreased testosterone levels in men.
  (b) Greater prevalence of genital abnormalities in males at birth.
  (c) Male sperm counts decreased by 50% in Copenhagen in the last 50 years and by 40% in the last 20 years only in Paris.
  (d) A huge 150% increase in breast cancer in women since 1960.
- Our eyes evolved for far field vision but thanks to man's invention of writing and then TV and the PC we are 3 times more likely to be short-sighted, a telling example of how our evolution is unable to keep pace with our rapidly changing environment.

The inescapable conclusion, however, is that we are becoming a genetic joke physically, part of an overall *reverse evolution* process.

DETERIORATING GENE POOL

In *The Descent of Man* Charles Darwin cited the work of his cousin Francis Galton more than ten times. Galton did much important scientific work, including proposing and defining the term *eugenics*, on which subject Darwin wrote:

> *We civilized men, on the other hand, do our utmost to check the process of elimination; we build asylums for the*

> *imbecile, the maimed, and the sick; we institute poor-laws; and our medical men exert their utmost skill to save the life of every one to the last moment. Thus the weak members of civilized societies propagate their kind.*

Carlo Cipolla (1974) pointed out that our population growth graph went almost vertical with the coming of the industrial revolution and implored that what we needed was 'quality not quantity,' a phrase the first author recalls his fifth grade teacher Miss Bachelard repeating often.

As Lynn and Vanhaven (2002) point out, however, we have dysgenic fertility trends so that the least intelligent people have the most children.

As part of that the none-too-intelligent but overpaid greedy executives whose businesses brainwash us to buy their often shoddy products can indeed afford to have children and buy them the right qualifications to carry on the family line in a capitalist fashion.

In contrast, many of the brightest children who struggle to come top at school will end up as scientists and engineers and the like, make relatively little money and struggle to afford a house and children, avoid divorce and stay sane enslaved as underpaid back room boys.

In addition, modern medical science is able to keep alive people with serious genetic disorders and there is concern in some quarters that this will lead to a deterioration of the human gene pool:

> *Many people are born each year with genetic defects that in the past would have hampered their reproductive potential. Now, medical treatment enables them to survive, reproduce,*

and pass on the defective genes. Followers of this view, such as the Nobel Prize winning geneticist H.J. Mueller, see this tampering with selection as a black cloud hanging over our future. Someday, Mueller says, all people will be born with one major genetic problem or another: diabetes, PKU, hemophilia.

M.L. Weiss, A.E. Mann,
Human Biology and Behaviour (1978).

The bottom line once again, therefore, is that we are into reverse evolution both mentally and physically, in part because eugenics became a dirty word because of ill-conceived attempts at reducing 'bad breeding,' for example:

(a) From 1907, 27 US states passed sterilization laws to prevent such people as epileptics, the feeble-minded, habitual criminals, and 'moral perverts' from having children. In most states these laws were not enforced but in California 10,000 people were sterilized by 1935.

(b) Other countries including Denmark, Germany, Norway, Sweden and Switzerland passed similar laws, in Sweden 60,000 young women being sterilized between 1935 and 1976.

(c) Eugenics was supposedly the justification for the massive extermination programs of the scientists and geneticists of the Third Reich, leading to the stigma attached to the word.

In the economically decaying West, having spent the best part of a century fighting socialism, we have now have gone too far in our quest for equality, insisting that regardless of sex, race or any other factor, we are all equal.

We have dumbed down our education systems, our political systems, and our 'consumer zombie' society in general in which we now breed 'willy-nilly,' perhaps with a quick copulatory act between yet another raft of mindless TV ads.

As our society regresses it is now, once again in history, more and more a fight for survival in an increasingly fierce economic rat race whilst the planet's resources and its environment gradually diminish in quantity and quality.

The first author's father, despite having had 3 children (he was the third!), believed in ZPG (zero population growth), quite correctly at that time.

Since then China has had its one-child policy which we might call NPG, and has become the world's second largest and strongest economy.

The first author, told by a woman he had made pregnant that the child would be "mildly retarded", consulted some experts who inferred that 'mildly' was really quite serious. He then persuaded the woman to have an abortion though 5 months pregnant. She did, about which he has no conscience.

David Galton concludes that: *Society as a whole should embrace the new* [eugenics] *technology and the opportunities if offers less timorously, or even with some measure of enthusiasm* (Galton, 2001).

ANIMAL FARM

Most, if not all, the terrorism, revolutions and wars in history have been about a "fair go" because it isn't really sane, for example, that just Buckingham Palace alone should have 650 rooms!

No doubt that sort of anomaly, along with hard times, helped inspire the French and Russian revolutions.

Few countries, if any, are still governed by monarchies and most have so-called democracy. These are not truly democratic, however, and are in fact corrupt capitalist oligarchies in which a few rich families, powerful bureaucrats and business leaders are able to make most of the input into the important decisions at all levels of government.

All too often our leaders fit the Peter Principle well, that is, they are incompetent. This is borne out by the results as we are always lurching from one disaster to another and constantly fed a load of bullshit saying we've never had it so good.

Lynn and Vanhaven note that in the richest nations the correlation of IQ with earnings is only 0.35. This is a low figure bearing in mind that high earnings should enhance performance. Indeed, if we do bear this in mind, then the real correlation would be a negative one showing that the fattest capitalist pigs have more animal cunning and greed and less intelligence.

George Orwell was a socialist, of course, and we think of capitalist pigs when we think of his *Animal Farm* and wish that we had *real democracy*, a topic we return to in the next and last 'solutions' chapter.

On being bossed around, it should be noted that it is not usually the truly superior person that runs the show. An example is how a baby's cry can automatically start lactation in its mother. This, of course, is just a survival mechanism, but it is also an exemplar of how rich bosses live off enslaved workers and it is not hard, of course, to relate their frequent whinges to those of infants, after all that is what they are paid megabucks to do, along with produce shit products which they hire expert brainwashers usually called advertising agencies to addict you to.

The bottom line is, therefore, that our leaders are usually greedy unethical pigs of pretty average intelligence, if that, thus being an important cog in the machinery of our *reverse evolution*.

CONCLUSION

A 'Cambridge man' like the first author, Ian Morris, author of the book *Why the West Rules - For Now*, opines that people everywhere are essentially clever chimps.

We guess is that the human race past its peak around the 1960s. WWII was long over and there was relative peace in the world, we had TV, tape recorders and transistor radios, and the first PCs were just a few years away. Then the world's human population was perhaps already about double that for comfort if everybody was to have a good standard of living that might be sustainable for the long term. Now it has more than doubled again to a clearly unsustainable level.

Overpopulation, overconsumption, pollution, global warming, resource depletion and land degradation are such serious problems that the survival of many species, including ours, is threatened.

Everywhere you look real standards are declining though we are usually told the opposite while incompetent and overpaid CEO's are simply looting the planet while they still can.

The heading for an article posted on the Internet is

*Beware of Corporate Media Brainwashing.
Through Corporate Media Brainwashing,
the World's Elite Disguises Their New World
Order Plan as it Dumbs America Down.*

The article is, in fact, a gripe about banks in the wake of the sub-prime lending crisis in the US, but it can be viewed as a reminder of what brainwashed consumer and believe any bullshit zombies we are.

19th century French lunatic asylums used to make money by having inmates perform for the public once a week. In Australia in recent years the treasurer has said year that his deliberately pessimistic national budget was in surplus but not reminded us that each time the national debt was continuing to rise.

This is the typical econobabble of economists and business leaders, stuff that would have been suitable in the public performances in 19th century French 'funny farms'.

Yet we brainwashed zombies accept such crap. No wonder that we are in *reverse evolution* and, as we slowly grow less intelligent we are, of course, blissfully unaware of it and too busy trying to survive the 'rat race' to care even if we were.

Finally, a good and sometimes humourous example of consumer zombies can be found in the movie *Dawn of The Dead* with many scenes of hoards of zombies creeping around a huge shopping centre. In this story, however, the zombies are not looking to buy anything, they are simply looking for a meal of human flesh from a 'non-zombie', who even if just bitten will ere long become a zombie too. This 'contagion' aspect of the story reminds one of the importance of imitative learning in the very young and social learning in teenagers and adults.

As for BW zombies – what better example than Muslim terrorists? In July 2016 the Australian media began to talk of "terror health checks", that is, checking suspected Muslim activists for mental health problems. As noted earlier in this chapter, thanks to centuries of interbreeding, most Muslims are 'retards' to a considerable degree, whilst anyone following this savage, vile and primitive religion in this day and age should be certified in some way, if not several, e.g. as somewhat insane, at risk of radicalization, and thus perhaps a terrorist risk etcetera. Then, for treatment of their mental health the only sensible course would be to give them radical prefrontal lobotomies using the simple 'drilling holes from the side' method of Freeman and Watts discussed in Chapter 7.

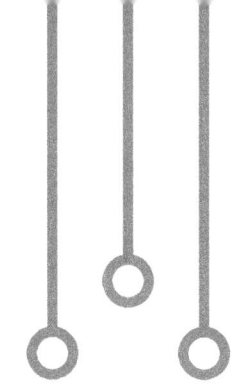

Chapter 16
KEEPING YOUR BRAIN ACTIVE

Neural Darwinism. *A term coined by Nobel laureate Gerald Edelman, this describes the process in which neurons that receive constant stimulation grow and those that do not atrophy.*
MS Sweeney, The Complete Mind (2009).

INTRODUCTION

Unhealthy arteries not only means development of atherosclerosis, and with it the risk of heart disease, but also increased aging of the brain, the cerebral cortex losing up to 30% of its neuronal activity with aging, though dendrites lengthen to compensate in part for this.

Therefore to reduce both physical and mental aging one should be at pains to establish a sound diet, diet supplement, exercise and relaxation routine along the lines discussed in many books to normalize cholesterol and homocysteine levels, including plenty of antioxidants to reduce DNA mutations and thence cancer risk (Mohr, 2012b, 2013, 2015).

A truly healthy lifestyle will also reduce the effects of any harmful food substances and any genetic disadvantages you may have concerning, for example, predisposition to heart disease or breast cancer.

Research in recent decades has shown that *neurogenesis*, the growth of new neurons by cell division, occurs in birds, tree shrews, primates, and humans, whilst the nervous systems of some fish and amphibians continue to grow in size throughout life. Neurogenesis may have been lessened in primates to retain past learning more efficiently, but humans can create neurons in brain areas such as the hippocampus, amygdala, and cerebral cortex for new learning (Cozolino, 2002).

MEMORY LOSS WITH AGE

Jane Durga at Wageningen University in the Netherlands gave 818 people aged 50-75 800 mg of folic acid (about 3 times the RDA) a day, or a dummy pill. Three years later the supplement users did as well as people 5.5 years younger on memory tests, and as well as people 1.9 years younger on cognitive speed tests (Holford, 2009).

As this improvement no doubt related to reduction of homocysteine levels, homocysteine being one of the main villains in both atherosclerosis and neural pathway deterioration, other homocysteine-lowering nutrients such as B6 and B12 should be likely to reduce brain aging as well and, indeed, studies are in progress on this issue (Holford, 2009).

As noted in the Chapter 5, antioxidants improve IQ in children. They also reduce memory loss with aging, much of which is owing to reduced liver function, and antioxidants reduce the 'detox burden' on the liver (which may include excess alcohol).

Well-known now, DHA and EPA oils improve brain function. The herb ginkgo biloba is also helpful and a double-blind placebo-controlled French trial found that giving 320 mg a day to 60 to 80 year-olds improved cognitive processing speed to that of healthy young adults (Holford, 2009).

Acetyl-L-carnitine (ACL) boosts energy production in the brain, improves the brain's glutamate receptors responsible for learning, and may stop formation of lipofucian, an "age spot" in neurons that interferes with memory (Gottlieb et al., 1990).

ACL is expensive and glutamine, the most abundant amino acid in the cerebrospinal fluid surrounding the brain, is an alternative. One US study of healthy volunteers found glutamine enhanced problem-solving ability.

Phospholipids are also helpful in reducing age-related problems. Acetylycholine is derived from phosphatidylcholine or pure lecithin and deficiency of this is probably, after high homocysteine levels, the main cause of declining memory with age, and Holford (2009), who calls acetylcholine "the memory molecule," recommends 5 to 10 gm of (commercial) lecithin to maximize mental function.

Gottlieb notes that 300 mg/day of another phospholipid, phosphatidyl serine (PS), has been found to reverse the chronological age of the outside layers of neurons by up to 12 years (Gottlieb et al., 1990).

Thus, to combat memory loss with age take[5]:

- Folic acid and B12, and also B6 and B1, B2, B3.
- Lecithin [5 - 10 gm], phosphatidyl choline (pure lecithin) or phosphatidyl serine. Linseeds will help absorption of lecithin (Mohr, 2012b, 2013, 2015).
- 1000 mg DHA and EPA, i.e. two fish oil capsules.
- Antioxidants A, C [3 gm], E [100 IU/decade of age], selenium and zinc.
- Glutamine [5 - 10 gm].
- Ginkgo biloba, 160 – 320 mg.
- ACL, 250 – 2,000 mg.

Finally, sustained stress is harmful to the brain[6] so relaxation and exercise (including mental exercise) will help reduce memory loss with age.

ALZHEIMER'S DISEASE

Supplements required for this are, of course, similar to those of the preceding section:

- Folic acid [10 mcg], B12 [250 mcg] and B6 [20 mg] to reduce homocysteine levels.
- Lecithin (+ linseeds for absorption) to provide phospholipids. Firshein (1998) recommends phosphatidyl serine dosage of 150-300 mg/day.
- Omega-3 from fish oils.
- Turmeric.
- Antioxidants as in the preceding section.

---

[5] Daily dosages recommended by Holford (2009) shown in [ ] brackets.
[6] Because the stress hormone cortisol shrinks dendrites (Holford, 2009).

- DHEA [15 mg], a precursor to testosterone and oestrogen.
- N-acetyl cysteine which is converted into the brain's primary antioxidant glutathione.
- Hyperzia serrata [200 mg], a moss which is an ancient Chinese remedy. This helps keep the neurotransmitter acetylcholine in circulation.
- ACL, 500 – 2,000 mg/day.

Turmeric's active ingredient is anti-inflammatory curcumin which breaks up plaques in Alzheimer's patients' brains (Holford, 2009).

PARKINSON'S DISEASE

The conventional treatment for Parkinson's disease is the drug L-dopa which is a direct precursor of the neurotransmitter dopamine which is linked to mood and behaviour.

As with Alzheimer's, also a neural issue, homocysteine levels are linked to Parkinson's and B6 plays an additional role independent of it's homocysteine-lowering one in preventing Parkinson's.

Indeed, Geoffrey and Lucille Leader tested patients with Parkinson's and found that "literally 100 percent of them had nutritional deficiencies based on tests that measure what is going on in the cells" (Holford, 2009).

Antioxidants help prevent free-radical damage to brain cells, slowing progression of Parkinson's disease, a 7-year pilot study finding that 3 gm C and 3,200 IU of E delayed the need for drug therapy by up to 2 or 3 years (Holford, 2009). This study published in 1992 used alpha-tocopherol; much better results would be expected with the much more potent tocotrienol forms of vitamin E.

Coenzyme Q10 is also helpful, being one of the most important antioxidants for protecting mitochondria, and a US study of 80 patients found that 1200 mg of CoQ10 slowed loss of motor function by 44%, 300-600 mg slowing it by 20% (Holford, 2009).

Thus useful supplements for Parkinson's disease include:

> B6, folic acid and B12.
> CoQ10 [1200 mg].
> Magnesium.
> C [3 gm], E [3,200 IU], selenium and zinc.

In addition plenty of protein should be had, perhaps some of it as supplements, because protein is converted with the aid of B6 to L-phenylalanine.

This, with the aid of folate, magnesium, manganese, iron, copper, zinc and C, is converted to L-tyrosine which the same substances convert to L-dopa which is used in drug form for conventional treatment (Holford, 2009).

B6 and zinc then convert L-dopa to dopamine, C converts this to noradrenalin, which B12, folate and niacin then convert to adrenalin.

It also helps to reduce stress levels, avoid environmental and other toxins, and reduce auto-intoxication from constipation by taking magnesium, perhaps as cheap Epsom Salts, magnesium also being helpful for muscle, arterial and brain function.

Finally, according to Gottlieb et al. (1990), Parkinson's patients have low levels of the hormone DHEA (dehydro-epaindrosterone) and medically supervised supplementation

(10 mg/day for women and 25 mg/day for men) may reduce symptoms.

DISEASES INVOLVING THE NERVOUS SYSTEM

Homocysteine not only attacks arteries, perhaps being the initial instigator of atherosclerosis, but also nerves and neural pathways in the brain. Many of the supplements cited in this chapter should be helpful in treating MS, in particular B12, injections of which totally eliminated symptoms in one patient (Firshein, 1998), and perhaps vitamin D now being trialled for MS treatment.

The authors also believe it likely that trigeminal neuralgia and Carpal tunnel syndrome may be caused by the cyst-like fibrolipid plaques of atherosclerosis. Initially these extend inside arteries, but with further growth they bulge outside the artery, perhaps interfering with adjacent nerves in the face, in the case of trigeminal neuralgia, or adjacent nerves in the hand in the case of Carpal tunnel syndrome which "results from median nerve entrapment as it passes through a tunnel in the wrist" (Walther, 1988).

Vitamin B6 deficiency has been found to cause the symptoms of carpel tunnel syndrome and it has been found that B6 dosage of 2 mg/day reduced symptoms, whilst 100 mg/day of pyridoxine for 12 weeks has been found to "correct" the condition. Applied kinesiology treatments involving appropriate manipulations of the hand and wrist have also been found helpful (Walther, 1988).

Carpal tunnel syndrome may also result from trauma to the hand such as stopping a fall with the hand extended, from regular 'wear and tear' in occupations such as carpentry or typing, the latter being a classical cause with heavy old-fashioned typewriters which required significantly more pressure to operate them than modern PC keyboards.

Shingles is an acute and painful inflammation of the spinal nerve ganglia, often associated with a prominent, itchy and painful rash around the middle of the body, and sometimes on the face, neck, arms and legs as well. The rash usually goes after 2-3 weeks, sometimes leaving scars, but the pains which are known as post-herpetic neuralgia can persist for much longer. Therapies for shingles include acupuncture, aromatherapy, reflexology, 'visualization' (of the rash vanishing), and hydrotherapy. Such treatments, and also 'colour therapy', acupressure, yoga and massage are helpful for trigeminal neuralgia and carpal tunnel syndrome (Shealy, 1999)

STROKES

A stroke occurs when a blood clot or ruptured blood vessel cuts off blood flow to the brain, which requires about 20% of the body's oxygen supply. Without oxygenated blood, brain cells die, resulting in loss of cognitive and/or motor functions.

There are four types of stroke:

[1] Thrombotic strokes - when an artery supplying the brain is blocked by fatty deposits.
[2] Embolic strokes - when a fatty clot forms elsewhere in the body, moves and gets stuck in a brain blood vessel. Types [1] and [2] account for 80% of strokes.
[3] Haemorrhagic strokes occur when an artery ruptures in the brain, usually as a result of high blood pressure.
[4] Transient ischemic attacks or TIA's are a temporary obstruction with mild and temporary symptoms.

Table 16.1. Stroke symptoms.

Damaged brain region	Symptoms
Right hemisphere	Weakness or paralysis on left side; confusion; disorientation; denial of paralysis; impaired judgment/reasoning; emotional instability
Left hemisphere	Weakness or paralysis on right side; reduced vision for objects to right; impaired thinking; difficulty speaking or understanding others; depression
Cerebellum	Impaired balance; nausea, vomiting; dizziness; extreme weakness of arm and leg on same side as cerebellum injury
Brain stem	Unstable BP & pulse, leading to coma; difficulty swallowing, pronouncing words; vertigo & impaired walking; weakness or paralysis on both sides

Table 16.1 shows the effects of stroke-induced damage to different regions of the brain (Sweeney, 2009). When a stroke cuts off blood to part of the brain, neurologists can estimate the location of the damage by the patient's symptoms.

AGING OF THE SENSORY SYSTEM

The senses become less acute with age as a result of changes in the sense organs as well as in the brain. Minimum levels of stimulation, called thresholds, are required before the brain perceives a sensation. Thresholds increase with age, requiring greater stimulation before sensations register so that the aging brain is slower in both IQ tests and in life in general.

The working memory of the brain also decreases, so that an abundance of lights and sounds can overwhelm the elderly brain so that, for example, driving in heavy traffic becomes difficult for the elderly (Sweeney, 2009).

The eyes and ears, the primary means of information gathering, suffer most from aging:

[a] Common eye diseases in the elderly include glaucoma, cataracts, and macular degeneration. The eyes also tend to become dry, eye muscles become less efficient, and the lenses lose clarity.
[b] A high proportion of the elderly suffer some degree of hearing loss, and many older people require hearing aids.

MENTAL ILLNESSES

Many of the supplements noted in earlier sections are helpful with mental illnesses, including B-vitamins, vitamin C, phospholipids, fish oils, magnesium, and zinc.

Several other supplements are also helpful, including niacin, manganese, and chromium (Holford, 2009).

THE IMPORTANCE OF SLEEP

One study showed that sleep-deprived adults had significantly reduced cognitive function.

Getting plenty of quality sleep, which is said to have a "dishwasher effect" on the brain, is also important because in old age we tend to sleep only about circa 6 hours per night (with 20% of this REM sleep) whereas mature adults get about 8 hours/night (again with 20% REM), whilst infants get about 14 hours/night, with 40% of this being REM sleep to help the young brain develop (Sweeney, 2009).

Many children and adults suffer from sleep disorders including (obstructive) sleep apnoea, insomnia, sleep hypoventilation, restless legs syndrome, sleep talking, and sleepwalking. The prevalence of sleep apnoea, which interferes with breathing, has increased because many more people are obese, but there are new remedies for sleep apnoea such as facial attachments to aid breathing.

CONCLUSION

Sound programs for diet and diet supplements including plenty of antioxidants, exercise, and relaxation will all help combat some of the key causes of aging such as reduced immune function, atherosclerosis, deterioration of collagen and thence skin, DNA mutations, and memory loss which can begin to occur as early as the mid-40s.

For relaxation, sitting in a comfy chair listening to quiet relaxation music, perhaps involving nature sounds, is far preferable to noisy music, movies or sporting crowds. Indeed, scientific research has shown that listening to pleasurable and relaxing music causes a short-term increase in the ability to solve spatial problems, and may also increase cognition at many levels, from simple perceptions to deeper thoughts (Sweeney, 2009).

B vitamins, phospholipids, fish oils, antioxidants, amino acids, glutamine, magnesium, hormones, turmeric, ginkgo and hyperzia serrata help deal with neurological problems, along with getting plenty of sleep and sound diet, exercise and stress reduction regimes.

Chemicals have also been developed that 'turn on' brain growth factor genes which don't change brain size, but may slow the neuronal wear and tear of aging, perhaps enabling humans to retain a greater percentage of their original memory capacity well past middle age (Lynch & Granger, 2008).

Finally, thinking young won't hurt, along with plenty of continuing learning to keep the brain in some sort of shape, noting the equation for real IQ given in Chapter 6.

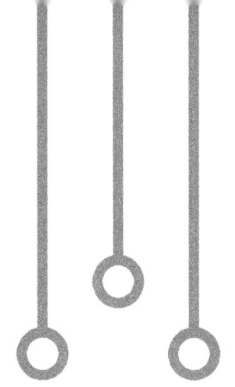

Chapter 17
THE RELATIVITY OF INTELLIGENCE

The contraction in length predicted by the theory of relativity has never been proven. Indeed, many 'disproofs' of this contraction have been produced - - - observer-based length correction is merely a sort of parallax correction. In fact, objects do not contract in absolute terms as a result of their speed, however great. Thus predictions of infinitesimal size and infinite mass as a particle gets close to the speed of light are absurd. These same predictions, however, are the basis of the [assumed] 'singularity' of the Big Bang.
G. A. Mohr, Richard Sinclair & Edwin Fear,
The Evolving Universe (2014).

INTRODUCTION

Einstein is assumed to be ever so clever, yet according to the present authors in the recent book quoted from above, the Theory of Relativity is full of errors, but when he moved onto tensor calculus Einstein was able to fool mathematicians of his day, and of today as well, in part because the mathematical fraternity, as with religions, believe and pass on to following generations the same BS.

In the next two sections, however, we shall discuss the matter of 'relative intelligence' before giving a few examples of what Real IQ, as defined in Chapter 6, we might guess a trio of famous people to have had.

HYPERBOLIC PLOT FOR TEST SCORES

Figure 17.1 shows a simple rectangular hyperbola of marks m (/100) that a person scores in a test, exam, or IQ test, the

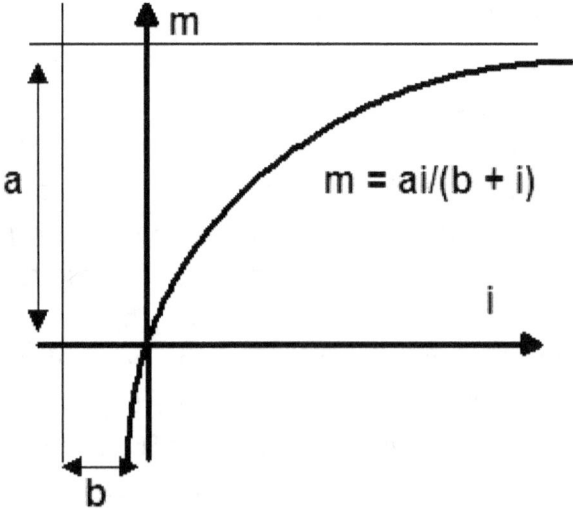

Figure 17.1. Hyperbolic plot for scores in tests.

horizontal axis being for *i*, or intelligence – and perhaps we should emphasize that this should be *real IQ* (RIQ) as defined in Chapter 6.

The equation for this hyperbola is:

$$m = ai/(b + i). \tag{17.1}$$

and we will assume that the constants have values $a = 200$ and $b = 204$, giving the results:

$$m = 99 \text{ for } i = 200$$
$$m = 65.8 \text{ for } i = 100$$
$$m = 39.4 \text{ for } i = 50$$

These values are not quite as we'd like them. The first is OK, but the marks for the next 2 cases are a bit high, but one cannot do much better with this simple type of curve in giving some sort of resemblance to the results that might be expected but for the third case – with RIQ = 50 one's score would be more like 10, if that, unless the test was very simple indeed.

The main point, however, is that according to Mohr's 10th Law (Mohr & Fear, 2015), *everything* should be given a score but the top score, be it 10 or 100, is not permitted because perfection is impossible in the real world. Indeed, this is normal practice, in Victoria's matriculation examinations top scores of 99.8 appearing in most years in some subjects, but scores of 100/100 are never given.

RECEPTION AND COMPREHENSION

Figure 17.2 shows curves in which how well a perceived 'object' is in turn 'received', 'understood, and 'remembered'

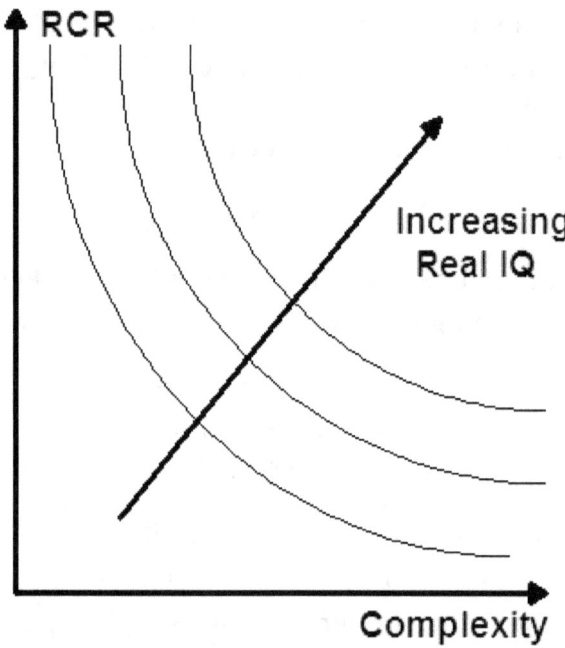

Figure 17.2. Curves of reception-comprehension-remembering (RCR) vs. complexity of the object being perceived.

is related to the complexity of the object and the Real IQ of the perceiver – the 'higher up' curves being for people with greater Real IQ.

The curve for how likely the object is to be remembered was discussed in Chapter 8 and its equation is:

$$p = an/(b + n).$$

where p is the probability of the object being remembered and n the number of repetitions or hearings of a person's name it takes us to remember a 'typical' newly encountered person's name, this corresponding, of course, to n rehearsals in the short term memory buffer of the Atkinson-Shiffrin model of memory discussed in Chapter 1 (see Figure 1.2).

Applied to the memory of a single person we set $a = 1$ and a typical result might be $b = 3$, $n = 3$, giving $p = 0.5$, or 50% memory retention after three repetitions. Here p is either:

(a) How well an item is learnt. People's names might be a good example of this. Ourselves, we often think one needs about three repetitions of such things to remember them.

(b) How much of a 'block' of information is learnt. An example might be a list of names where, because of *interference*, words at the beginning (the *primacy effect*) and end (the *recency effect*) are remembered best.

For a slower learner, on the other hand, b might double to 6 so we need $n = 6$ to get $p = 0.5$ or 50% learning.

Applied to conditioning of the populace by advertising, p is the proportion of the population affected and larger values of the asymptote b which flatten the curve might occur when there are two or more competing advertisers in the market. In politics this highlights the advantage of dictatorship.

In education it perhaps highlights the importance of avoiding conflicting messages so that it is often best to learn one subject at a time, and if this is done on a vicarious manner and perhaps later in life (not too much later!) so much the better might the subject be learnt.

The bottom line here, however, is that Figure 17.2 illustrates the obvious, namely that those with higher RIQ are better learners, whilst the examples above of 3 reps for perhaps the 'average' person, and 6 for a slower learner, show that we have here another way of measuring 'effective' or 'real' IQ.

ETHNICITY AND IQ

According to Lynn (2006) average IQ levels of the indigenous populations in different regions of the world vary greatly, being 105 for China, Japan and Korea, 100 for Europe, 90 for Northern Canada, 85 for the rest of North and South America, and also North Africa and India, and only 67 for sub-Saharan Africa and 62 for the Australian Aborigines.

According to Mackintosh (2011) the latter levels are perhaps too low but, however, he notes that three studies of the San Bushmen of southern Africa found their average IQ to be only 54, attributing such low levels to environmental factors and malnutrition, and noting that there has been some improvement in the IQ levels of such populations.

The score attributed by Lynne to Asians, on the other hand, may be too high, other studies indicating IQ levels only marginally above 100.

Many studies have shown significant differences in IQ between different ethnic groups within the same nation, blacks in the USA rating up to 15 points lower than whites, but Mackintosh (2011) notes that there is little evidence that this difference is genetic in origin.

FAMOUS EXAMPLES OF REAL IQ

We believe that IQ test scores tend to be on the generous side, and it is easy to find claims of IQ's of 160+ for well-known people such as actors, along with claims of 190-250 for other people still alive today, and a 'suggested' IQ of 250-300 for William James Sidis (1898-1944) who started grammar school at age 6 and completed in just 7 months.

IQ tests vary greatly in difficulty and it is not difficult to find IQ tests that may give scores differing by circa 50%, so that one might, for example, score 150 on an easier IQ test, but only 100 on a more difficult one. Then, of course, IQ tests must have varied greatly over the last century of so, making accurate historical comparisons of IQ impossible. Claims of very high IQ made for some people, therefore, are questionable.

Mensa entry in Australia is based on IQ >= 140 and we expect their IQ tests are on the easy side as otherwise their membership would be minimal. Therefore we can't/won't give scores >140, largely because we believe in 'Real IQ' (RIQ), as defined in Chapter 6.

Having commented in the first section about Einstein and his 'ridiculous theory of relativity', we will guess his RIQ at circa 120 – 130. This is generous if one bears in mind that his school teachers had low opinions of his intelligence and prospects of achieving much, and if one realizes that his period working in a patent office gave him an excellent opportunity to get ideas from the work of other people, leading to his famously productive year of 1905. In addition, his early works are said to have been "laughed out of Physics conferences."

Generally, however, Einstein is believed to have had an IQ of 160-180, one in 3.4 million people having an IQ of 160, or some 2059 people in the world's approximate present population of 7 billion. 0.1% of the population has an IQ of 145, however, or 7 million people out of 7 billion.

The idea for relativity, of course, simply came from the Lorentz-Fitzgerald contraction equation, the form of which is simply applied three times to give a presumed variation of mass, length and time (the three fundamental dimensions M, L and T) with the object's speed relative to that of light (v/c), i.e., a kind of parallax phenomenon only. Thus Appendix A of *The Evolving Universe* (Mohr, Sinclair & Fear, 2014) gives an example of the first author's calculation (without relativity) of the deflection of light by the sun so famously taken to be the first proof of the Special Theory of Relativity.

Then Appendix B of the same book gives an example of the first author's work on his *large curvature correction* in structural mechanics, demonstrating that one can do OK without having to be silly enough to talk about curved space time etcetera.

And finally Appendix C of *The Evolving Universe* presents in light humour the 'Ridiculous Theory of Relativity', giving a table of 11 examples of the errors and BS involved in the Special Theory of Relativity and early writings about it.

Moving to a second example of real IQ, we would give Isaac Newton a Real IQ of 140+ at his peak, but as he deteriorated 2 nervous breakdowns in Cambridge, and perhaps gallons of booze etcetera, his IQ would have gone downhill a fair bit by the time he quit Cambridge at 42 and became MP for Cambridge and took charge of the Royal Mint where he came up with the idea of the 'gold standard' (involving the weight of the gold) to counter the then widespread practice of 'rimming' the gold coinage of the time.

Stephen Hawking, therefore, wrote of Newton being a nasty person, and perhaps that may have been true in his

Royal Mint days when it was noticed he had strange habits, like those in his Cambridge days noted in an earlier chapter, for example getting up at 5 AM and turning up at the mint soon thereafter expecting to see things happening.

As a final example we would guess Hawking's RIQ at circa 120 (popular opinion has him at circa 150) when he was a bright youngish student, but much less with the ravages of amyotrophic lateral sclerosis (ALS) [the technical term – more commonly known as motor neuron disease (MND)] from age circa 25 onwards.

It was easy for Hawking to become famous sitting in Newton's chair with his first simplistic popular market book *A Brief History of Time* having been very successful, in part because of Simon Mitton's suggestion that adding a second equation to the book [other than $E = mc^2$] would halve the sales.

The scientific community in general, however, feels that Hawking has never really done anything much except for playing 'armchair commentator' waffling about such topics as the Big Bang Theory which the present authors, like many others, do not subscribe to.

The first author (GAM) had a bad time with Cambridge Clod Mitton over his first book effort in 1979 - being asked by a stupid anonymous review to double the size of the book – thus under 'virtual contract' he did so PDQ and was then knocked back, not by Mitton, but by the CUP 'Syndicate' or Board.

Nevertheless, he kept adding new work and the 'tome', as he came to call it, grew more and more extensive, but it was knocked back by CUP 2 or 3 more times. Eventually it was published by OUP, but by this time he had been on the dole since 1985, having "walked the plank" when a new Cambridge Maths PhD boss at Auckland Uni. bullied him into doing so.

Without an OK last job referee he never got another job, despite being interviewed many times for positions ranging from Lecturer through to HOD, Dean and even CEO of a tertiary institute. This was, at least in part, because the nasty ex-boss, who was nominated as a 'referee', was backstabbing him, as he realized in hindsight when 'adding up' comments he heard during interview processes over the years.

After a seminar in which the first author spoke about his Lambda-Beta transformation which converts Lagrange multiplier-constrained FEM problems into more compact penalty factor-constrained ones (Mohr & Caffin, 1985; Mohr, 1992), the Cambridge clod new HOD piped up afterwards:

WE couldn't understand what you were talking about.

The real truth, however, is that the new HOD was a typical Cambridge clod and 'up himself' halfwit – so of course he couldn't understand other than trivial maths because he was living in the past by decades as Cambridge clods usually do.

As for the first author's IQ, he recalls doing 3 IQ tests of spatial, verbal, and maths IQ from a book by then well-known psychologist Hans Eysenck in 1970 (at age 24) and scoring best on the maths one. He redid that maths test circa 1996 (at age 50) and did circa 15 IQ points better. The actual scores, however, are being kept secret, but the increase does back up the definition of Real IQ in Chapter 6.

As a final note on the inclusion of 'creativity' in our definition of Real IQ in Chapter 6, one of the best examples of this was Alexander Graham Bell who researched in areas ranging from telephone systems to medicine and aeronautics. Better still, Thomas Edison held a staggering 1,093 US patents plus others in the UK, France and Germany, and it is he who invented the word 'Hello' as a greeting to be used on the phone, whereas Bell had favoured using 'Ahoy'.

Finally, it should be noted that:

(a) The effect of family environment on children's IQ scores declines as they grow up, according to many geneticists eventually declining to zero.
(b) Genetic influences on IQ increase as children grow older, correlations being about 0.50 in children and adolescents, but according to some geneticists increasing to 0.80 in older adults (Mackintosh, 2011).

Chapter 18
CONCLUSIONS

*A neurotic is a man who builds a castle in the air.
A psychotic is the man who lives in it.
And a psychiatrist is the man who collects the rent.*
Lord Webb-Johnson, British surgeon.
In *Look*, October 4, 1955.

I have no great intelligence, I have imagination.
The late John H. Argyris, CBE, World Hons Mult.,
Former Chairman of the World Innovation Foundation.
Said to the first author by phone from Stuttgart circa 1996.

LANGUAGE

Chapter 1 discussed the human brain: its evolution, its structure, the associated nervous system, neurotransmitters, the brain's storage capacity, the Atkinson-Shiffrin information processing model of memory, and the four types of long-term memory, that is, *procedural, declarative episodic,* and *semantic*.

What really sets homo sapiens sapiens apart is his enlarged cerebral cortex and therefore Chapter 2 discussed how we developed and understand language, how different languages are connected, how infants learn language and vocabulary growth, also discussing the important learning processes of imprinting, modelling, and group modelling.

LEARNING

Chapter 3 discussed classical conditioning, operant conditioning, behaviour shaping, memory reinforcement, electro-chemical effects in the brain, memory structure, a simple Finite Element model of memory, long-term potentiation, and 'classical brainwashing.'

Chapter 4 presents three quantitative methods of measuring attitudes, and also the 'contact hypothesis' of ethnic conflict, mere exposure research, giving examples of measuring attitudes using the method of equal-appearing intervals and Guttman scaling, also discussing widely used Likert scaling.

INTELLIGENCE AND PSYCHOLOGY

Chapter 5 discussed how to raise smarter children by:

[1] Having only one or two children.
[2] Providing an 'enriched' learning environment as in the classical rat experiments that resulted in larger brains.
[3] Encouragement as in the 'teacher expectancy effect'.
[4] Providing better nutrition, including antioxidants.
{5] Avoiding dietary neurotoxins.
[6] A program of 'IQ building'.

[7] Early use of small learning groups.
[8] Such techniques as 'Superlearning' with relaxing music and "You can do it!" encouragement.
[9] Home schooling, at least in part.
[10] Early introduction to algebra and calculus.

Chapter 6 discussed biology, biochemical learning and evolution, enriched environments, IQ building and IQ tests, and the important concept of 'Real IQ.'

Chapter 7 discussed human psychology and psychiatric disorders and practice, concluding that drugs such as Valium and those for ADHD are over prescribed, thus doing a great deal more harm than good in the long run.

EDUCATION AND LIFE SKILLS

Chapter 8 began with a brief history of the education system of, then discussing the advantages or early learning; 'learning curves'; thinking via images, symbols, concepts and rules; creative thinking; the need for a 'condensation' of the school system; the need for less 'fragmentation' in education; TAFE and University courses, many of which are seen to be mainly for 'money making' purposes; and concluded by discussing the many problems in the education systems of today.

Chapter 9 discussed the importance of learning life skills such as understanding the 'time value of money', the hierarchical nature of most workplaces, and how to get on in life by 'networking' and using such techniques and 'stroking' to get on with people, and observing body language etc. to gauge who one's friends and enemies are.

THE CONSUMER SOCIETY

Chapter 10 discussed the mass media, including radio, TV, movies, newspapers and the Internet, noting how we tend to be 'brainwashed' into our beliefs (including religion and politics) from an early age.

Chapter 11 discussed advertising techniques and strategies, the 'CAB' model of psychological responses, the important *reception-yielding model* of attitude formation, how advertising targets *basic needs* and *metaneeds*, addiction, 'push and pull' marketing, the ubiquitousness of modern advertising, religious advertising, and new trends in marketing, concluding that we have been reduced en masse to *consumer zombies* and that, thanks to our exponentiation or our population since the industrial revolution, we are putting the planet and ourselves in peril through pollution, resource depletion, and global warming.

Chapter 12 asks *Have You Been Brainwashed?*, using an example of Likert Scaling to illustrate how one can assess this, and concluding with the first author as a "pathetic example".

Chapter 13 discusses the psychology of habits, giving examples of habits both bad and normal that may be acquired by imitative and/or social learning, formal teaching, of the 'brainwashing' of the media and advertising.

HUMAN CONFLICT AND REVERSE EVOLUTION

Chapter 14 discussed human conflict and Mohr's simple attitudinal model of conflict which uses the equation:

$$A^{\star\star\star} = A + B + C + D + S - (R_N - 12) + (R_P - 12)$$

to numerically evaluate a person or group's attitudes towards another group, here the terms being:

A^{***} = final, overall attitude.
A = initial or basic attitude.
B = attitude towards the *behaviour* of the group in question.
C = the positivity or negativity of *contact* with the group.
D = the degree of difference between the two groups.
S = the societal attitude of 'group 1' towards the other group.
R_N = degree of approval for negative responses to 'group 2'.
R_P = degree of approval for positive responses to 'group 2'.

Tabular numerical examples of evaluation of all these terms are given. Then 'psychopathic leaders' are discussed, along with Cattell's 16 personality factors and scaling of these, concluding with other factors that contributed to human conflict, these being: hierarchical factors, social norms, economic factors, growing populations, proximity and competitiveness.

Chapter 15 then discussed our *reverse evolution*, as evidenced by small but significant decreases in IQ observed over the last century, arguing that this is a result of overpopulation, careless breeding (particularly consanguineous breeding amongst Muslims), a worsening environment, poor diet, lower standards in education, the 'brainwashing' that reduces us to 'consumer zombies', a deteriorating gene pool, evolutionary physical decline (e.g. baldness, obesity, the growing need for glasses), and the 'animal farm' nature of human society, led as it usually is by greedy and none too intelligent people historically including, of course, alpha male types just as in the case of chimpanzees and apes.

KEEPING YOUR BRAIN YOUNG

In line with Mohr's *Real IQ* introduced in Chapter 6, Chapter 16 discussed how to keep your brain young, that is, keep on learning later in life, keeping healthy both physically and mentally and ensuring IQ enhancing nutrition and, if need be, nutrition to prevent memory loss with old age and combat such ailments as Alzheimer's and Parkinson's diseases.

THE RELATIVITY OF INTELLIGENCE

Chapter 17 discussed how the marks we might get in an IQ test or exam will depend on our 'Real IQ', and how the efficiency of perception, understanding, and remembering information depends both on the complexity of the information and, of course, our 'Real IQ', concluding with a few examples of famous people regarded by history as clever.

KEY ISSUES OF LEARNING AND BEHAVIOUR

Man's disastrous history of conflict should not continue. We are now deep into *World War 3* (Mohr, Fear & Sinclair, 2015) with no end of it in sight. It is perhaps, appropriate, therefore, to further elaborate and summarize Mohr's attitudinal model of conflict (outlined in Chapter 14) in the next two sections.

MOHR'S ATTITUDINAL MODEL OF CONFLICT

In Chapter 14 a basic 'five-value' attitudinal model of conflict was given:

$$A^{**} = A^* + fS = A + xB + yC + zD + fS \qquad (18.1)$$

where
- A = initial attitude, $A^\star$ and $A^{\star\star}$ = 'overall' attitude
- B = attitudes towards behaviours of the second party,
- C = contact history between the two parties,
- D = degree of difference between the parties considered [note that positive values of D = similarity],
- S = view of society's attitudes towards the second party and
- f, x, y, z are scaling coefficients that indicate the relative importance of the terms.

To complete the model the effect of contact upon group differences can be written as:

$$C^\star = C + d\,D, \text{ where } d = \text{scaling factor} \quad (18.2)$$
$$D^\star = D + c\,C, \text{ where } c = \text{scaling factor} \quad (18.3)$$

so that 'positive differences' (i.e. similarities) increase positive contact, and positive contact increases 'positive differences' (i.e. similarities), the positive and negative scoring used here (e.g. see Table 14.1) being similar to that used for the 'five-factor' model of personality (Larsen & Buss, 2002).

Equations 18.2 and 18.3 involve a 'positive feedback loop' which can be shown by writing

$$D^{\star\star} = D^\star + c\,C^\star = (D + c\,C) + c\,(C + d\,D) \quad (18.4)$$

Then if both scaling factors are 0.5 and the initial values of C and D were both scores of 5 (the range of possible scores being -10 to +10 as in Table 14.1), the result of Equation 18.3 is

$$D^{\star\star} = 5 + 5/2 + 5/2 + 5/4 = 11.25$$

and the outcome is 1.25 higher, i.e., the increase in $D^{\star\star}$ is 25% greater than without the 'feedback' of increased D also increasing C.

Finally, note that, though a little confusing at first, the notion of 'positive differences' being similarities does help shift thinking from negative to positive.

ASSESSMENTS FOR DIFFERENT TYPES OF CONFLICT

If the simple attitudinal analysis of Tables 14.1 and 14.2 is undertaken for each of the areas of human conflict discussed

Table 18.1. Totals for the equation: $A^{\star\star} = A + B + C + D + S$
A =initial attitude, B =behaviour, C =contact, D =differences, S =societal attitudes. Max/min for A, B, C, D, S = 10/-10.

Conflict type	A	B	C	D	S	$A^{\star\star}$
Gender	0	+4	-2	-8	-2	-8
School bullying	-2	-2	-1	-3	0	--8
Work bullying	-2	-2	-2	-5	0	-11
Tribal/territorial	-4	-3	-3	-2	-4	-16
Imperial	-6	-6	-5	-6	-5	-28
Religious	-4	-2	-4	-6	-6	-22
Ethnic	-4	-4	-4	-6	-4	-22
Societal groups	-2	-2	-3	-5	-2	-14
Political	-3	-1	-1	-4	-6	-15
World War	-6	-8	-8	-4	-8	-34
Terrorism	-5	-6	-6	-5	-6	-28
Revolution	-5	-6	-3	-4	-4	-22

in the first author's recent book *The History & Psychology of Human Conflicts* (Mohr, 2014b), totals for a hypothetical person for each of these areas might be as shown in Table 18.1.

Total scores A^{**} for gender conflict, and school and workplace bullying, are from -8 to -11 or 'mildly negative' scores because conflict in these areas is on a minor scale.

Scores for tribal/territorial, political, and societal groups range from -14 to -16, or 'medium negative' scores.

Scores for imperial, religious, ethnic, terrorist, and revolutionary conflict range from -22 to -28, or 'high negative' scores, reflecting the severity of conflict often involved in these areas.

Finally, the score for world war is -34 because of the escalation of the level of conflict that occurred in the two world wars of the last century.

CONCLUSION

With human conflict continuing around the globe, and World War 3 continuing unabated thanks largely to Islamists and jihadists, and our exponentiating population resulting in pollution, resource depletion and global warming, our long term existence is threatened, as pointed out in the recent book *The Doomsday Calculation* (Mohr, 2012c).

The algebraic attitudinal model of conflict first presented in the recent book *The History & Psychology of Human Conflicts* (Mohr, 2014b), and represented briefly here, might in small measure indicate that human conflict can be reduced by changing human attitudes in a positive way, rather than the very negative and inciteful propaganda used, for example, by leaders of Muslim extremist and terrorist organizations.

This is no easy task, however, as people are brainwashed with religious mumbo jumbo from an early age. As the recent book *World Religions* makes clear, however, without exception religions were invented by greedy men seeking power, influence and money (Mohr & Fear, 2015). Muhammad, for example, having been expelled from Mecca, invented his religious mantras and lies of talking to God in the desert to gather followers to help in his jihad to overtake Medina, and then Mecca, in following centuries Muslims taking over much of the world by force.

As former intelligence analyst Paul Monk wrote in reviewing the book *The Mind of Islamic State* by Robert Manne in the Weekend Australian of November 5, 2016:

> *Islam did not arise or spread by peace or persuasion, nor did Muhammad preach that it should do so. It arose as a religion calling for the violent overthrow of all non-Muslim religions and principalities, in order that the "truth" might prevail. For several centuries, its adherents strove by all means at their disposal to conquer the whole of Europe and Asia.*

He went on to say that the Ottomans and now modern jihadists *"renewed these wars of conquest"* in many parts of the world based on the *"dangerous assumption that Islam is the 'final revelation' and that sooner or later the world must and will become Muslim – through jihad and as the 'will of Allah'."*

We cannot do away with religions, unfortunately, so to at least reduce Islamic jihad around the world, therefore, a revised edition of the Koran that removes frequent mention of such evils and jihad is urgently needed.

As for intelligence, the equation for Real Intelligence given in Chapter 6 illustrates that it is, indeed, possible to increase one's intelligence through continued learning in later life.

Indeed, drugs that selectively enhance the brain's ability to collect, assemble, and encode information have been developed and tested on rats, monkeys and humans. The new drugs improve communication between cortical neurons, allowing brain regions to build larger than normal networks and improve access to other regions (Lynch & Granger, 2008).

Finally, to conclude on a positive note, we believe that it is important in life to have HOPE for, when one looses all hope, life will seem not worth living. Thus students thrive on encouragement and hope, as exemplified by the 'teacher expectancy effect', whilst people suffering from depression can be helped greatly if they are given HOPE.

Mankind's disastrous history of conflict seems unlikely to end and we face other threats as a result of overpopulation, resource depletion, climate change etcetera. The authors HOPE we can solve some of these problems, however, and thus increase our chances of avoiding the extinction forecast for many animal species, including ourselves (Mohr, 2012c).

As noted in earlier chapters of the present book, we should push for *real democracy*, as outlined in Chapter 20 of *The Doomsday Calculation* (Mohr, 2012c), rather than the highly oligarchical and antiquated Westminster system that still governs much of the Western world today, and only then, perhaps, might there be any real chance of avoiding increasing global catastrophes and perhaps extinction.

☺☹☺☹☺☹☺☹☺☹☺☹☺☹

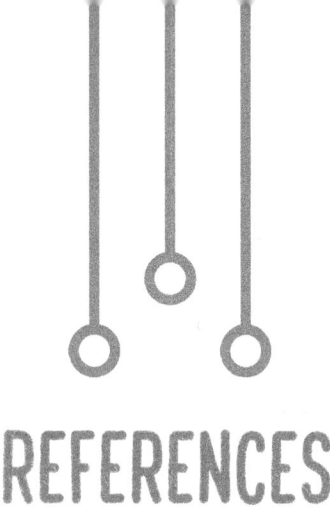

REFERENCES

Atkinson RC, Shiffrin RM, Human memory: A proposed system and its control processes. RW Spence, JT Spence (eds), *The Psychology of Learning and Motivation, Vol. 2,* Academic Press, New York (1968).

Atrens D, Curthoys I, *The Neurosciences and Behaviour: An Introduction,* 2nd edn, Academic Press, Sydney (1982).

Bell R, Hall, R, *Impacts: Contemporary Issues & Global Problems,* The Jacaranda Press, Milton QLD (1991).

Ben-Menashe A, *Profits of War, The Sensational Story of the World-Wide Arms Conspiracy,* Allen & Unwin, Sydney (1992).

Bradley RH, Caldwell BM, Early home environment and mental test performance in children from 6 to 36 months, *Development Psychology* 12 (1967) 93-97.

Burt C, The distribution of intelligence, *British Journal of Psychology* 48 (161-174) 1957.

Callaghan G, Taller, Wider, *The Weekend Australian Magazine,* April 5-6, 2008, pp 13-17.

Campos L, McCormick P, *Introduce Yourself to Transactional Analysis, A TA Primer,* 4th edn, Transactional Pubs, Berkeley CA (1974).

Cantwell, A, *The Cancer Microbe,* Aries Rising Press, Los Angeles (1990).

Carter P, *IQ and Psychometric Tests* 2nd edn, Kogan Page, London (2007).

Carter R, *Mapping The Mind,* Phoenix, London (2000).

Cipolla, CM, *The Economic History of World Population*, 6th edn, Penguin, London (1974).

Collins AM, Quillian MR, Retrieval time from semantic memory, *Journal of Verbal Learning and Verbal Behaviour* 8 (1969) 240-247.

Cozolino L, *The Neuroscience of Psychotherapy, Building and Rebuilding the Human Brain*, W.W. Norton & Co., NY (2002).

Craughwell, Thomas J, *How Smart Are You?, Test Your IQ*, Black Dog & Leventhal, New York NY (2012).

Cuthbertson I, article on TV documentary program 'Men in Danger', *The Weekend Australian*, Review p 28, March 29, 2008.

Darwin, Charles, *The Expression of the Emotions in Man and Animals*, Harper Collins (Fontana), London (1999).

Davies B, *An Introduction to Clinical Psychiatry*, Melbourne University Press, Melbourne (1971).

de Bono E, *Lateral Thinking for Management*, Pelican, Harmondsworth (1982).

Delgado JMR, *Physical Control of the Mind: Towards a Psychocivilized Society*, Colophon Books (Harper & Row), New York (1971).

Eagly AH, Chaiken S, *The Psychology of Attitudes*, Harcourt Brace Jovanovich, Orlando FL (1993).

Egerton Eastwick RW (ed.), *The Oracle Encyclopaedia*, George Newnes, London (1896).

Fancher RE, *The intelligence men: Makers of the IQ Controversy*, WW Norton, New York (1985).

Firshein R, *The Neutraceutical Revolution*, Riverhead Books, New York (1998).

Forbes HD, *Ethnic Conflict: Commerce, Culture, and the Contact Hypothesis*, Yale University Press, New Haven (1997).

Foss, DJ, Hakes, DT, *Psycholinguistics, An Introduction to the Psychology of Language*, Prentice-Hall, Englewood-Cliffs NJ (1978).

Galton D, *In Our Own Image, Eugenics and the Genetic Modification of People*, Little Brown & Co, London (2001).

Gottlieb W et al. (editors), *The Doctors Book of Home Remedies*. Bookman Press, Melbourne 1990.

Govoni N, Eng R, Morton G, *Promotional Management: Issues and Perspectives*, Prentice-Hall, Englewood Cliffs NJ (1988).

Holford C, Colson D, *Optimum Nutrition For Your Child*, Piatkus, London (2008).

Holford C, *New Optimum Nutrition For The Mind*, Basic Health, Laguna Beach CA 2009.

Insight vol. 7, part 91, Marshall Cavendish, London (1982).

Larsen RJ, Buss DM, *Personality Psychology, Domains of Knowledge About Human Nature*, McGraw-Hill, NY (2002).

Lieberman JA, *Shrinks, The Untold Story of Psychiatry*, Little Brown & Co, NY (2015).

Likert R, *New Patterns of Management*, McGraw-Hill, New York (1961).

Lindzey G, Hall CS, Thompson RF, *Psychology*, 2nd edn, Worth, New York (1978).

Lynch G, Granger R, *Big Brain, The Origins and Future of Human Intelligence*, Palgrave Macmillan, Houndmills, Basingstoke (2008).

Lynne R, Vanhanen T, *IQ and The Wealth of Nations*, Praeger, Westport CT (2002).

Lynn R, *Race differences in intelligence: An evolutionary analysis*, Washington Summit, Augusta GA (2006).

Mackintosh NJ, *IQ and Human Intelligence*, 2nd ed., Oxford University Press, Oxford (2011).

McCormack MH, *What They Don't Teach You at Harvard Business School*, Fontana/Collins, London (1986).

McGuire WJ, A syllogistic analysis of cognitive relationships, in *Attitude Organization And Change*, CI Hovland and MJ Rosenberg (eds.), Yale University Press, New Haven (1960).

Meadows DH, Meadows DL, Randers J, Behrens WW, *The Limits to Growth*, Pan, London (1974).

Mohr GA, Caffin DA, Penalty Factors, Lagrange Multipliers and Basis Transformation in the Finite Element Method, *Civil Engineering Transactions of The Institution of Engineers, Australia*, Vol. CE27, No. 2, May 1985.

Mohr GA, *The Finite Element Method for Solids, Fluids, and Optimization*, Oxford University Press, Oxford (1992).

Mohr GA, *A Course in Management Science* - unit MP12, International Arts & Sciences College, St Kilda, Melbourne (1995).

Mohr GA, *The Pretentious Persuaders*, Horizon, Sydney (2012a).

Mohr GA, *Curing Cancer & Heart Disease*, Xlibris, Sydney (2012b).

Mohr GA, *The Doomsday Calculation*, Xlibris, Sydney (2012c).

Mohr GA, *The War of the Sexes*, Xlibris, Sydney (2012d).

Mohr GA, Heart Disease, Cancer & Aging, Proven Neutraceutical and Lifestyle Solutions, Horizon, Sydney (2013).

Mohr GA, *Elementary Thinking*, Xlibris, Sydney (2014a).

Mohr GA, *The History and Psychology of Human Conflicts*, Horizon Publishing Group, Sydney (2014b).

Mohr GA, Richard Sinclair & Edwin Fear, *The Evolving Universe: Relativity, Redshift, and Life From Space*, Xlibris, Sydney (2014).

Mohr GA, Fear E, *World Religions, The History, Issues & Truth*, Xlibris, Sydney (2015).

Mohr GA, *The 8-Week+ Program to Reverse Cardiovascular Disease*, Book Venture, Ishpeming MI (2015).

Mohr GA, Edwin Fear & Richard Sinclair, *World War 3: When and How Will It End?*, Inspiring Publishers (2015).

Mohr GA, Edwin Fear, *The Brainwashed: From Consumer Zombies to Islamism & Jihad*, Inspiring Publishers (2016).

Morgan CT, King RA, Robinson NM, *Introduction to Psychology*, 6th edn, McGraw-Hill, Tokyo (1979).

Newcomb TM, Persistence and regression of changed attitudes, *Journal of Sociological Issues* 19 (1963) 3-14.

Niblett WR (ed.), *Higher Education: Demand and Response*, Tavistock Publications, London (1969).

O'Guinn TC, Allen CT, Semenik RJ, *Advertising and Integrated Brand Promotion*. Thomson South-Western, Mason OH 2006.

Ostrander S, Schroeder L, *Superlearning*, Delacorte Press/Confucian Press, New York (1979).

Packard V, *The Waste Makers*, Pelican, Harmondsworth, London (1963).

Packard V, *The People Shapers*, Nelson, Melbourne (1978).

Parkinson CN, *The Law*, Schwartz, Melbourne (1980).

Penn, *Microtrends, The Small Forces Behind Today's Big Changes*, Allen Lane, London (2007).

Perlmutter D, Colman C, *Raise a Smarter Child by Kindergarten*, Broadway Books, New York (2006).

Peter LJ, Hull R, *The Peter Principle*, Souvenir Press, London (1969).

Przemieniecki JS, *Theory of Matrix Structural Analysis*, McGraw-Hill, New York (1968).

Ripps LJ, Schoben EJ, Smith EE, Semantic distance and the verification of semantic relations, *Journal of Verbal Learning and Verbal Behaviour* 12 (1973) 203-210.

Robertson I, *Sociology*, 2nd edn, Worth, New York (1981).

Rosenfeld A, *The Second Genesis: The Coming Control of Life*, Pyramid Communications, New York (1972).

Sampson A, *The Arms Bazaar*, Coronet Books, London (1977).

Sargent M, *Drinking and Alcoholism in Australia: A Power Relations Theory*, Longman Cheshire, Melbourne (1979).

Schauss A G, Nutrition and behaviour, *J App Nutr* 35 (1983) 30-35.

Schmidt-Nielsen K, *Animal Physiology: Adaptation and Environment,* 2nd edn, Cambridge University Press, Cambridge (1979).

Selmes C (ed.), *New Movements in the Study and Teaching of Biology,* Temple Smith, London (1974).

Shealy CN (editor), *The Complete Illustrated Encyclopedia of Alternative Healing Therapies,* Element, Shaftesbury, Dorset (1999).

Skodal M, Skeels HM, A final follow-up study of one hundred adopted children, *Journal of Genetic Psychology* 75 (1949) 85-125.

Solomon MR, *Consumer Behaviour: Buying, Having and Being,* Allyn and Bacon, Boston (1992).

Sternberg RJ, *In Search of the Human Mind,* 2nd edn, Harcourt Brace College Publishers, Orlando FL (1998).

Sternberg S, High speed scanning in human memory, *Science* 153 (1966) 652-654.

Sweeney MS, *Brain, The Complete Mind, How it Develops, How it Works, and How to Keep it Sharp,* National Geographic, Washington D.C. (2009).

Sykes CJ, *Dumbing Down Our Kids: Why American Children Feel Good About Themselves But Can't Read, Write or Add,* St Martin's Griffin, New York (1995).

Taylor FW, *Principles of Scientific Management,* Harper, New York (1911).

Teasdale T, Owen D, A long-term rise and recent decline in intelligence test performance: The Flynn Effect in reverse, *Personality and Individual Differences* 39(4), 837 - 843 (2005).

Teasdale T, Owen D, Secular declines in cognitive test scores: A reversal of the Flynn Effect, *Intelligence* 36(2), 121-126 (2008).

Thomas M, *As Used on the Famous Nelson Mandela, Underground Adventures in the Arms and Torture Trade,* Ebury Press, London (2006).

Thomas J, Hughes T, *You Don't Have to be Famous to Have Manic Depression: The Insider's Guide to Mental Health,* Michael Joseph, London (2006).

Ungar G, Desidero DM, Parr W, Isolation, identification and synthesis of a specific behaviour inducing brain peptide, *Nature* 238 (1972) 198-202.

Vander AJ, Sherman JH, Luciano DS, *Human Physiology*, 6th edn, McGraw-Hill, New York (1994).

Vernon PE, *Intelligence and Attainment Tests*, University of London Press, London (1960).

Walther DS, *Applied Kinesiology, Synopsis*, Systems DC, Pueblo CO (1988).

Weinberg R, *One Renegade Cell*, Phoenix, London (1999).

Weiss ML, Mann AE, *Human Biology and Behaviour, An Anthropological Perspective*, 2nd edn, Little Brown, Boston MA (1978).

White M, *Rivals, Conflict as the Fuel of Science*, Vintage, London (2002).

Youngson RM, Schott I, *Medical Blunders*, Robinson, London (1996).

www.ingramcontent.com/pod-product-compliance
Lightning Source LLC
Chambersburg PA
CBHW071220080526
44587CB00013BA/1440